I0764049

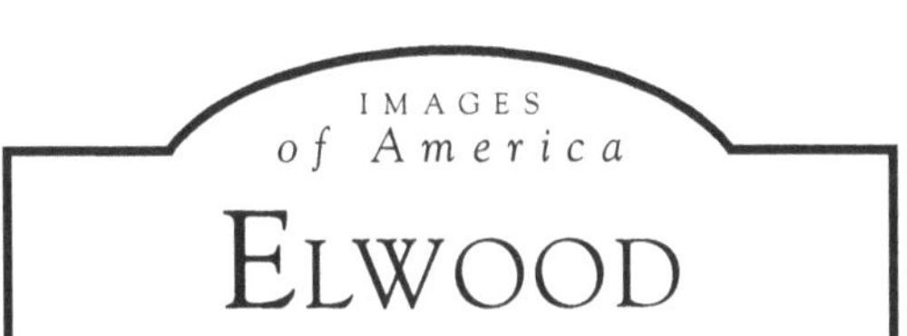
IMAGES
of America
ELWOOD

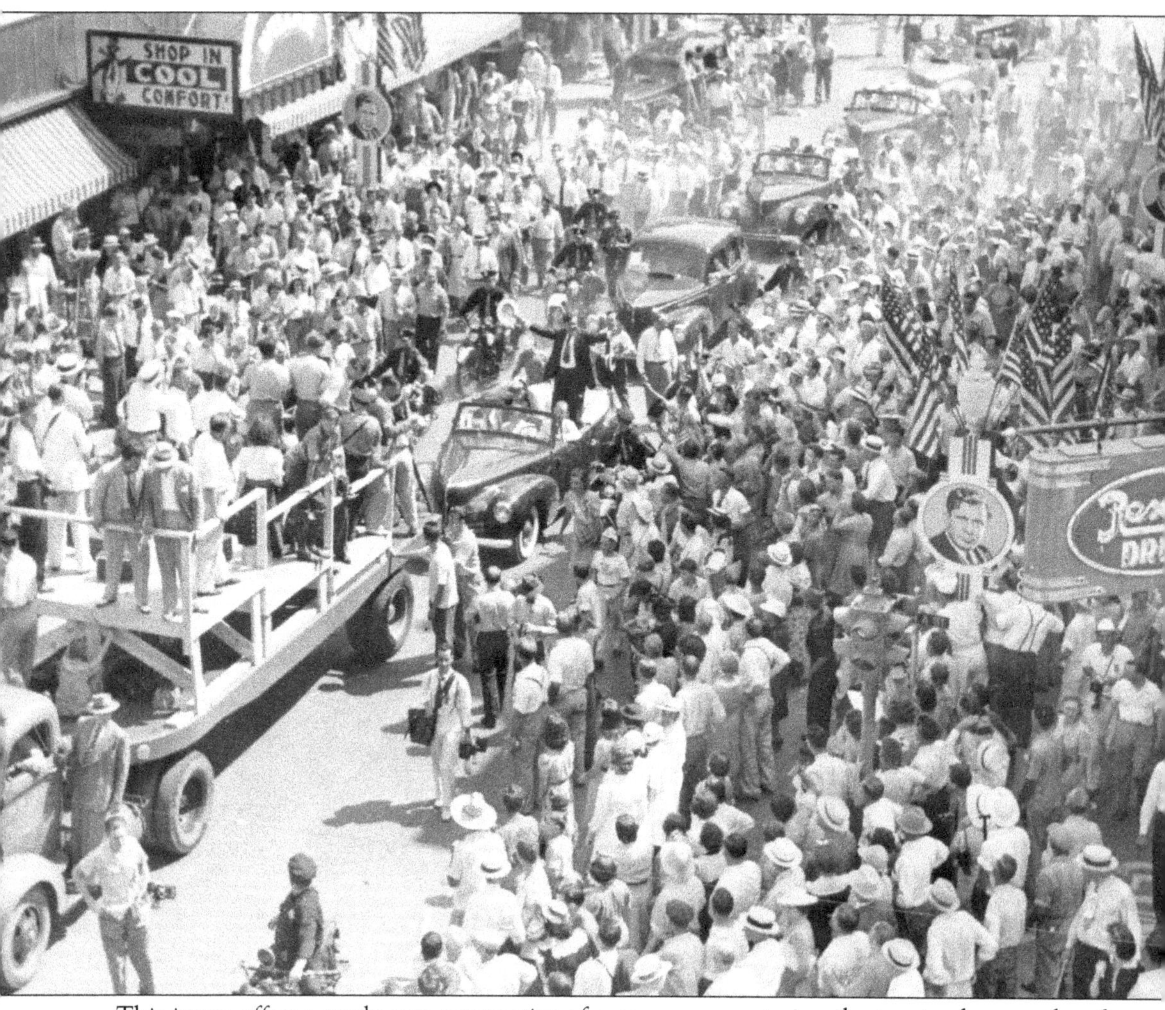

This image offers a rarely seen perspective of cameramen capturing the iconic photographs of Wendell Willkie parading north along Elwood's Anderson Street on Saturday, August 17, 1940. Greeted that day by an estimated 250,000 supporters, Willkie had returned to his hometown to accept the Republican Party's nomination as the candidate for US president, challenging two-term incumbent Franklin Roosevelt in the coming November's election. (Courtesy Elwood Heritage Center.)

On the Cover: Youthful Elwood entrepreneurs man their front-yard souvenir stand, selling a Willkie sticker to one of the quarter-million visitors flooding the city on August 17, 1940. Seizing the opportunity, scores of Elwoodites, even kids, turned their homes into hotels and their yards into tourist stops, selling hot dogs, soft drinks, and souvenirs. (Courtesy Elwood Heritage Center.)

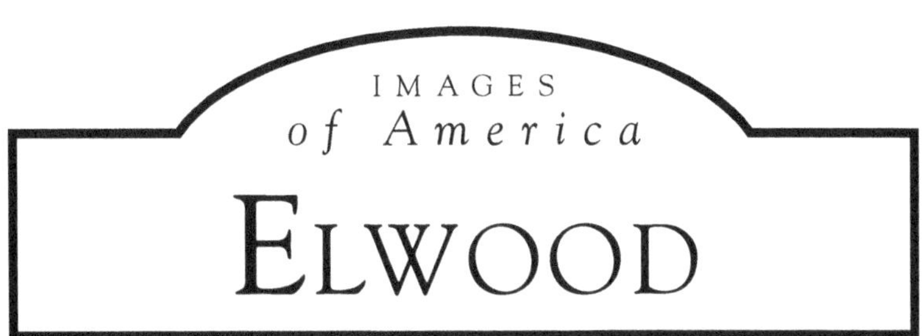

Janis Thornton and Marcy Fry
for the Elwood Chamber of Commerce
Foreword by Mayor Todd Jones

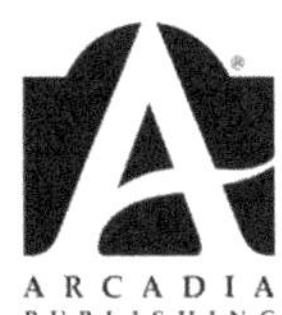

ISBN 978-1-4671-0340-4

Published by Arcadia Publishing
Charleston, South Carolina

Library of Congress Control Number: 2018963195

For all general information, please contact Arcadia Publishing:
Telephone 843-853-2070
Fax 843-853-0044
E-mail sales@arcadiapublishing.com
For customer service and orders:
Toll-Free 1-888-313-2665

Visit us on the Internet at www.arcadiapublishing.com

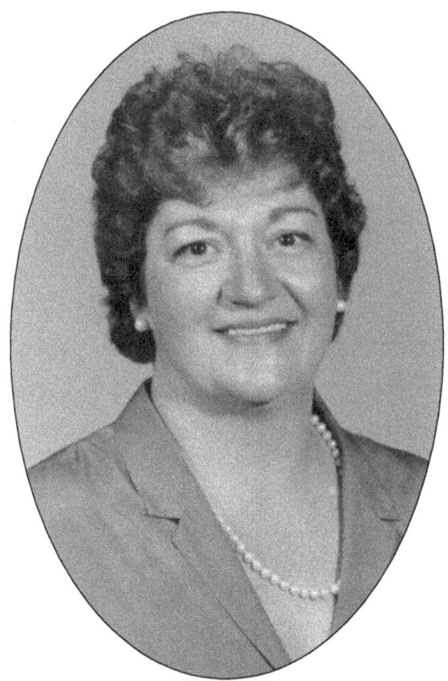

As executive director of the Elwood Chamber of Commerce, Barbara Armstrong set the bar high, meeting every challenge with courage, intelligence, and grace. We dedicate this book to her.

Barbara J. Armstrong
1936–2015

Contents

FOREWORD

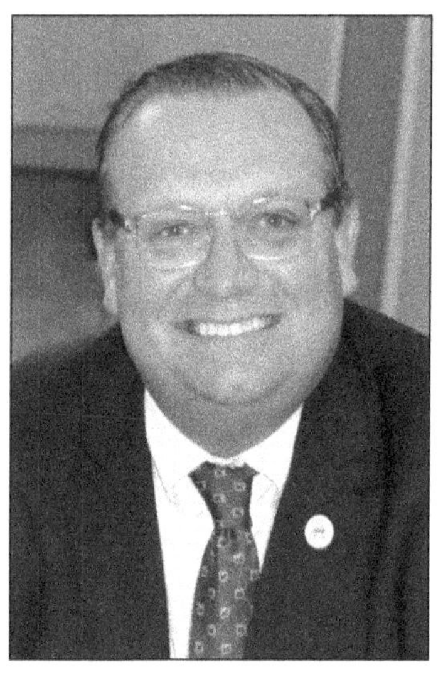

Born and raised in Elwood, I've had the opportunity to witness firsthand what it's like to grow up in a small city, a city where neighbors help neighbors, homes fly the American flag with great pride, generations choose to raise their families, and everyone knows your name.

I learned as a young boy that with hard work and dedication, there was nothing I couldn't do. I could be anything I wanted to be and live anywhere I wanted to live. My roots run deep, and I cannot recall a time when I wanted to live anywhere but my hometown. Today, my wife, Susie, and I raise our four children Addie, Ava, Ivy, and Lucas in the very city I grew up in. I am certain that I would not be the man that I am today if it were not for the role models, mentors, and friends that I had as a result of living in Elwood, and I am excited to be able to offer that same opportunity to my children.

To be asked to write the foreword for this book was a tremendous honor. The pictures contained on the following pages are so much more than photographs. They are the memories of a city that, over the years, has endured so much yet stood so strong. These pages hold snapshots of the rich history that Elwood is known for. They represent who we are and where we came from.

As mayor of Elwood, I have a unique view of a city on the move. I feel an enormous sense of pride as I watch the positive changes turning into positive momentum. Together with business owners and citizens, my administration has worked diligently to continue to make Elwood the best choice to call "home" and to raise a family.

Elwood truly lives up to its nickname, "Heart of Hoosierland." Spend one day in our city, and you will feel the love and hometown pride our citizens hold deep in their hearts. Who knows, you may decide you want to call Elwood your home.

Welcome to Elwood!

—Mayor Todd Jones

Acknowledgments

Early in 2018, when we put out our first call asking Elwood citizens to help us produce a new Elwood history book by digging into their family albums, dozens of our neighbors answered. The content of the pages that follow is a testament to their response.

Among the contributors are the Elwood Heritage Center's Marjorie Pierce, Ranny Simmons, Mike Williams, and Jonathan Huffman, whose unbound knowledge of Elwood's past was indispensable. Jamie Scott and Todd Buckmaster of the Elwood Public Library made their archives available to us whenever we asked, and Sandy Burton and Bob Nash of the *Elwood Call-Leader* gave us space on their pages each time we issued a reminder about our photography needs.

We are deeply grateful to our many friends who allowed us to scan their precious vintage photographs: Kathy Amos, Jeanne Arehart, Beverly and Tom Austin, Lisa Baugher, Tena Beckley, Dave Berkemeier, Matt Boyland for the Elwood Fire Department, Ann Brewer, Jed Brown, John Carpenter, Dave and Cathy Case, Christy Clark, Carol Dever, Duane Etchison, the Dunnichay Family, East Main Street Christian Church, the *Elwood Call-Leader*, Elwood Community Schools, Elwood VFW, Karen Cole for First United Methodist Church, Dorcas Floyd, Eric Grogan, Randall Hall and Keith Israel of the Opera House, David and Linda Heflin, Ron Hinshaw, William Huneke, Bill Huntsman, Terry Jones, Todd Jones, Carolyn S. Julius, Rita Kelich, Judy Koehler-Newell, Marla and Sam Laudeman, Matt Leeson, Pam Lehman, Sue Loser, Madison County Historical Society, Theresa Mangas, Mick Melvin, Linda Moore, Ted and Deb Moser, Al Mottweiler, Ginny Noble, Cathy Ogden, Mike and Sherry Pace, Jeff Poe, Red Gold, Joe Rice, Carl Ritter, Earl and Tammy Savage, Steve, Pam and Mary Savage, Rose Schimmel, Stark County, Ohio, Historical Society, St. Vincent Mercy Hospital, Bobby Taylor, and Amy Seright Updike.

In most instances, photograph contributors are noted in the cutline. Photographs listing no source are from the chamber's own archives. We regret that due to space limitations, we could not use all the photographs submitted, but our gratitude to those who submitted them is no less.

—Janis Thornton and Marcy Fry
December 2018

INTRODUCTION

Long before European immigrants settled the land that would become Indiana, it was an unbroken wilderness of dense forests inhabited for millennia by native people.

When Indiana gained statehood in 1816, the natives still rightfully claimed two-thirds of the Indiana Territory. Two years later, a US government-appointed commission was tasked with negotiating land deals with the native nations. During that summer, a meeting between the commissioners and tribal leaders resulted in the Treaty of St. Mary's in which the natives agreed to cede nearly all their land south and east of the Wabash River. This spacious tract, dubbed the New Purchase, provided the land from which 37 counties were carved.

In January 1823, Indiana governor William Hendricks approved a charter for a forty-three square-mile region of the New Purchase to be designated Madison County. Pioneers from the east began arriving almost immediately to homestead the new territory, and 10 years later, Pipe Creek Township was organized on the northwest side of the county amid remarkably rich farmland.

Elwood got its start in 1852, when a general store opened near what is now the intersection of Main and Anderson Streets. The store was a crude structure filled with all the simple needs of a young community: barrels of sugar, salt, and vinegar, and bags of beans, rice, coffee, soap, nails, and hard candy. The next year, James Anderson, Mark Simmons, and J.B. Frazier laid out the town and named it Quincy. It was composed of three east and west streets—Simmons (now South A), Main, and Walnut (now North A); and one running north and south—Anderson Street. The original town plot shows six lots north of Main Street and two lots south.

When township residents decided to build a post office, they learned that Indiana already had a town named Quincy. As they sought a new name, they were unable to reach an agreement, until, according to local lore, someone pointed to J.B. Frazier's six-year-old son Elwood and said, "Why not?"

The town adopted the name in July 1869 and incorporated as a city in December 1872. At that time, the population totaled slightly more than 300 and had everything it needed: a flour mill, several stores, a bank, and a hotel.

The first railroad came through Elwood in 1856, when tracks for the Panhandle (which later became part of the Pennsylvania Railroad) were extended from Anderson to Logansport. After another 20 years passed, the Lafayette, Muncie & Bloomington line (which later would be part of the Nickel Plate, and today Norfolk & Western Railway) rolled through. The two systems triggered considerable growth in Elwood.

Although the city's development was steady, it was comparatively slow until 1886, when natural gas was discovered throughout east-central Indiana. Gas wells began springing up in Elwood soon after. Huge, flaming torches flickered round the clock, marking the presence of the fuel, and required nothing but a pipeline to supply consumers with efficient heat and lights.

Thanks to gas, Elwood's growth exploded, ushering expansion in all directions from its downtown crossroads and along the railroad lines. As the population multiplied, citizens advocated for a city government. The proposition was affirmed in April 1891, and the first election followed in June. William A. DeHority, a local banker and Indiana's first chief state accountant, was elected Elwood's first mayor.

Gas attracted many industries seeking cheap fuel. Manufacturing plants for Pittsburgh Plate Glass, MacBeth-Evans Glass, Elwood Furniture Company, American Tin Plate Works, and many others quickly settled in Elwood. Plants meant jobs, and workers throughout the state and beyond filled them. Retail stores and professional services, in turn, opened throughout the city to meet the needs of the workers and their families. Those newly minted businesses and services created even more jobs, and by 1909, Elwood's population topped 11,000.

Because everyone assumed the gas was inexhaustible, supply lines were left uncapped to allow the wells to burn continuously. As a result, almost as quickly as the gas boom appeared, it faded. Because local pumping stations supplied gas to communities as far away as Chicago, the pressure waned, and water began seeping into the wells. Residential neighborhoods suffered a reduction in pressure, as did the factories, which had constructed their own pipelines. As moisture spread through the pipelines, the supply became undependable; thus residents, businesses, and factories had no choice but to find alternative sources of power. By 1912, Elwood's gas service was supplied by Central Indiana Gas Company.

With the collapse of the gas era, Elwood's industries that had depended on the fuel began to vanish. Many felt the city's future was doomed. However, local citizens were determined to save their beloved hometown by recreating it.

Elwood was already rich with assets—robust buildings and business properties that could be refurbished for other uses, a large and reliable workforce, a strong infrastructure, and an enterprising, united community. Thus, community leaders teamed up. They encouraged local people to launch new businesses, and they reached out to industries from other cities and states to relocate there.

Consequently, in 1930, Monticello Manufacturing moved to Elwood; in 1935, Continental Can opened a plant there; and that same year, National Trailer Company took over the old MacBeth-Evans site. And those were only the starters. Many others—such as St. Clair Glass, Frazier Canning Company, Lewis Small Company, and G.I. Sellers and Company—followed. By the start of World War II, Elwood was booming again.

The boom continued long after the war ended, with the local population and economy growing steadily each year. But, with the advent of big box stores, shopping malls, and superhighways in the mid-1960s, Elwood experienced a shift. Its population began to slip, and Elwood's uptown began to fade.

Today, Elwood citizens find it difficult to imagine horse-pulled buggies plodding along the gas-lit mud streets, plank sidewalks, wood-frame buildings, and the rumble of passenger trains rolling through. Few Elwoodites remain who remember the sugary taste of the Sweet Shop treats, or standing in line at Mangas Cafeteria for Sunday dinner, or cheering Wendell Willkie at Callaway Park, or exchanging waves with the beautiful Tomato Festival queen as her float passed them by, or shopping for bargains at Leeson's, or taking in a Hollywood film from the front seat of their car at the Elwood Drive-in Theatre, or rolling a strike at Ballard Bowl, or boarding a Chicago-bound train at Pennsylvania Station, or digging into a roast beef sandwich at Wolff's Tavern, or strolling along Anderson Street on a Saturday night and greeting old friends long departed, and a million other cherished memories from days gone by.

Thanks to the city's rich past, today's Elwood is characterized as "the Heart of Hoosierland," and it has a long, bright future to look forward to. We are proud to present this book and hope its pages rekindle fond memories and spark poignant reflections. Images of America: *Elwood* is our gift to help you experience what was, what is, and what is yet to come.

—Janis Thornton and Marcy Fry
for the Elwood Chamber of Commerce

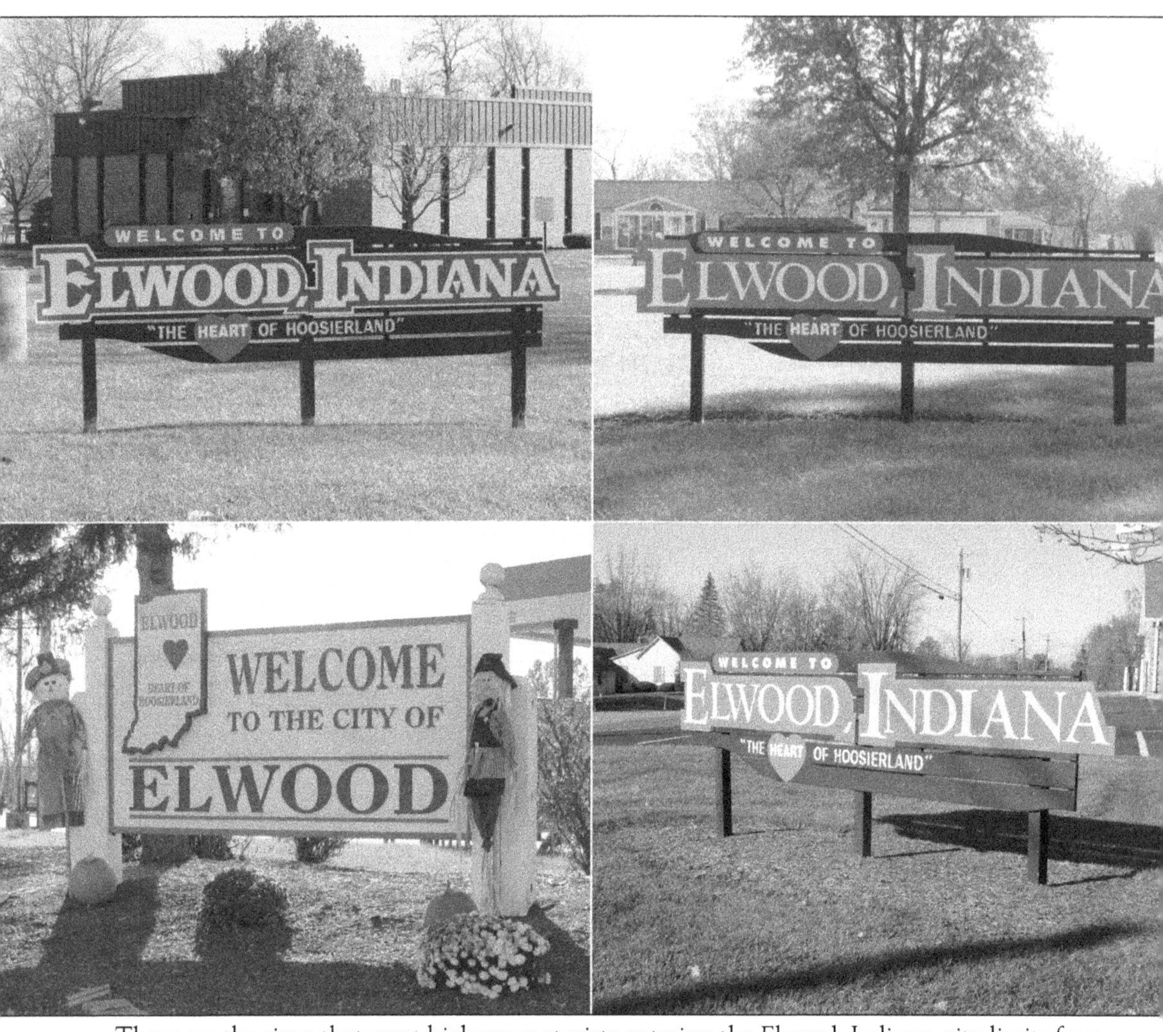

These are the signs that greet highway motorists entering the Elwood, Indiana, city limits from all compass points. The Elwood Chamber of Commerce adopted "the Heart of Hoosierland" as its motto in the early 1960s, and the community has embraced it ever since.

One

Founding and Early Years

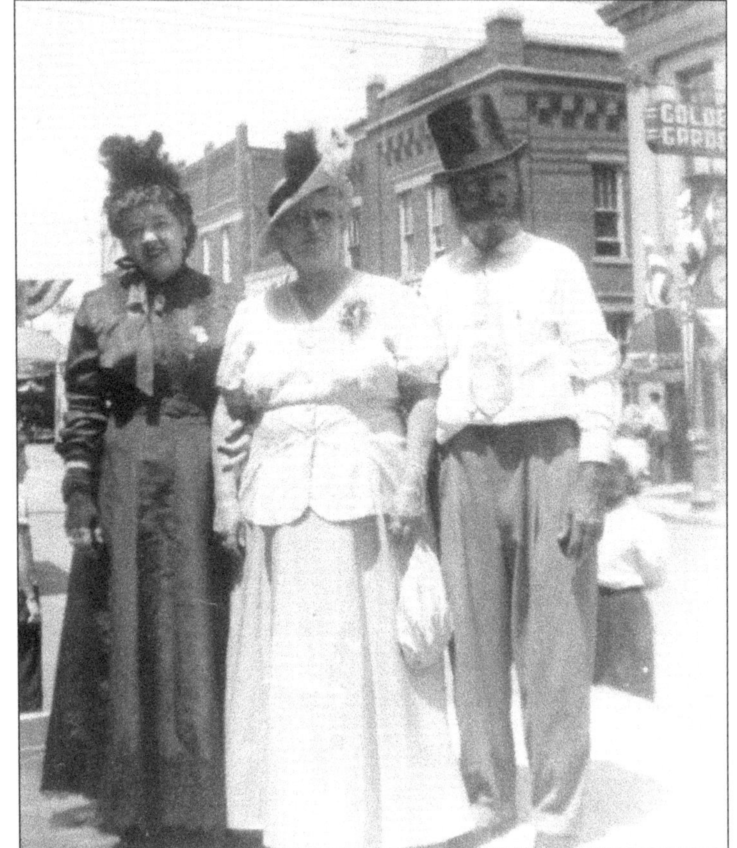

Pearl and Lawrence Lynas (center and right), along with an unidentified woman (left), pose in their turn-of-the-century costumes on the reviewing stand located in the 100 block of South Anderson Street in June 1952, during Elwood's centennial celebration. Lawrence was proud of his beard, boasting that he had not shaved since January 26 of that year. (Courtesy Pam Lehman.)

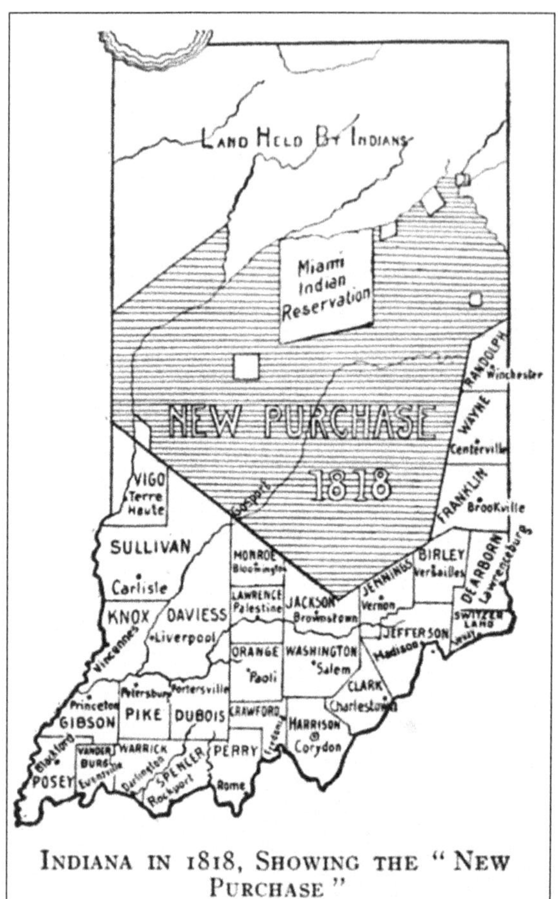

INDIANA IN 1818, SHOWING THE "NEW PURCHASE"

When Indiana joined the union, its native people owned two-thirds of the land. In 1818, state leaders and native tribes met in St. Mary's, Ohio. The result was the Treaty of St. Mary's, in which the tribes agreed to sell most of their land to the state. The spacious tract, dubbed the New Purchase, provided the area in which 37 counties, including Madison County, would be formed.

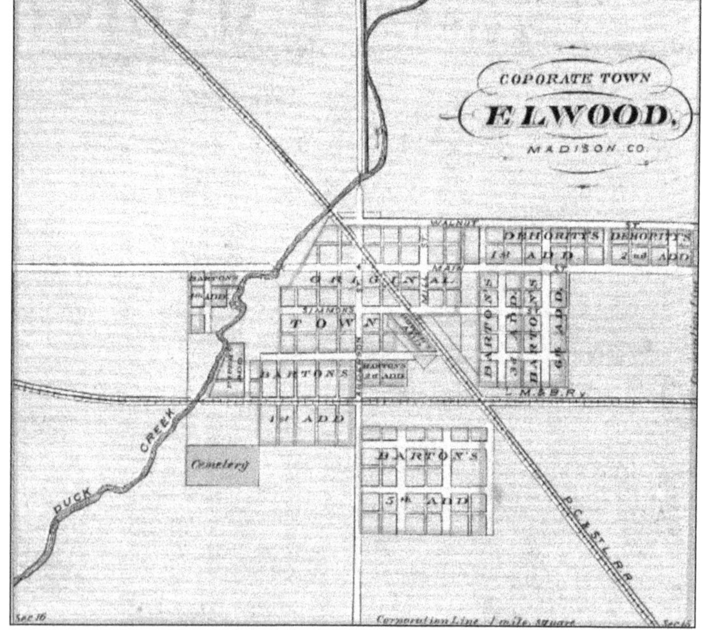

In 1853, founders James Anderson, Mark Simmons, and J.B. Frazier laid out the town, still known then as Quincy. They designated one north and south street to be named Anderson Street, and three east–west streets, which they named Main, Simmons (now South A), and Walnut (now North A) Streets. (Courtesy David Rumsey Map Collection, www.davidrumsey.com.)

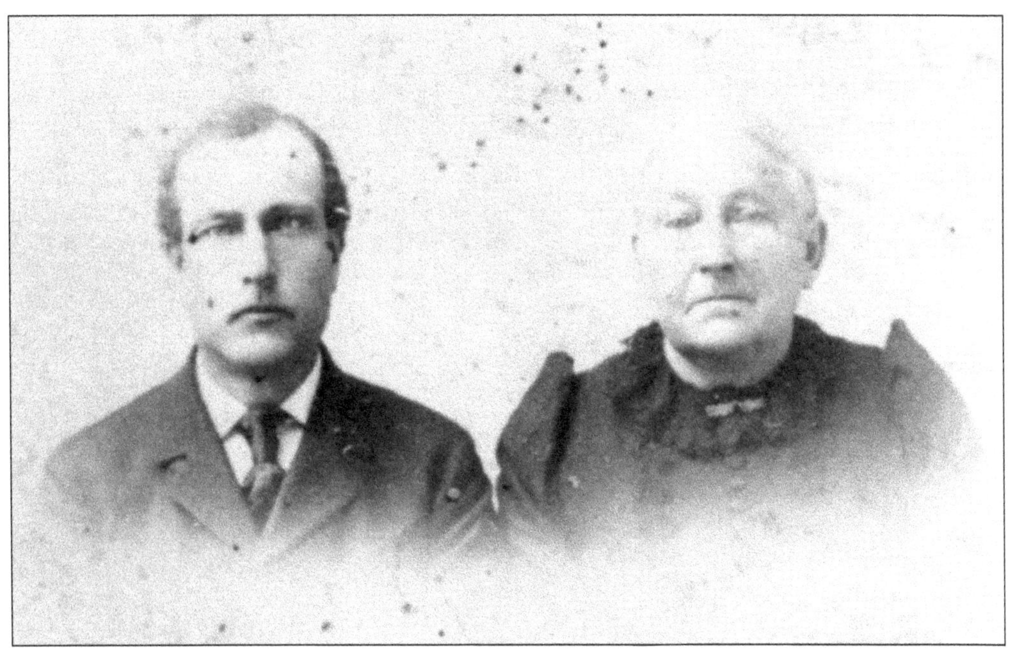

Pictured are Melvin Simmons and his mother, Elizabeth, son and wife of Elwood founder Mark Simmons. According to family lore, Melvin was born in 1850 in a log cabin built on the same stretch of land now occupied by the Elwood Chamber of Commerce. (Courtesy Ranny Simmons.)

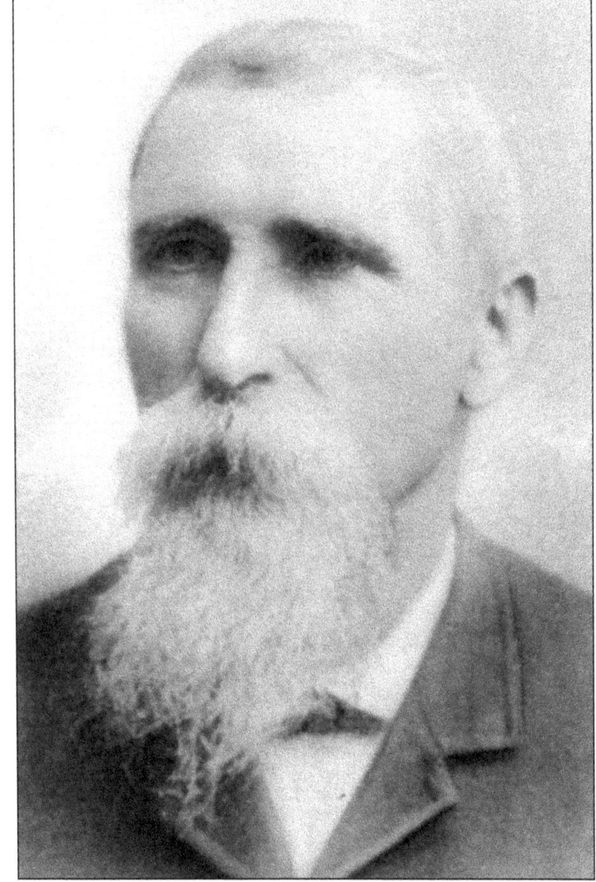

James M. Anderson, one of the town's founders, was a land speculator. He migrated to Indiana when the state was in its infancy, settling first in Wayne County. After a few years, he moved to Greenfield and, later, to Elwood, where he died in 1858.

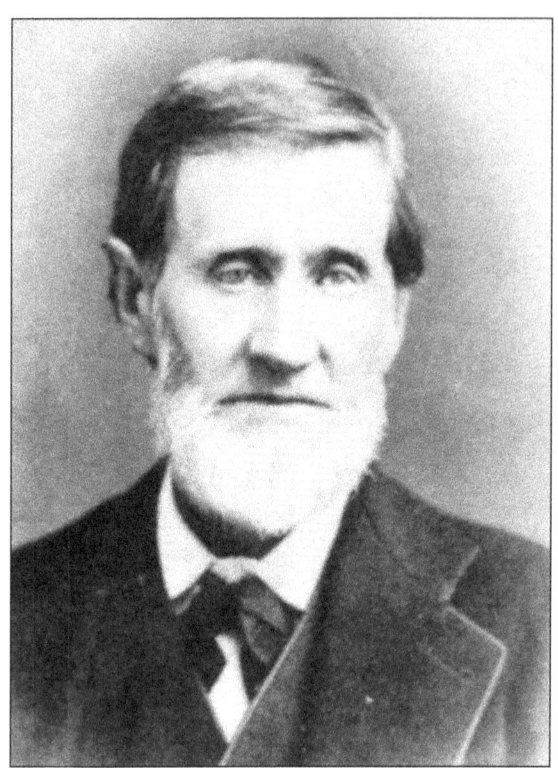

Dr. Bediah Tharp Calloway was born in Wayne County, Indiana, in 1824. He settled in Quincy in the early 1850s with his wife, Mary Ann. He built Elwood's first brick building in 1873 for a dry-goods business and retired from his medical practice in 1882. Afterward, he organized Elwood's first bank, serving as its president until his death in 1899. Dr. Calloway was beloved throughout Elwood.

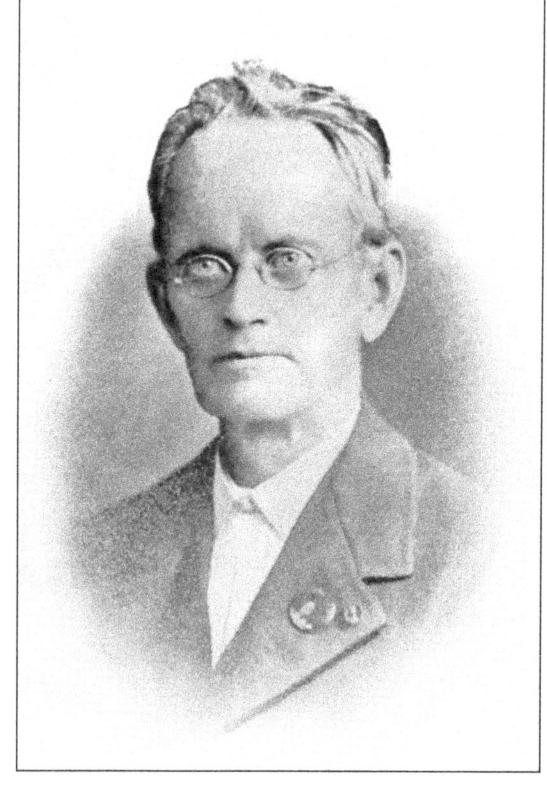

Capt. Richard Largent "R.L." Leeson was born in Wayne County in 1826. When the Civil War started, he joined the 68th Indiana Infantry and participated in numerous battles, including Chickamauga, Chattanooga, and Orchard Knob. After the war, he settled in Elwood, opening his first store in 1877. He died on September 23, 1906. The afternoon of his funeral, all the Elwood stores closed in a show of respect. (Courtesy Matt Leeson.)

Gustav Kramer, pictured with his family, emigrated from Germany to America in 1853, settling in Quincy in 1862. After a successful career in timber and ice, he helped build Elwood's brick streets and sewers, and the Kramer business block, including the famous Opera House. When Kramer passed away on September 8, 1908, the *Call-Leader* reported that "he died with the happy smile of a child upon his lips." (Courtesy the Opera House.)

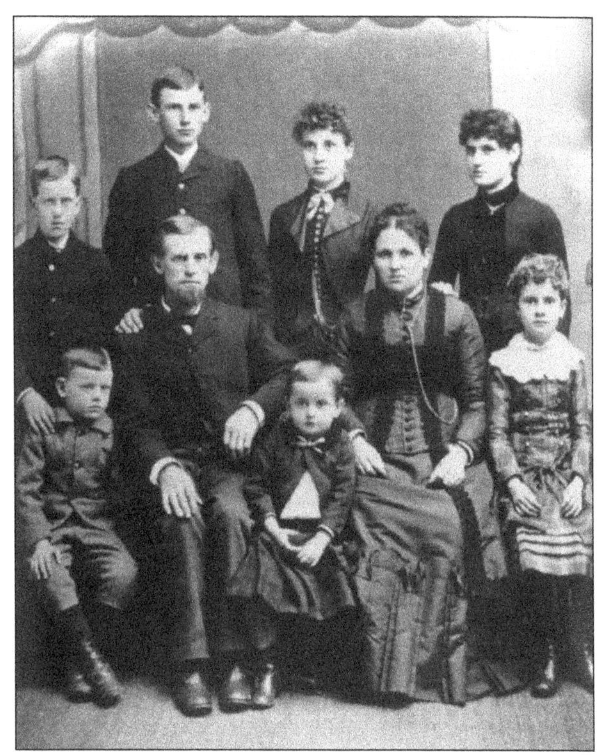

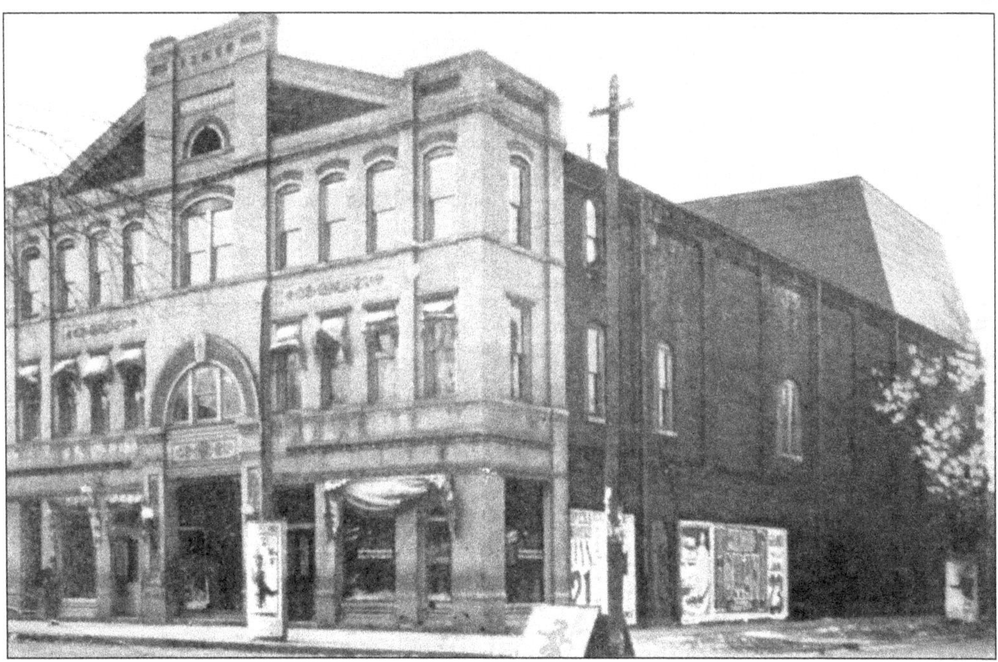

The Opera House, built in 1891 by Gustav Kramer, presented touring operas and vaudeville shows, featuring the likes of Agnes Herndon and James Whitcomb Riley. It also hosted high school graduations, parties, weddings, and other community events. Current owner Randall Hall and manager Keith Israel, Gustav Kramer's great-great-grandson, restored the facility's original charm and beauty, and it is again a popular site for dinners and parties. (Courtesy Elwood Public Library.)

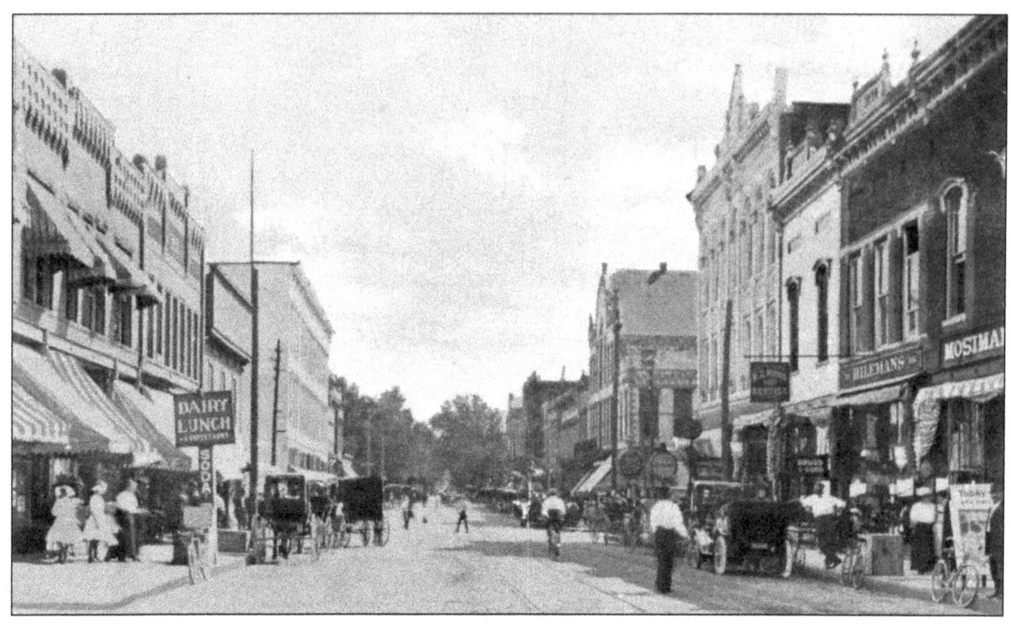

Both photographs capture a southward view of Elwood's uptown from the vantage of Main and Anderson Streets. Above, around 1905, a lone automobile is parked in front of Hileman's, while dozens of bicycles and horse-drawn carriages line the street. The movement of the bicyclist and the pedestrians suggest a busy, warm day in a bustling city. Notice the brick street, the streetcar tracks, Mosiman & James, W.Z. King Dentistry, the Opera House, and Leeson's. Below, around 1940, a similar view suggests an equally busy day, long after the brick street was paved, covering the obsolete tracks. Motorized vehicles have long replaced the horse and carriage; and merchants have stepped aside for the likes of Kroger's and Commons Drugs, while the Opera House and Leeson's remain irreplaceable. (Above, courtesy Eric Grogan; below, courtesy Dave Berkemeier.)

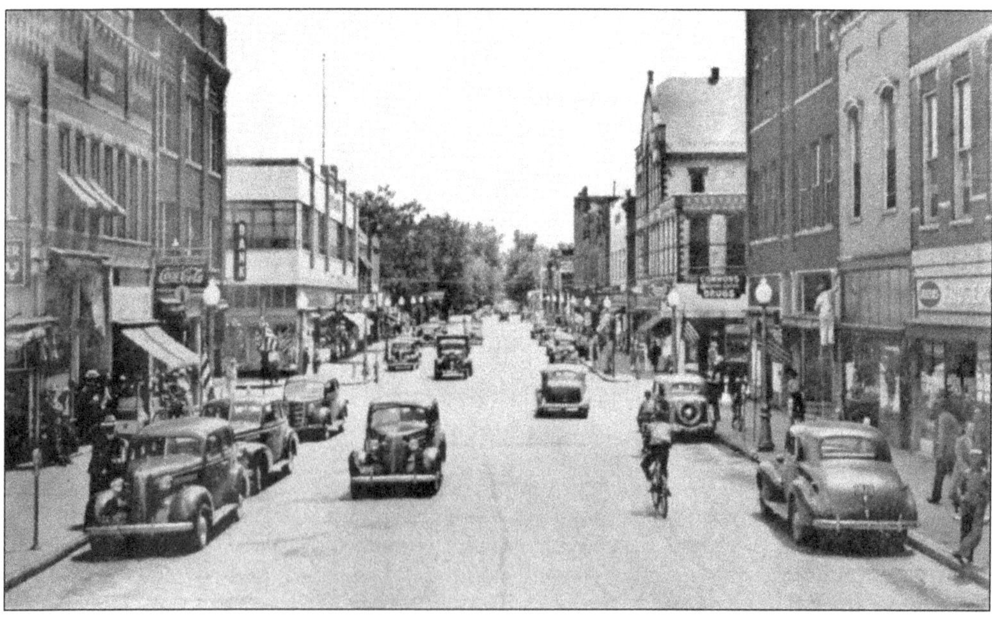

Two

Business and Industry

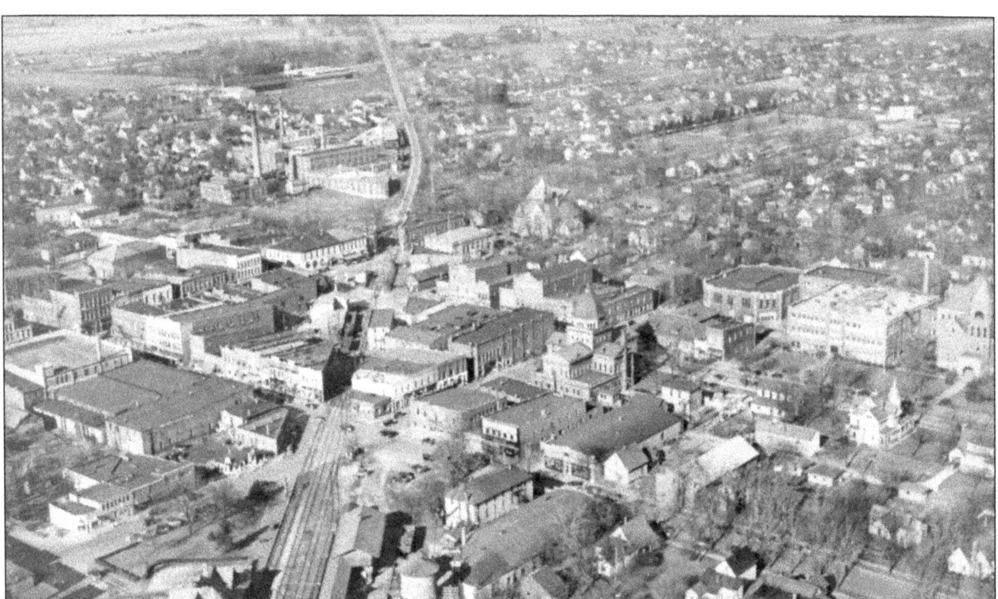

This aerial photograph overlooking Elwood was shot in 1937 by pilot Don Orbaugh from his plane. The view looks north, with the Pennsylvania Railroad track as the focal point. Many landmarks that no longer exist are shown, such as the smokestacks of the Continental Can Company in the upper left portion and the old Elwood High School on the far right. (Courtesy Ann Brewer.)

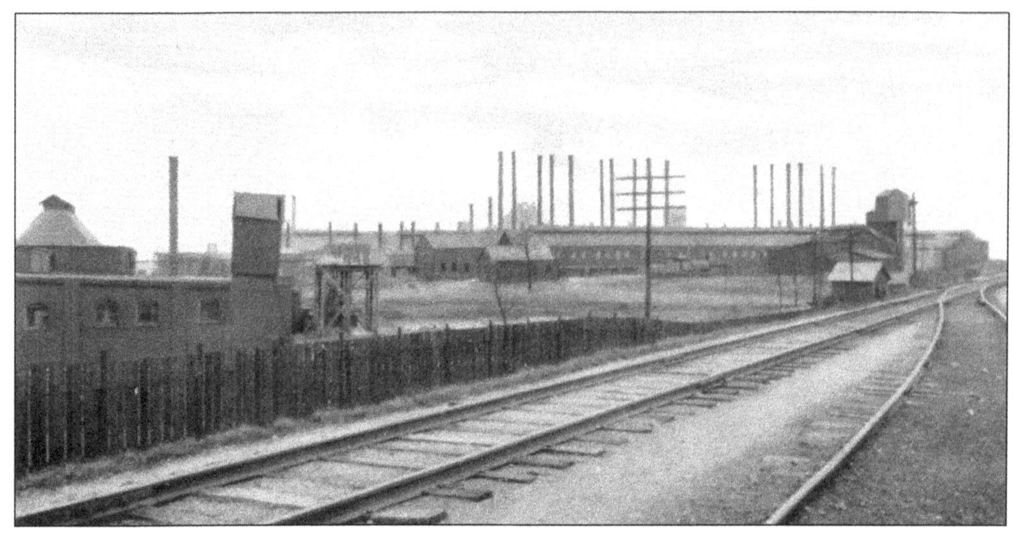

The first Tin Plate plant in America opened in Elwood on September 13, 1892, powered by the area's seemingly limitless supply of natural gas. Celebrating the occasion, thousands of people from Elwood and Central Indiana lined the streets in a driving rain to watch the celebratory parade plod through the muddy streets. At 1:30 p.m., Ohio governor and future US president William McKinley, an advocate for American industries and protective tariffs, stepped onto the balcony of the Opera House and delivered an impassioned speech to the jubilant crowd below. Within 20 years, the Tin Plate was the largest such plant in Indiana. After the Tin Plate's 20th anniversary, it merged with Carnegie-Illinois Steel Corporation. The merger created Indiana's largest factory and brought rapid growth to Elwood. (Both, courtesy Elwood Heritage Center.)

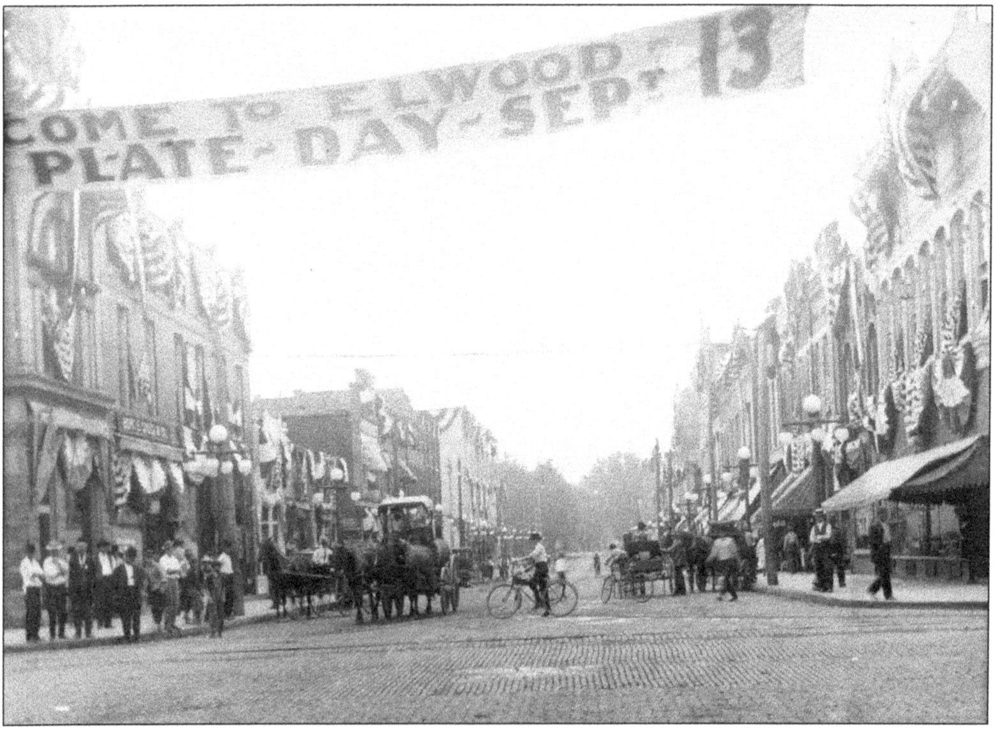

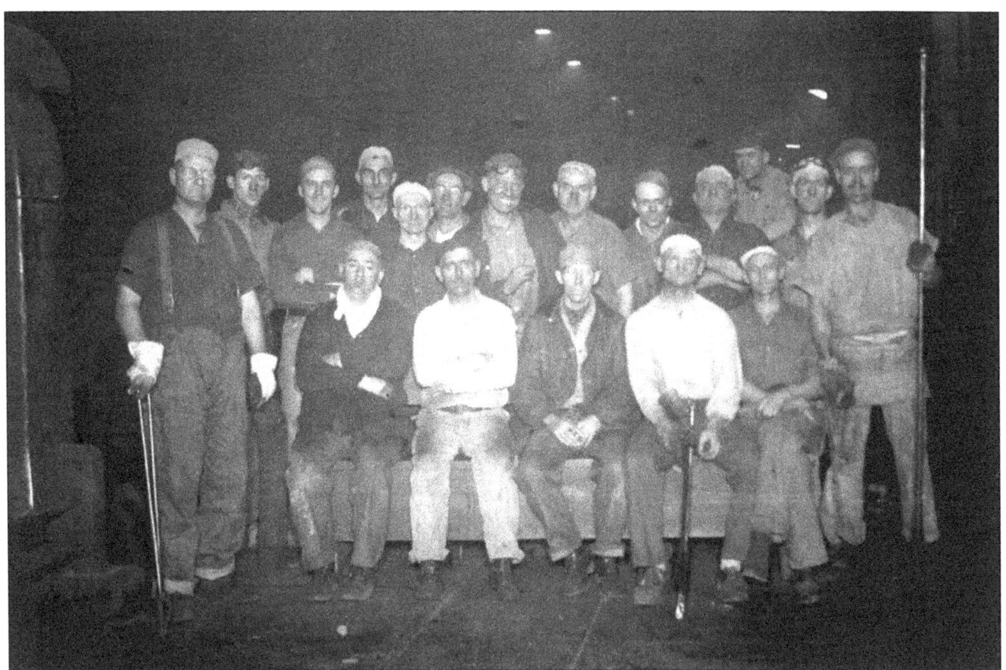

By 1908, the declining gas boom was taking a toll on the mill, and mills in other states began rising to prominence. The Tin Plate's inland position also hindered its production, and in 1938, the mill announced its closing. The largest factory in Indiana was vacated as its employees transferred to other mills elsewhere. The Hot Mill crew in the c. 1935 photograph above includes the following men: Blondie Sheets, standing first from left; Verlin Quick, standing fourth from left; C.V. Thumma, standing sixth from left; and Ted Sowash, standing ninth from left. The crew pictured below, around 1920, is unidentified. (Above, courtesy Rose Schimmel Stiner; below, courtesy Earl and Tammy Savage.)

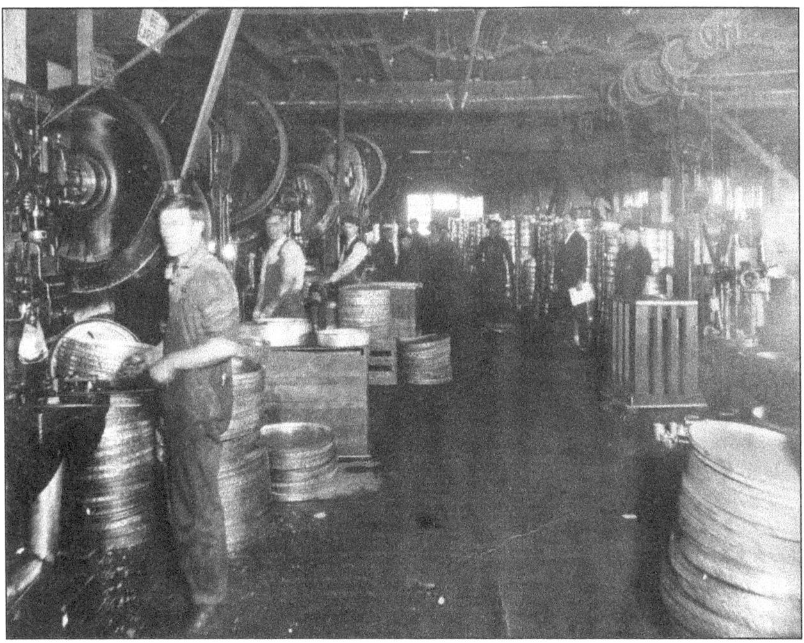

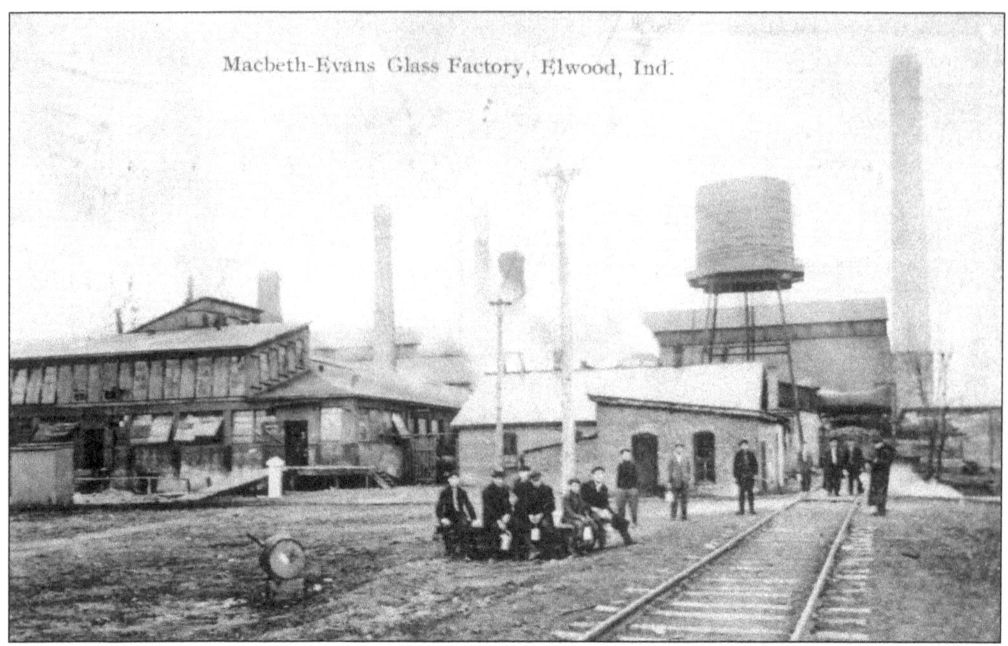

Elwood, surrounded by an abundance of sand suitable for producing glass, as well as a seemingly limitless supply of natural gas, was the perfect place for glass manufacturing businesses to locate and flourish. In 1890, a total of 365 glass craftsmen from Pittsburgh relocated to Elwood to work the city's first glass factory, MacBeth-Evans. (Courtesy Eric Grogan.)

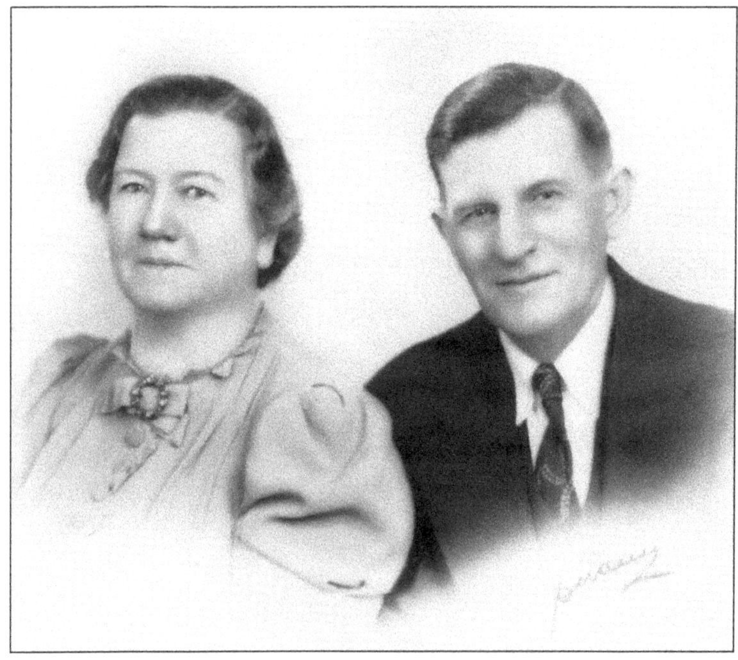

John "Pop" St. Clair, a French immigrant residing in Missouri, heard about the MacBeth-Evans plant in Elwood and moved his wife, Ellen, and kids there in 1903 to work for the company. But over time, the natural gas supply dwindled and so did production at the glass factories. The closure of MacBeth-Evans was a direct link to the opening of St. Clair Glass Works. (Courtesy Joe Rice.)

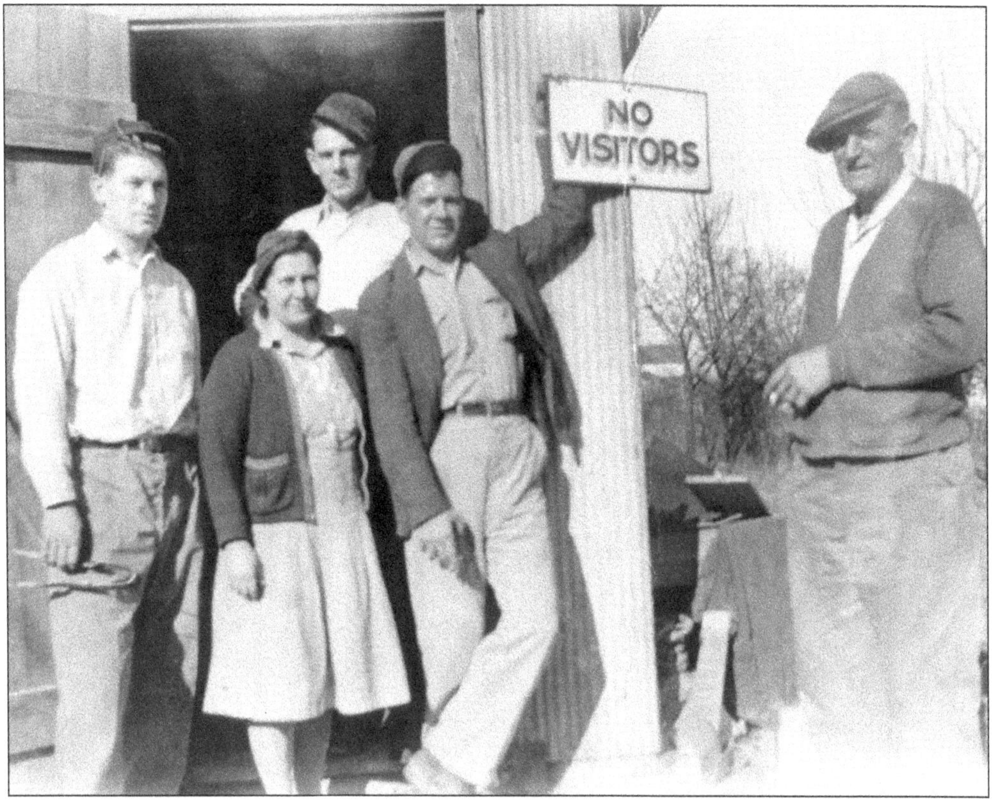

This photograph was snapped in 1942 outside the entrance to the St. Clair Glass Works manufacturing building, located behind the St. Clair family home at 408 North 5th Street, Elwood. From left to right are Joe St. Clair, Marie Hirsch, John St. Clair Jr., Ed St. Clair, and John "Pop" St. Clair. (Courtesy Joe Rice.)

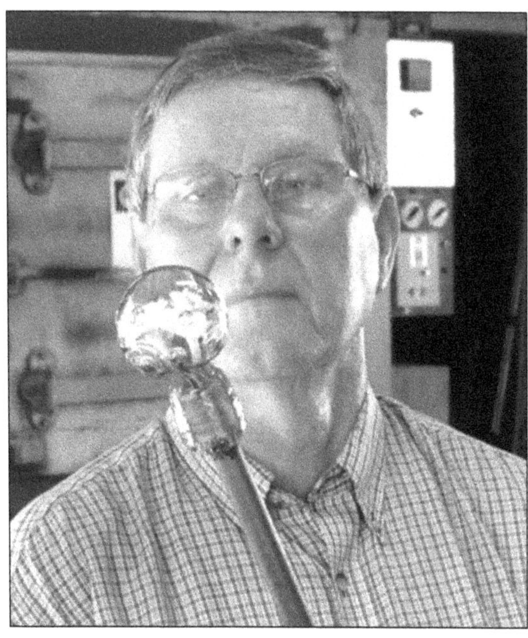

After MacBeth-Evans closed in 1938, Pop and Ellen's son, Joe, set the wheels in motion to fulfill his parents' dream. St. Clair Glass Works opened in 1941. Soon, connoisseurs of artistic glass praised the flawless St. Clair crystal. Pop died in 1958, and Joe took charge. After Joe died in 1987, his nephew and Pop's grandson, Joe Rice, pictured, stepped up to carry on the family tradition.

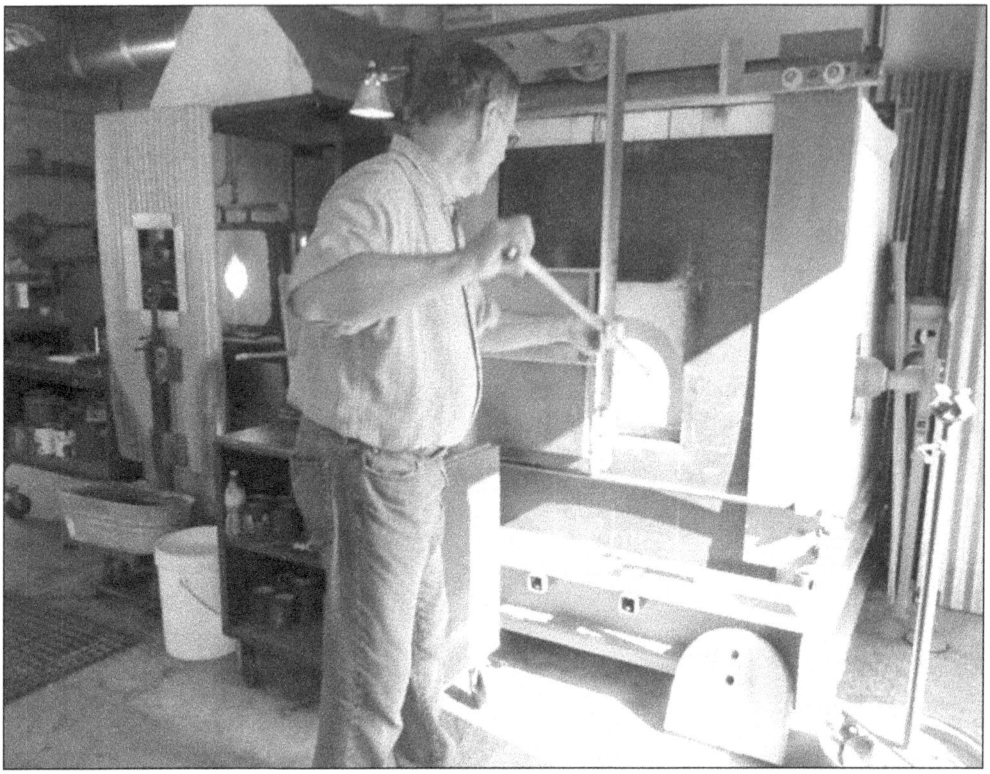

Joe Rice began working at the family glass business in 1962, when he was 12. After his uncles, Joe and Bob St. Clair, died, Rice purchased the House of Glass factory and, in 1988, launched a new era of the St. Clair tradition. It was the fulfillment of a dream that he continues today.

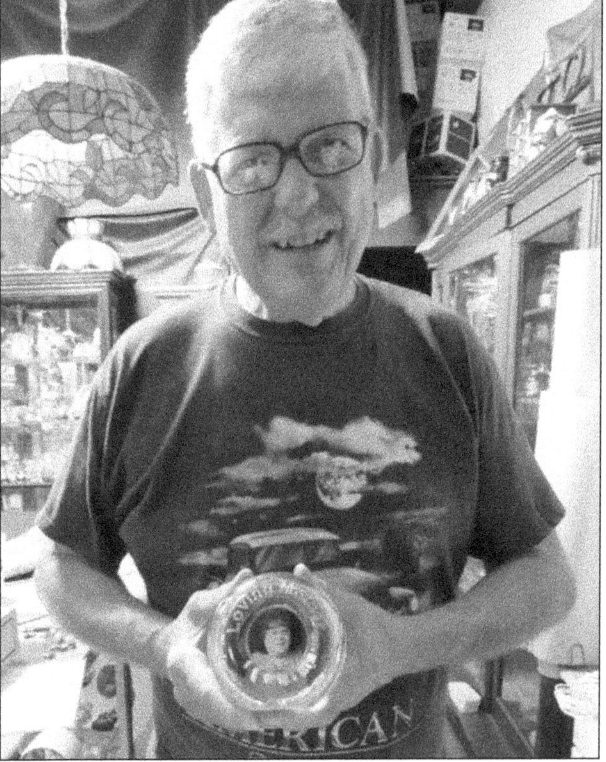

After the death of Elwood glass artisan Joe St. Clair in 1987, local tinsmith Jeff Ball seized on an opportunity. Ready for a new career direction, he purchased some of the St. Clair equipment at auction and opened his Prestige Art Glass (now named Carol's Legacy Glass) factory and showroom in 1990. Since then, Prestige has carved an impressive niche in the specialty glass market.

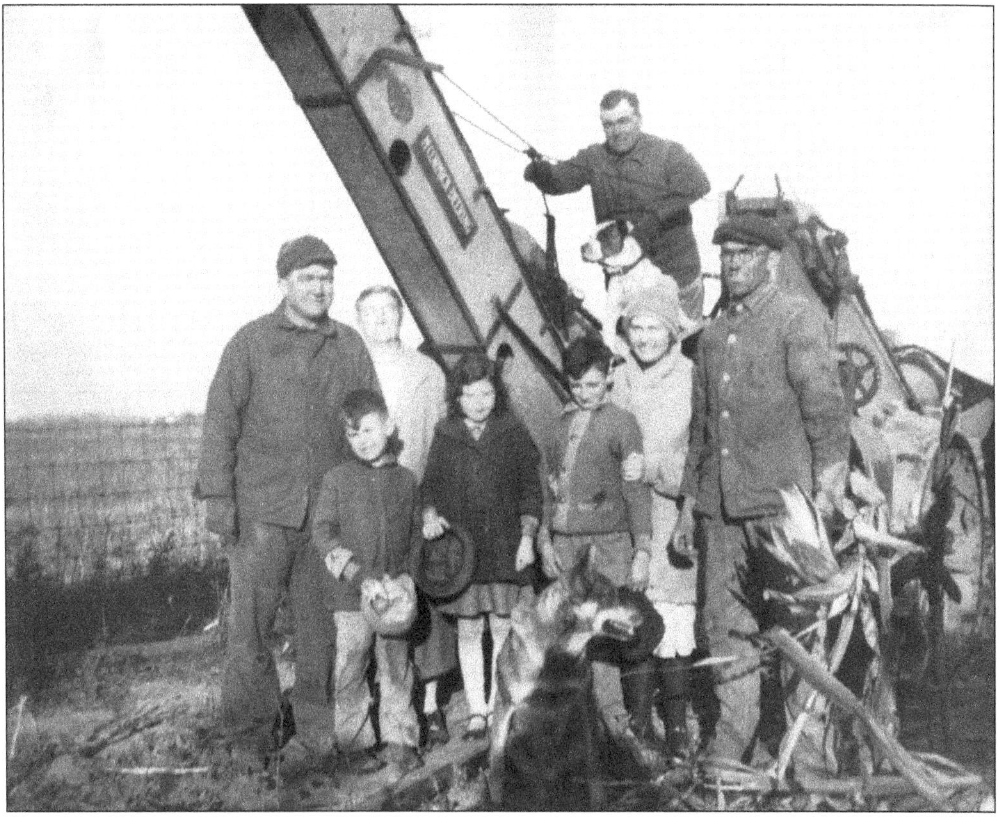

In 1930, the Procter brothers purchased one of the first mounting McCormick-Deering corn pickers in Indiana. Although it was intended for their own use, they soon built a business harvesting corn for other area farmers. From left to right are Elzie, Anna, and Murice Procter, Annabelle and Fred McCord, and Mamie and Harry Procter; in the back on the equipment is Roscoe Procter. (Courtesy Ted and Deb Moser.)

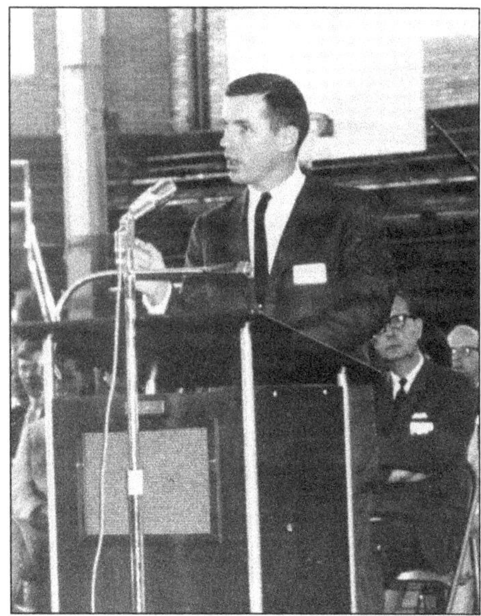

Michael Melvin speaks to Wendell Willkie High School students at their 1965 Career Day program. The annual event was an education, industry, and business project sponsored by the high school's guidance office. Melvin was president of Monticello Manufacturing Corporation, 2200 South J Street, which produced a wide assortment of items, including tools, household goods, and display frames. The company operated in Elwood from 1919 to 1966. (Courtesy Michael Melvin.)

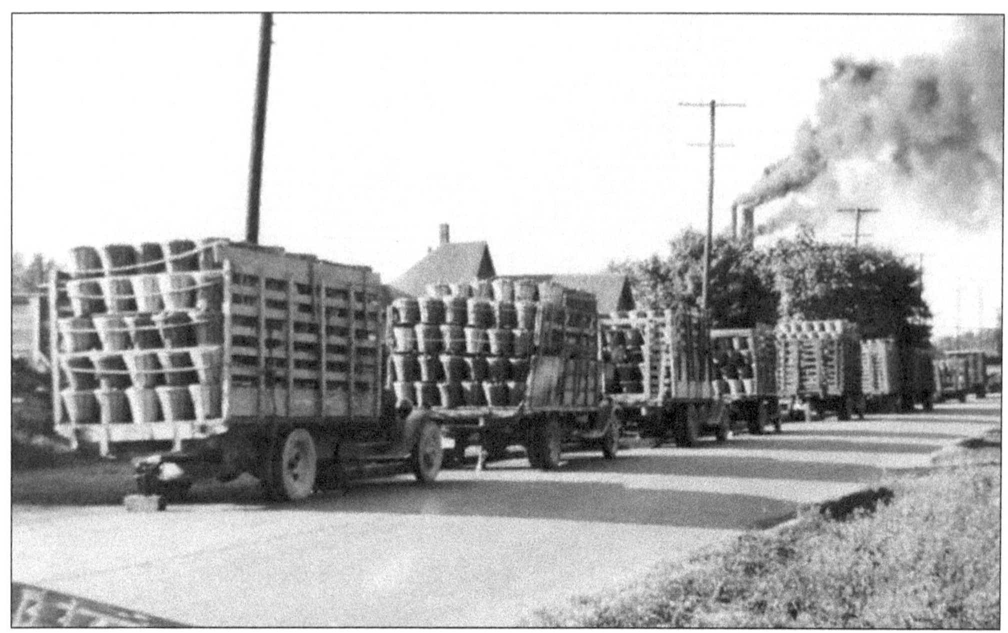

Trucks wait to unload at Frazier's, Elwood's first tomato canning plant, opened by O.B. Frazier in 1903. From the 1920s and 1940s, Indiana was the tomato capital of the world, and Elwood was the hub. At its peak, Frazier's was the area's largest operation, producing 500,000 cases of tomato products each season. The company closed its Elwood factory in the 1960s and relocated to Waverly, Louisiana. (Courtesy Elwood Public Library.)

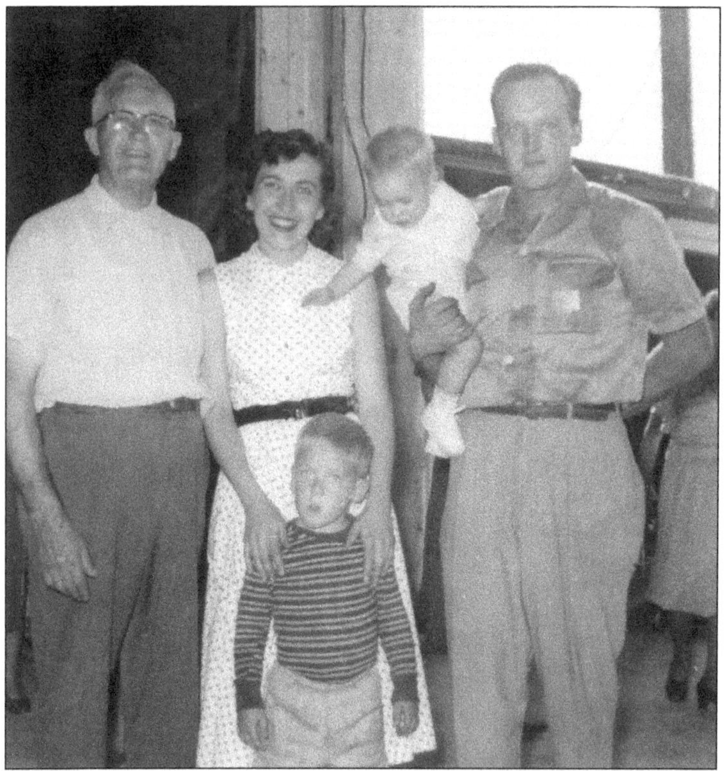

Grover Hutcherson (left), founder of an Orestes-based canning company that later became Red Gold, got his start at Frazier's. Here, he is shown with his daughter, Fran Reichert, her husband, Ernie, and their sons Brian (standing) and baby Gary. Hutcherson and his daughter purchased an abandoned cannery building in 1942, at the height of the war, and canned tomatoes for the troops, both stateside and abroad. (Courtesy Kathy Amos.)

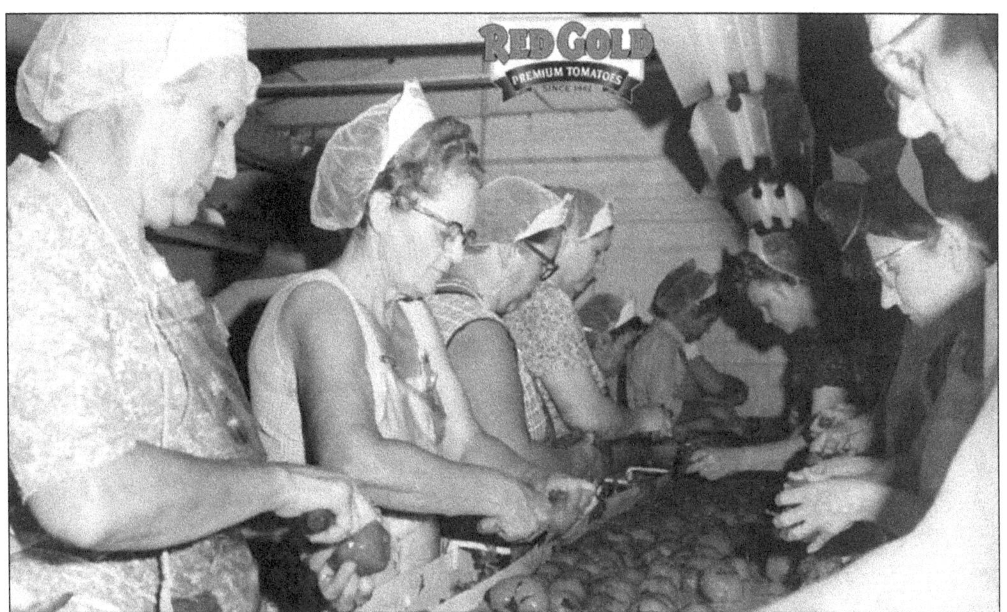

Red Gold workers, as shown in this 1959 photograph, demonstrate how more than 10,000 tons of tomatoes are processed for canning each season. Tomatoes are cored, peeled, washed, packed in cans, lidded, and cooked. Red Gold is the only tomato processing operation that remains in Indiana today. (Courtesy Red Gold.)

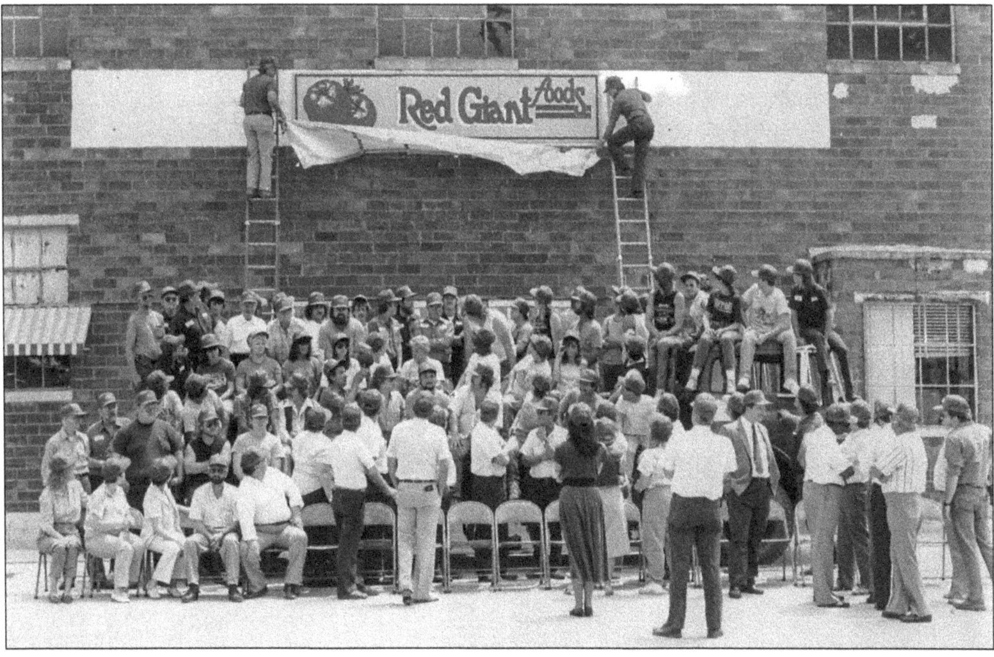

The Red Gold name was not used until the 1970s, when the brand was bought from another cannery. Brian Reichart became CEO in 1980, and Red Gold acquired Elwood-based Fettig Canning Company in 1981, making it possible for Red Gold to expand its production, increase its workforce, and make a greater contribution to Elwood's economy. Above, Red Gold employees replace Fettig's sign with their own. (Courtesy Red Gold.)

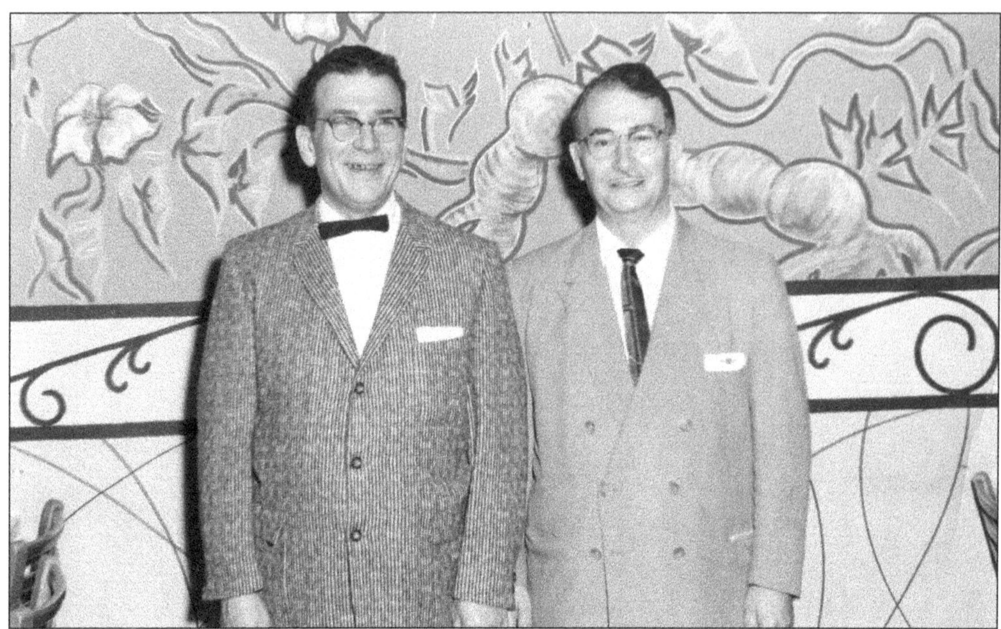

The Mangas brothers immigrated to America—Jack (right) in 1916, George (left) in 1922—joining relatives in Albany, Indiana. After their uncle taught them the candy and ice cream business, the brothers relocated to Elwood and, in 1928, opened their first enterprise, the Sweet Shop at 119 South Anderson Street. Its homemade candy, ice cream, and 25¢ fried chicken dinners made it an instant success. The shop moved across the street in 1933, where it expanded, providing a private room for meetings and "Bridge Room," with this caveat: "Only organizations of good repute will be allowed the convenience of the Bridge Room. As in the past, the Elwood Sweet Shop will not cater to rowdyism, and we want the people of Elwood to know they can come with their mothers, wives, sweethearts and children and fear no embarrassment." (Both, courtesy Theresa Mangas.)

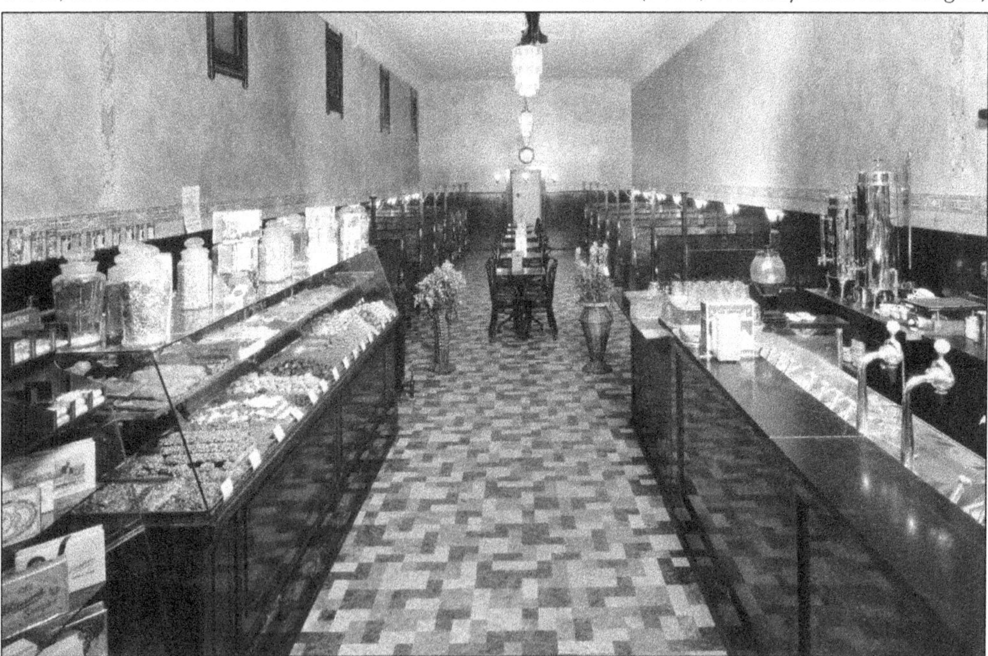

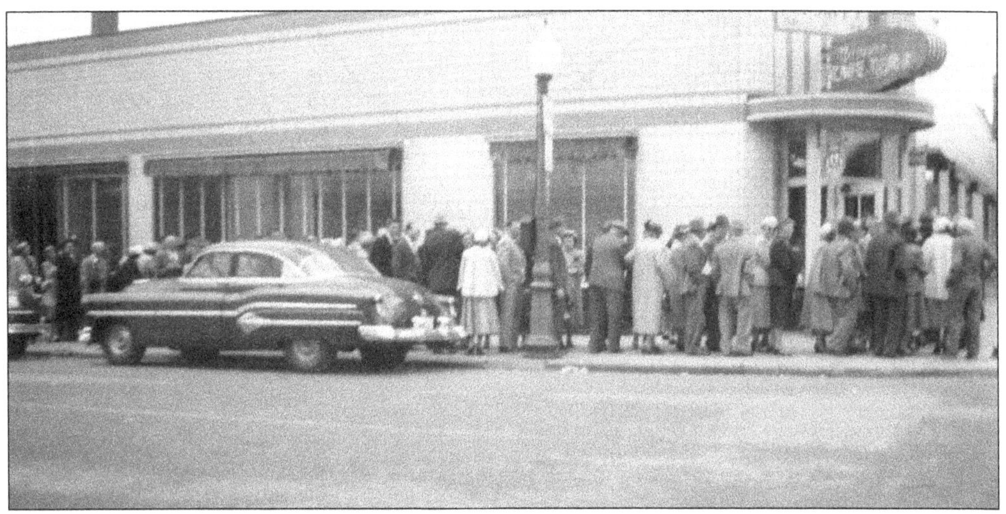

Jack and George Mangas opened Mangas Cafeteria in 1941 on the northwest corner of Anderson and Main Streets on the site of the former DeHority complex. Sundays and holidays were busiest, sometimes serving as many as 1,000 patrons, who would line up on the sidewalk to wait their turn. Elwood loved the cafeteria and the dignitaries it attracted. Over the years, Mangas Cafeteria welcomed the likes of Wendell Willkie, Robert Kennedy, Indiana governors, and Indy 500 driver Mario Andretti. The brothers sold the cafeteria in 1968 but bought it back four years later. In 1987, however, the families pulled out. The business changed hands several more times before Hook's Drug Store bought it and, in 1993, razed the building. Elwood mourned Jack's death in 1977 and George's in 2000. (Both, courtesy Theresa Mangas.)

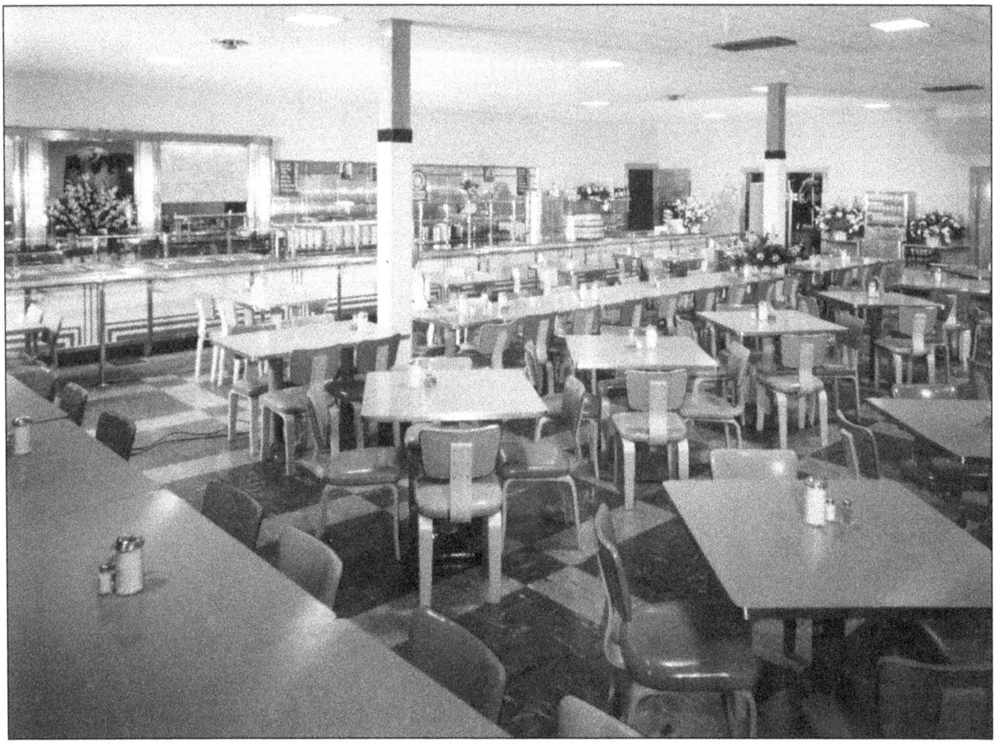

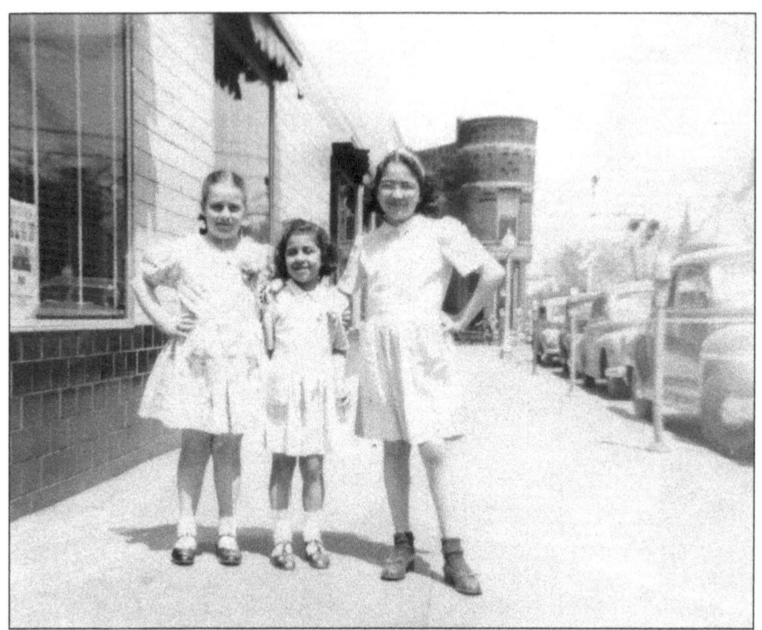

From left to right, Georgia Mangas, Martha Mangas, and Martha's big sister, Theresa, smile for their photographer on the east side of their parents' cafeteria on North Anderson Street. Growing up, all three girls helped out by working at the cafeteria. Today, Theresa still relishes the memories. (Courtesy Theresa Mangas.)

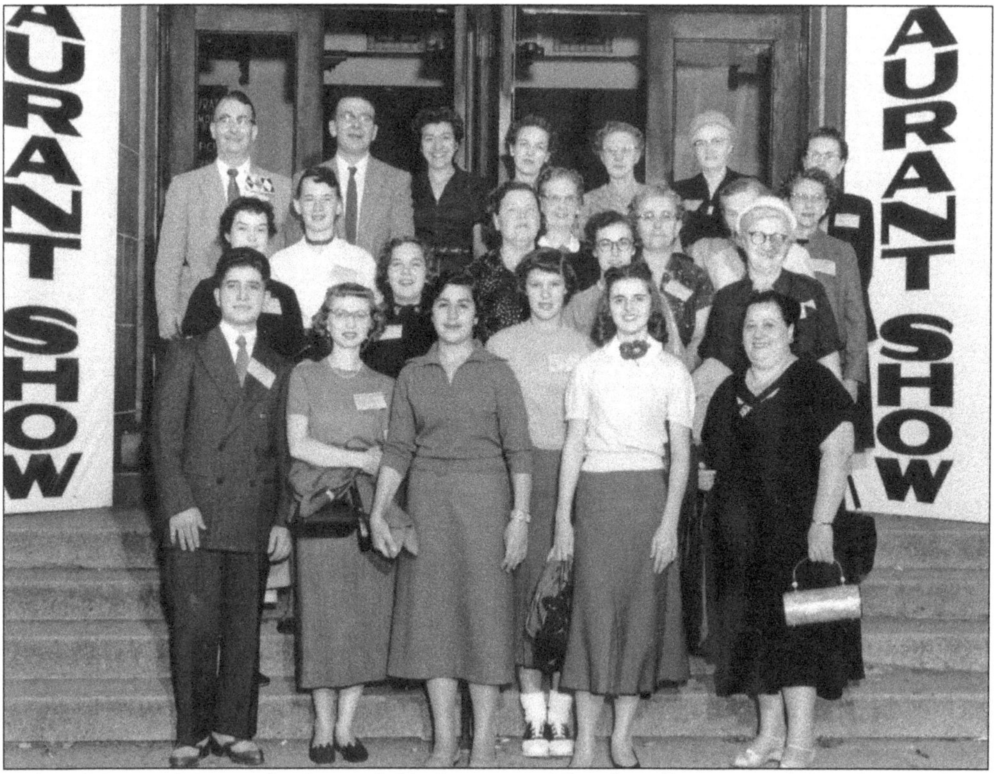

Jack and George Mangas (back row, left), their wives Theodora (first row, right) and Mary (back row, third from left), and several Mangas cafeteria employees posed for this photograph during the 1955 Indiana Restaurant Association Show at the Murat Temple in Indianapolis. The cafeteria was represented at the event many years. Jack served two terms on the association's board of directors. (Courtesy Theresa Mangas.)

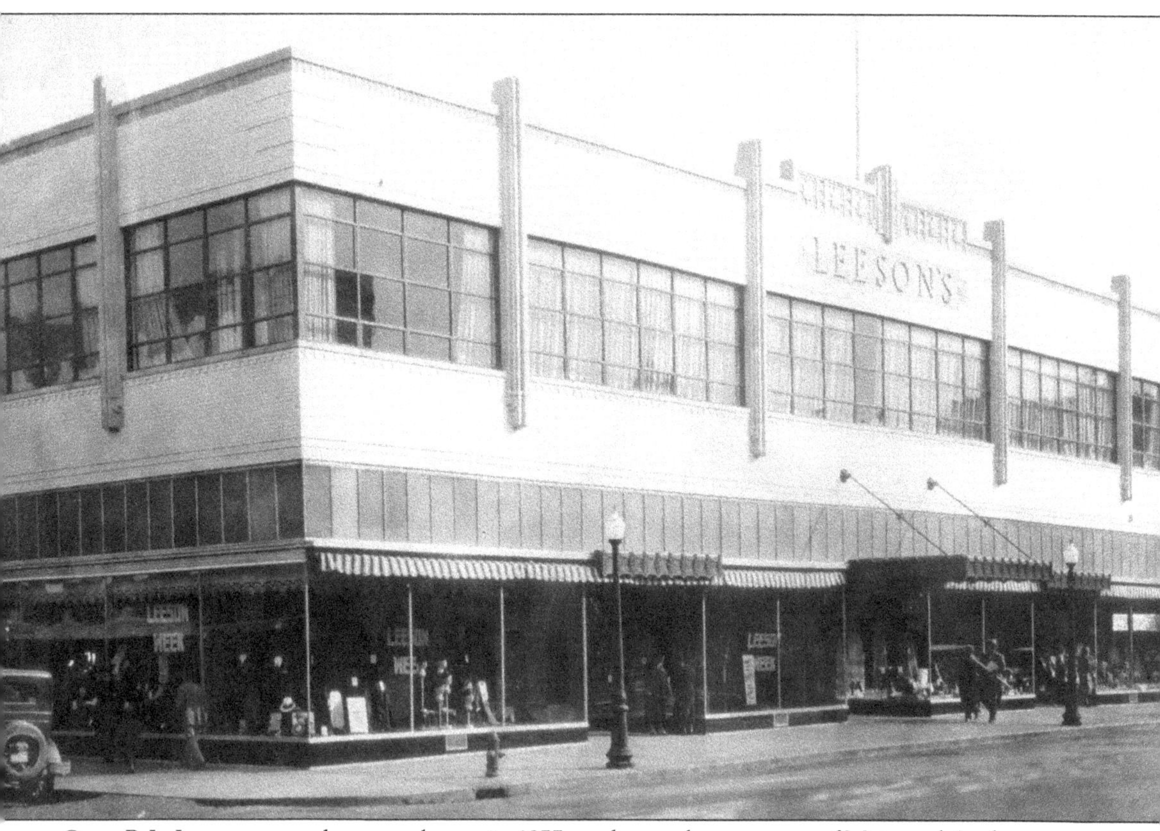

Capt. R.L. Leeson opened a general store in 1877 on the southeast corner of Main and Anderson Streets. The store was destroyed by fire a few years later, and Leeson relocated to 106 South Anderson Street. Steadily increasing business made expansion necessary, and Leeson erected a two-story building at Anderson and South A Streets. Leeson died in 1906, and his son, Wayne, took over, assisted by his sons, King and Lawrence. The store thrived, but on January 2, 1934, the city awoke to screaming sirens and raging flames. Leeson's was on fire again. As a bewildered Wayne eyed the smoldering ashes, a friend encouraged him to rebuild from the foundation to the roof and make it the kind of store he had always dreamed of. Wayne agreed. When he reopened, Leeson's was a modern, full-service department store, second to none in Indiana. Wayne's grandson David managed the family business after his father, King, died in 1970. Operating for 115 years, Leeson's shuttered for good in 1984. It was a sad day for Elwood.

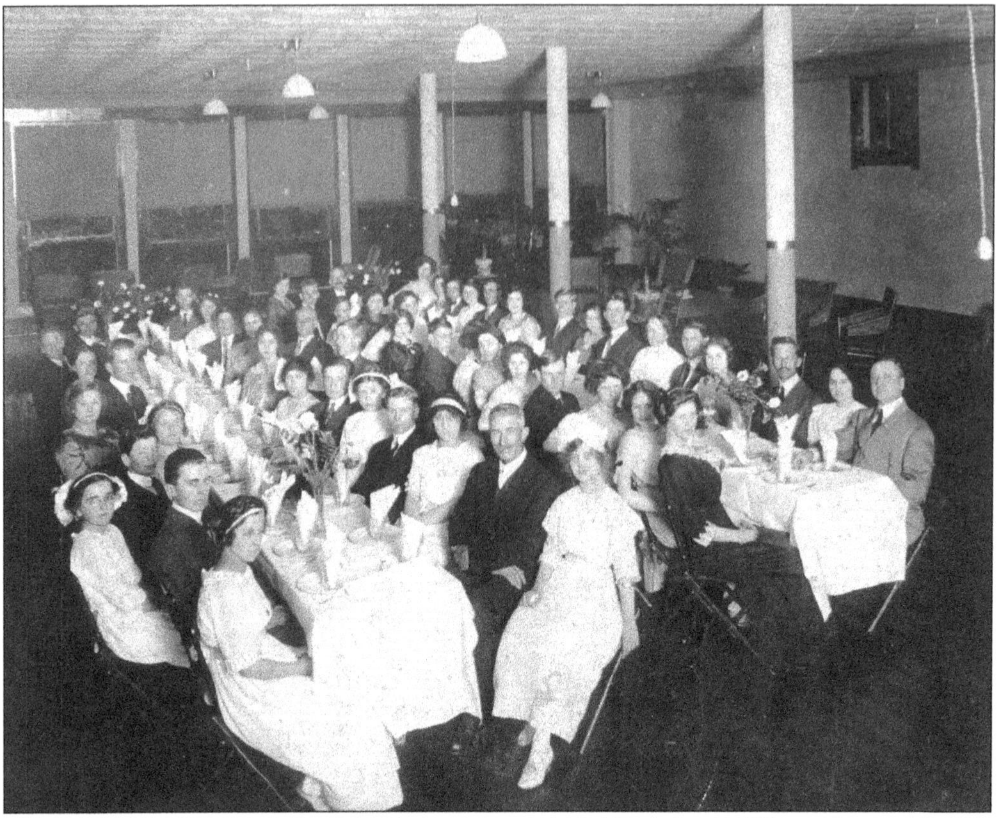

Chas. F. Wiley Department Store employees pose at their 1911 banquet. Wiley occupies the first chair on the far right. Wiley's was the second-largest department store in Elwood. The three-story brick building occupied the southwest corner of Main and Anderson Streets, known as the Callaway Block. Bennah Callaway and his sons, William and Henry, built the store in 1872 for their dry goods business. B.F. Wiley later acquired the site for a department store, which he turned over to his son William T. in 1896. William operated the store under the name W.T. Wiley & Co. for 10 years. In 1906, he sold the business to his brother Charles, who changed the name to Chas. F. Wiley Co. Department Store. Wiley's closed in the early 1920s. (Above, courtesy Elwood Heritage Center; below, courtesy Eric Grogan.)

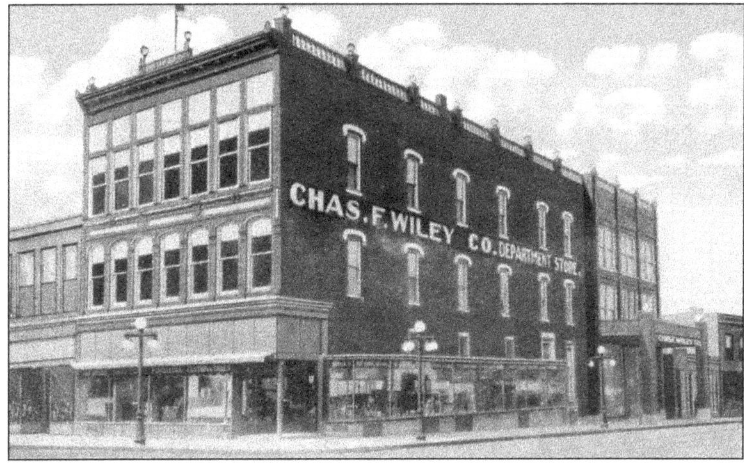

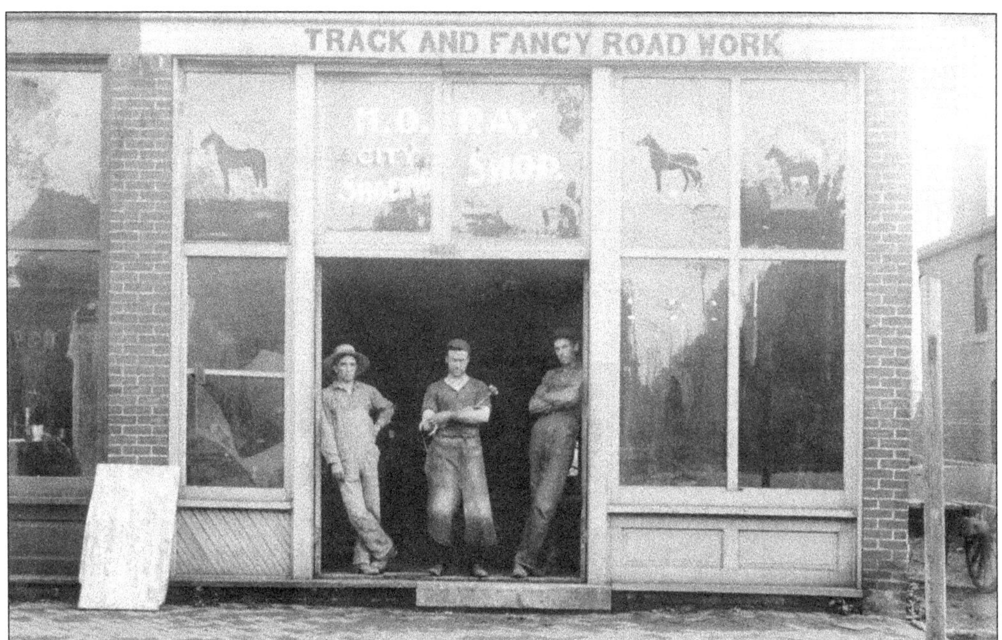

Herschel "H.O." Ray's City Shoeing Shop was located at 1441 South A Street. Ray, pictured in the center, offered general blacksmithing, shoeing, and repairs of any kind. Born in the Elwood area in 1886, Ray opened the shop in 1910 with his father, Jacob. It closed three years later, when Ray and his wife, Margaret, relocated to Michigan. (Courtesy Eric Grogan.)

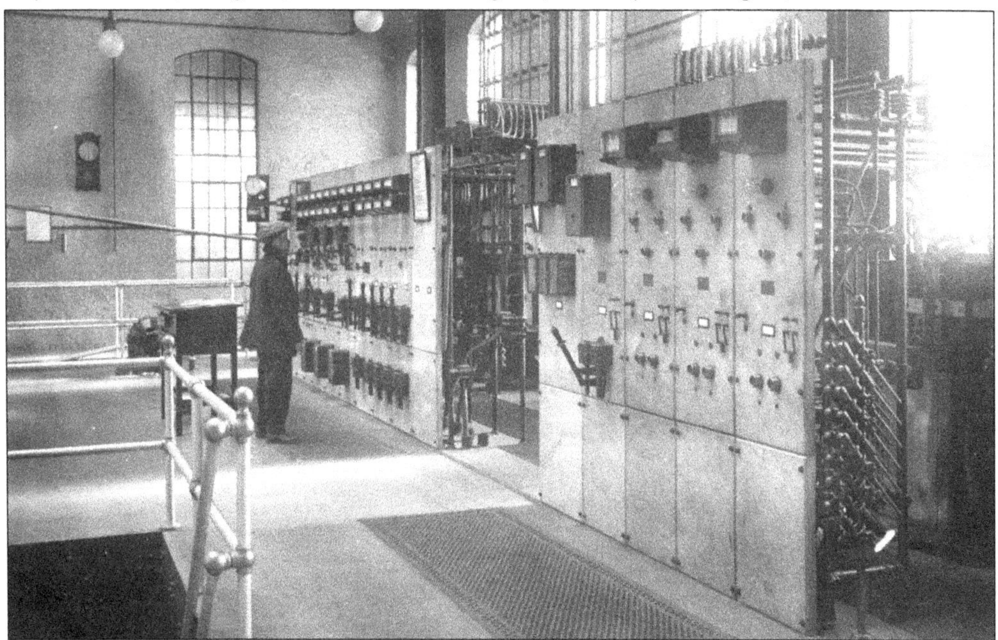

The Elwood Electric Light Company's first plant was located on the northeast corner of Sixteenth and North A Streets. After a boiler exploded in 1894, the plant was moved to Fourteenth and North A Streets. In 1911, the company was sold to American Gas & Electric, forerunner to today's Indiana Michigan Power Company. Dr. Daniel Sigler owned the first Elwood residence with electric lights.

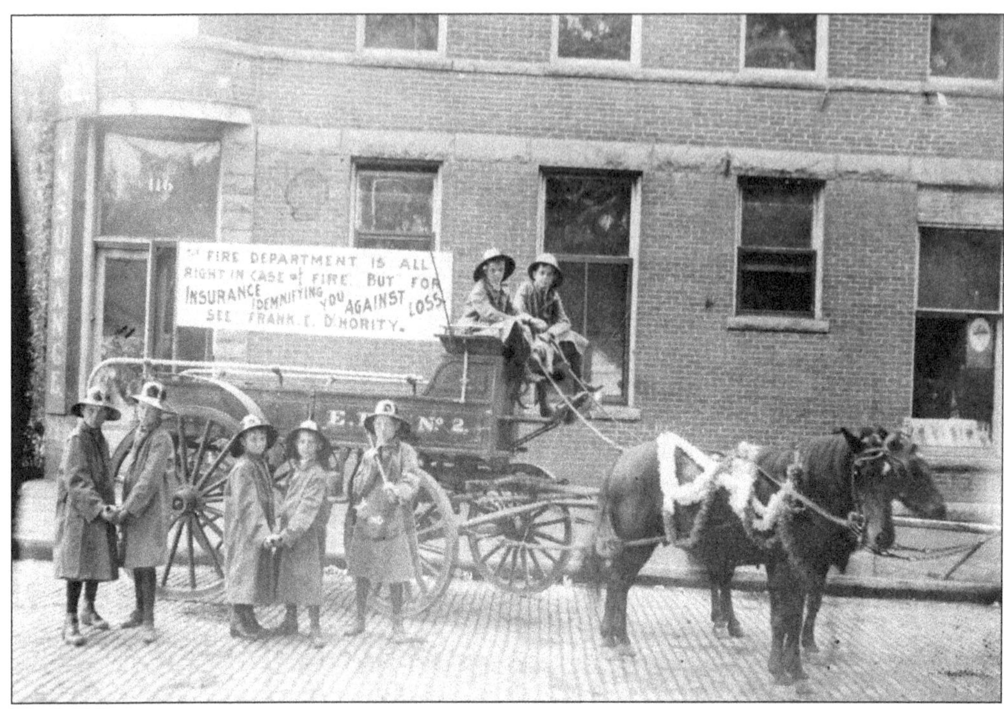

The above undated photograph was a promotional tool for the Frank E. DeHority Insurance Company. DeHority opened the firm on June 11, 1900, in a flat-iron building at 116 North Anderson Street, across from the current post office. When he opened his agency, it was the fifth insurance business in Elwood. After DeHority's son, Robert, joined the firm in 1931, he changed the firm's name to Frank E. DeHority and Son. Frank died suddenly in 1942 at age 67, and Robert carried on until his retirement in 1973. The photograph below, dated 1909, shows an unidentified woman standing in the doorway of the DeHority building. The sign in the window reads, "Fire, Lightning, Tornado, Boiler Accident & Liability Insurance." (Above, courtesy Sue Loser.)

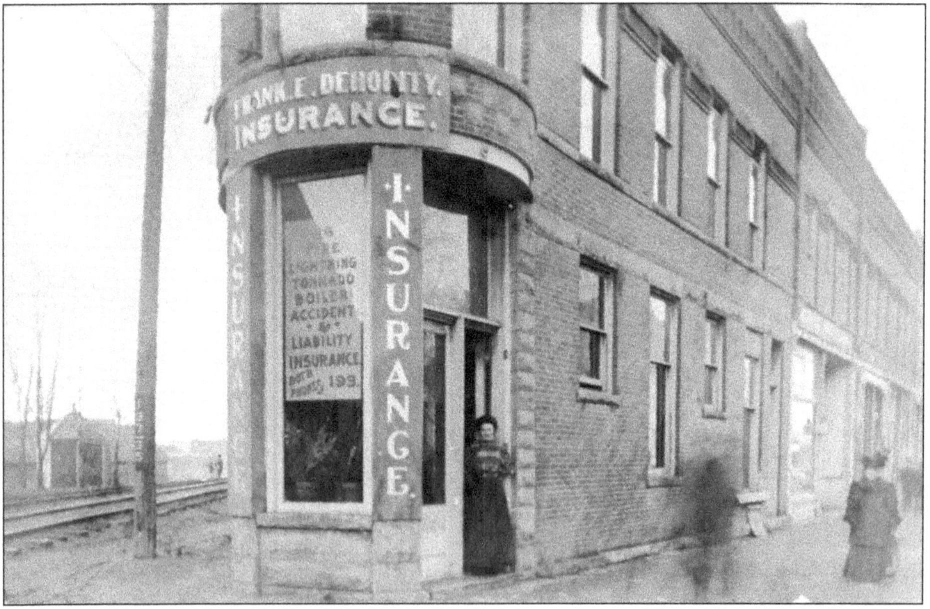

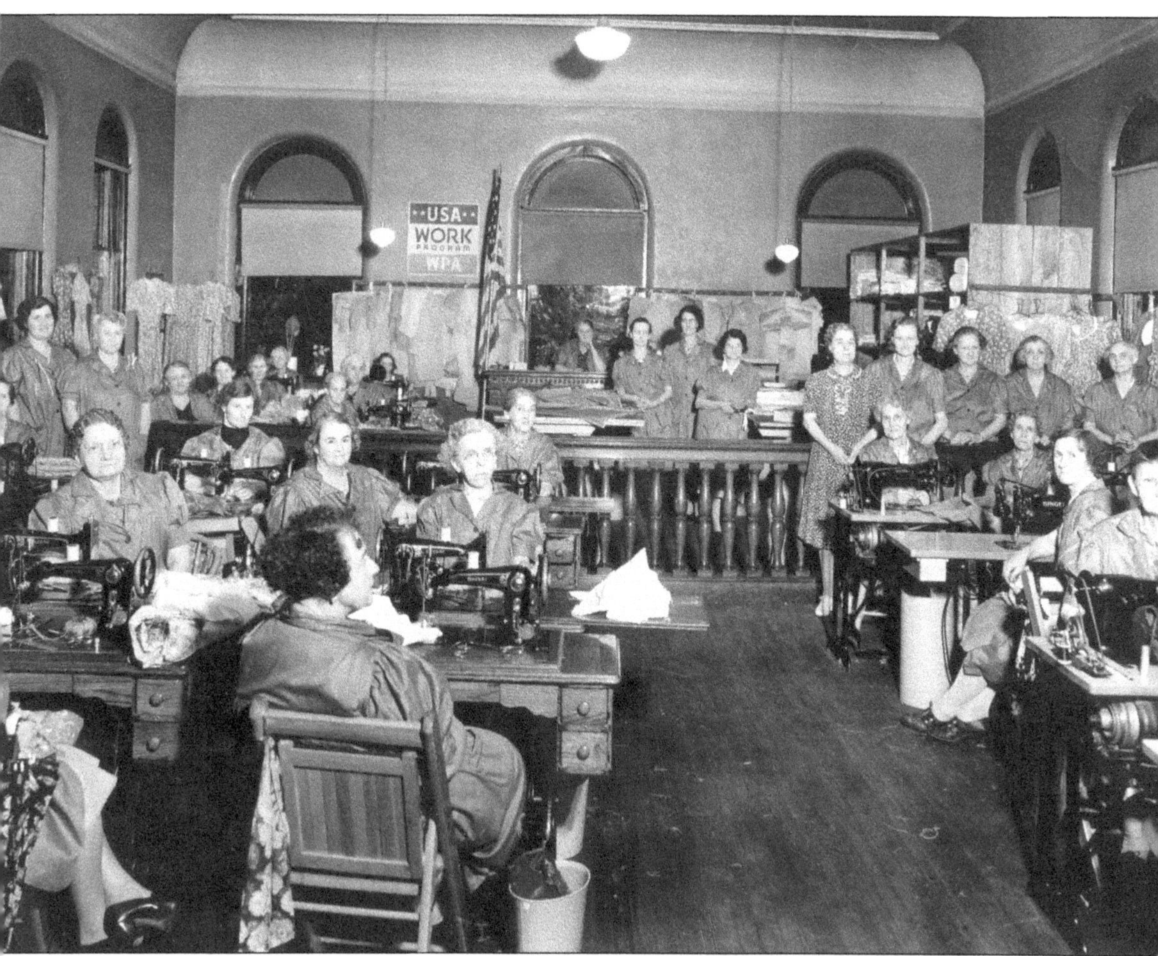

During the declining years of the Great Depression, the city operated a garment factory as a program of the Works Progress Administration (WPA). A sewing room, housed in the second-floor conference room of the city building, employed more than 40 women who made garments for the poor. Under the direction of supervisor Nora Carpenter, the women worked as cutters, seamstresses, and finishers to make clothing for infants, children, and men and women of all sizes. The hall was turned into a factory-like workroom, complete with sewing machines, tools, supplies, hundreds of patterns, bolts of fabrics, and spools of thread. The township trustee, Sam Welborne, whose office was up the hall from the sewing room, distributed the clothing to persons in need throughout the city. (Courtesy Elwood Heritage Center.)

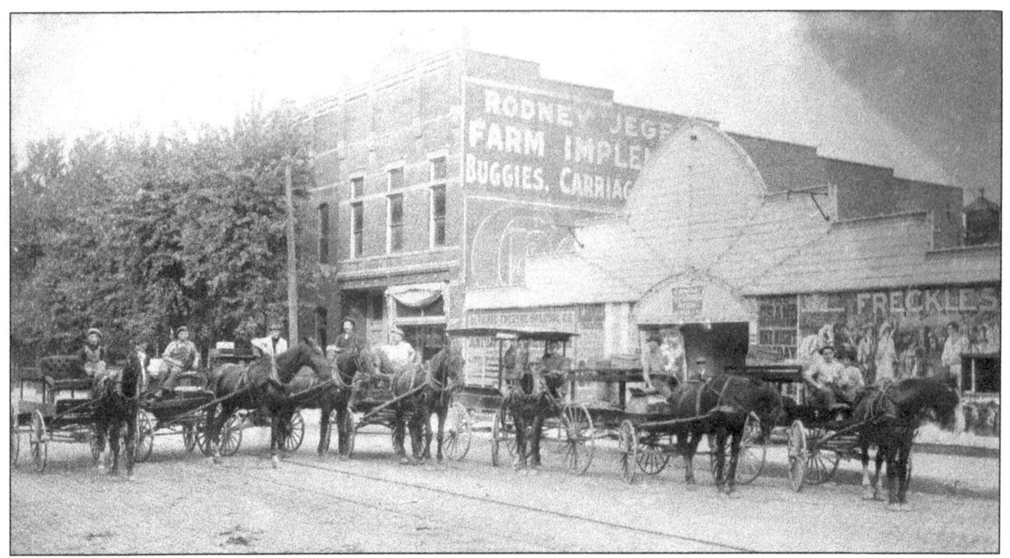

Drivers for John Keifer's Union Delivery Service line up October 8, 1914, at 321 South Anderson Street beside Keifer's Airdrome open-air theater, which he had converted into stables for the business. Keifer, who is shown standing in the entrance, delivered merchandise to customers of local retailers. The business closed in 1919. Keifer, however, remained a high profile Elwood businessman until his death in 1972. (Courtesy Mike and Sherry Pace.)

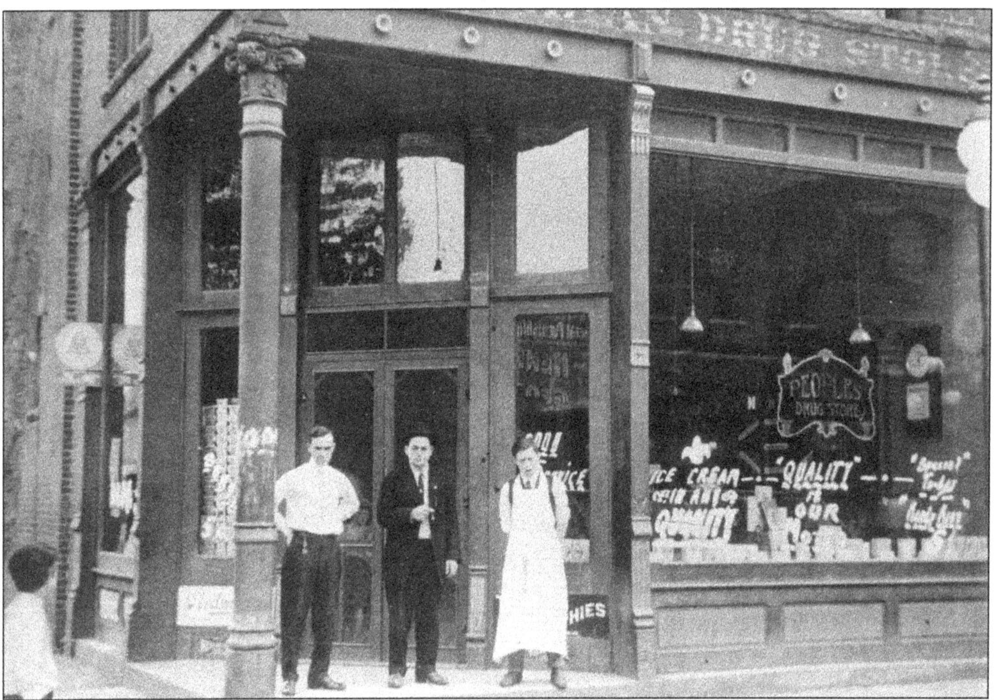

William G. Evans, left, purchased Peoples Drug Store at 16th and Main Streets in 1912 and operated it as Evans Drug Store until retiring in 1937. Besides selling typical pharmacy merchandise, Evans was an avid supporter of community activities and was elected to the Elwood City Council in 1948. He died in 1950. The man on the right is Bill Thumma. The other man is unidentified. (Couresy Elwood Public Library.)

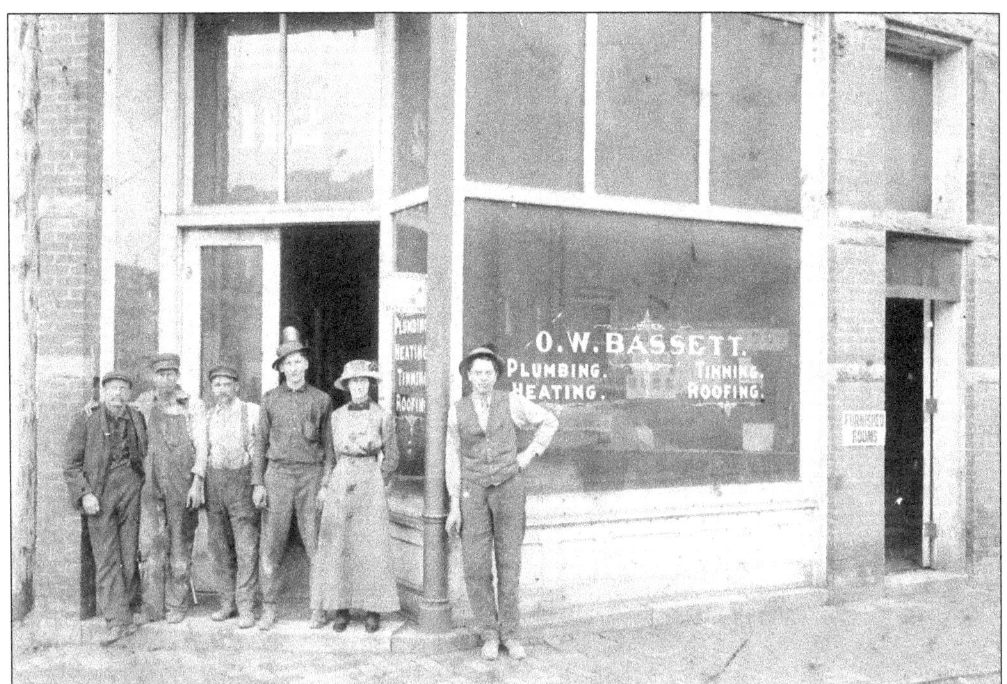

Stoner & Bassett—specializing in plumbing, heating, tinning, and roofing—opened in 1905 at 12 Chamness Avenue. When Stoner retired, O.W. Bassett moved the shop to 112 North Anderson Street, the former site of the Old Queen Saloon. Pictured from left to right are Grant Davis, unidentified, George Haines, Herman Pace, Garnet Pace, and Bassett. (Courtesy Mike and Sherry Pace.)

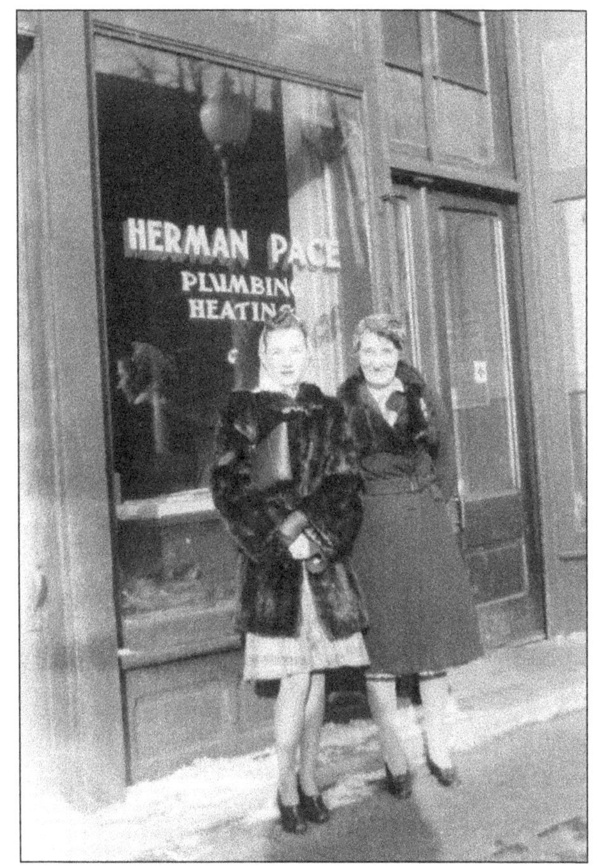

O.W. Bassett sold his business to George Haines in 1916. Haines joined the Navy in 1917 and sold the shop to Lee Stokes. In 1919, Herman Pace took it over and merged it with his own flourishing business at 315 South Anderson Street. When Pace retired in 1961, his son, Leroy, carried on. Shown here are Herman's daughter, Rosenell, and wife, Garnet, around 1943. (Courtesy Mike and Sherry Pace.)

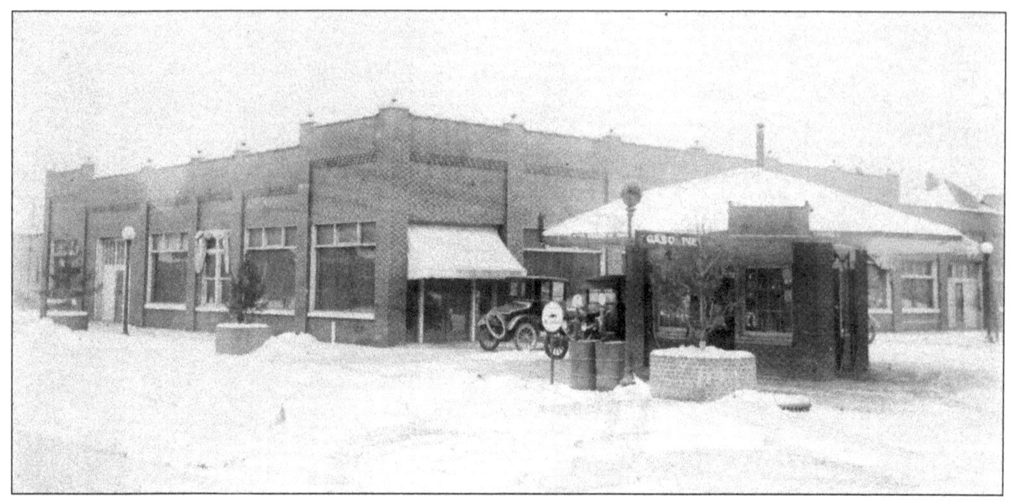

Firm Grinnell opened the little Mobile Oil service station in front of W.L. Abbot's Ford dealership, later B&O Motor Sales, in 1929. Children loved Grinnell's candy, sodas, and comic books, and regularly dropped by to stock up on their way home from school. After Grinnell's station was torn down in 1952, he maintained his contact with Elwood's kids and opened a toy store. (Courtesy Jed Brown and Sue Brewer.)

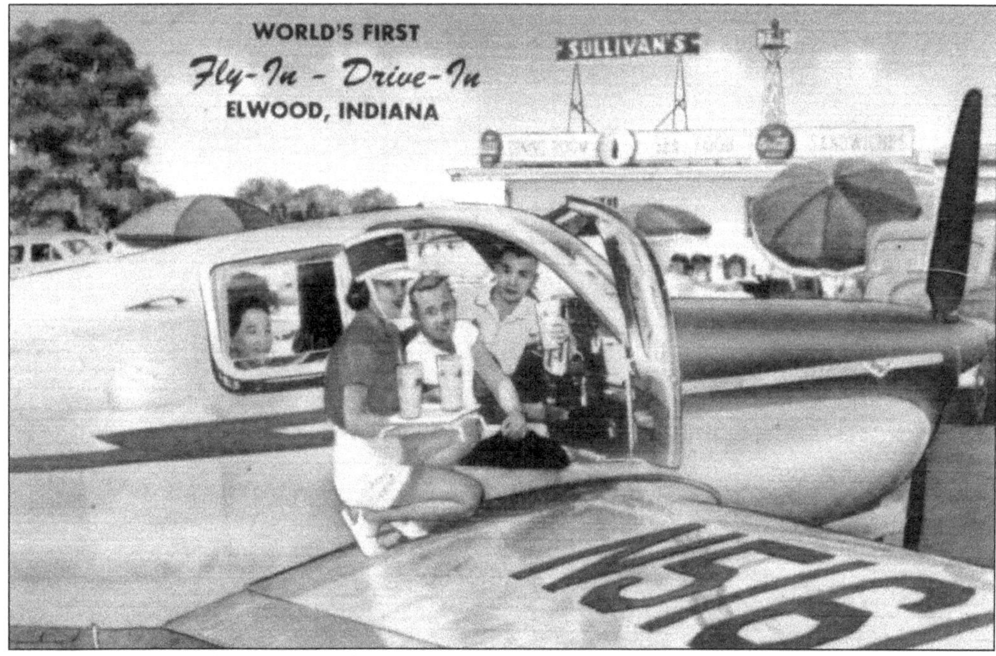

Sullivan's, the world's first fly-in drive-in restaurant, spread its wings in July 1955 at the Elwood Airport on State Road 37. On opening day, more than 50 pilots dropped in for a burger served by a friendly "plane hop." The restaurant was originally owned by Charlie and Ruth Sullivan and, over the years, remained a popular dining establishment for Elwood residents and area pilots. (Courtesy Ann Brewer.)

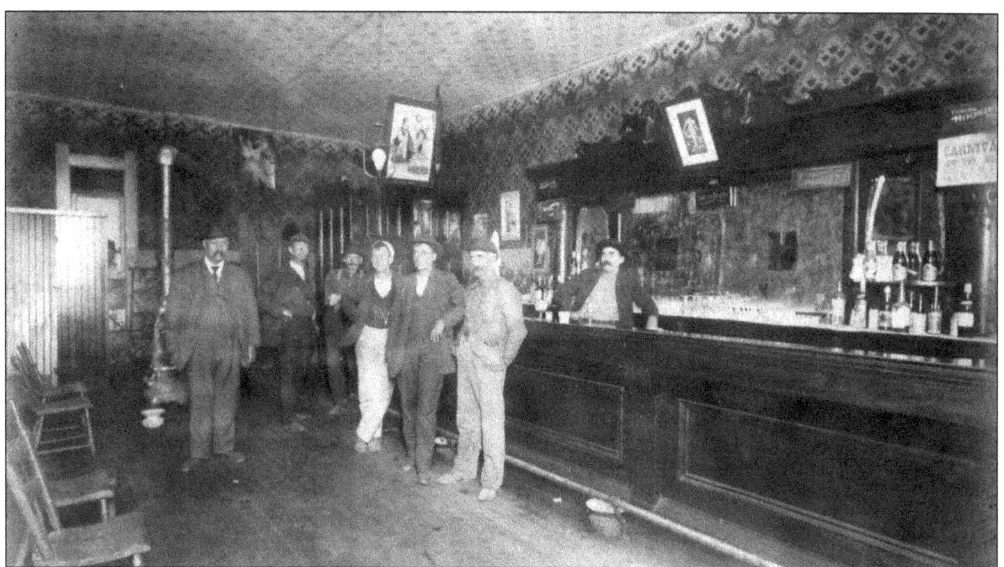

German immigrant Frederick Wolff arrived in Elwood in 1887 and opened a saloon on Main Street. In 1907, he moved it to 1449 South A Street, where it flourished for the next 102 years. Famous for its roast beef platters, Wolff's Tavern was an Elwood icon for decades. Although none of the men pictured could be positively identified, the gentleman on the left is likely Frederick Wolff. (Courtesy Ron Hinshaw.)

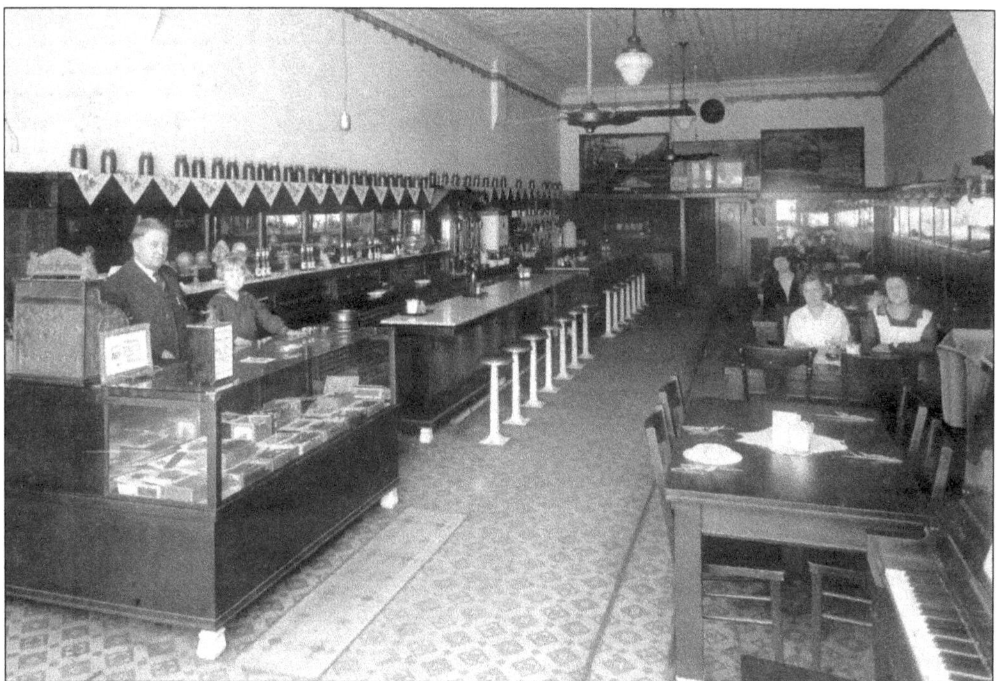

Joseph Lewton (left) poses with his young daughter, Wavian, behind the cash register at his Maine Restaurant, on 1517 East Main Street, around 1920. Lewton came to Elwood from Adams County around 1904 and was a restaurateur for the rest of his life. He died in 1924 at the age of 53. According to his obituary, nearly everyone in Elwood knew and liked him. (Courtesy the *Elwood Call-Leader*.)

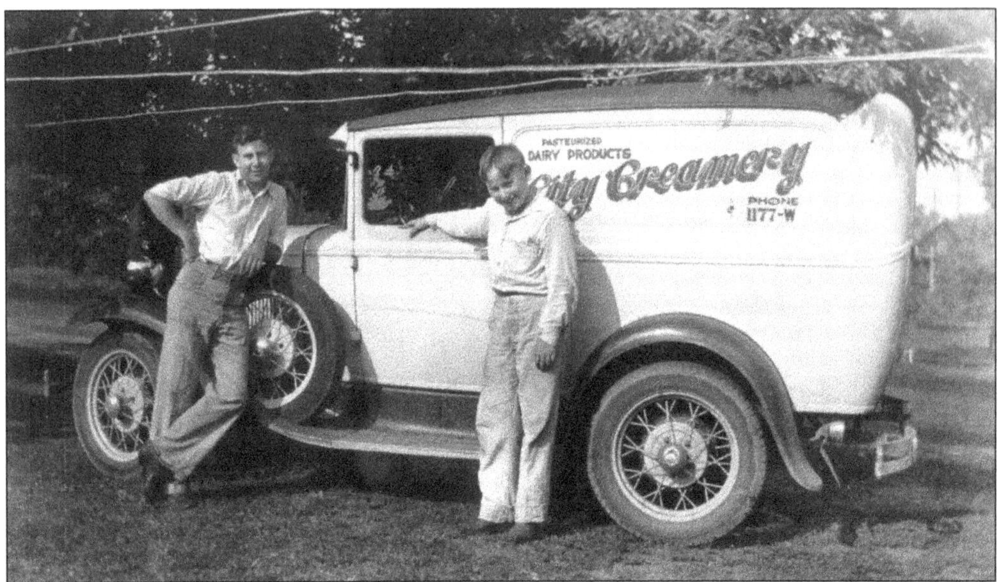

Don and Dick Orbaugh pose with City Creamery's 1929 Model A Ford delivery truck. Brothers Clyde and Paul Summers started the business in 1915 at 500 North 18th Street. At their busiest, they produced 30,000 gallons of pasteurized milk and 2,000 gallons of ice cream per month. City Creamery was purchased in 1985 by Sudy and Melissa Beeman, who renamed it Sudy's Creamery. (Courtesy Ann Brewer.)

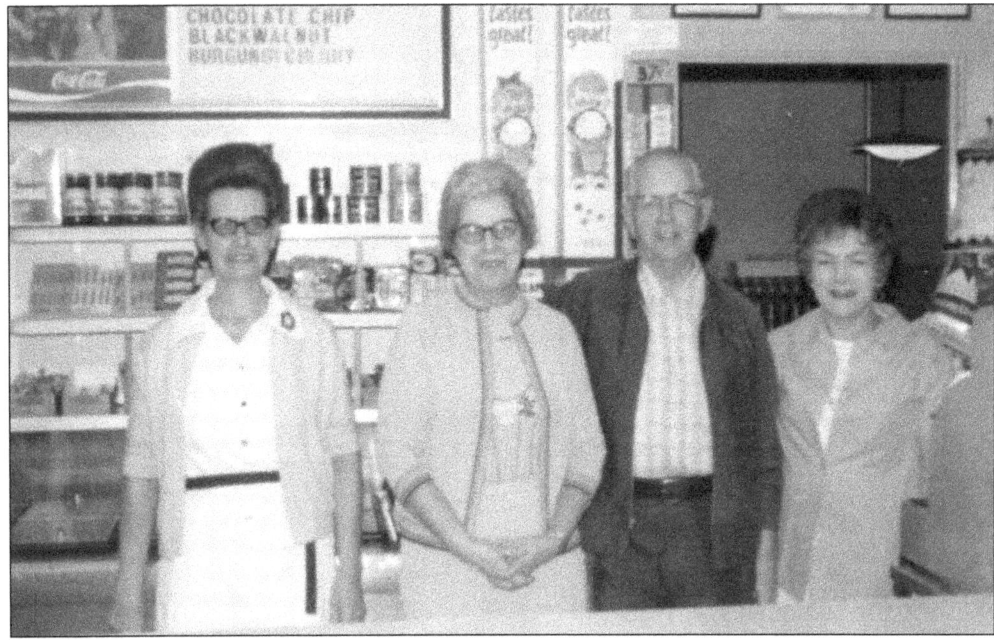

Pictured here from left to right are Lillian Towner, Marie Major, City Creamery owner Paul Summers, and Florence Havens. Summers's co-owner, his brother Clyde, died in 1958. Summers continued to operate the popular dairy until 1985, when he sold it to Sudy and Melissa Beeman and retired. Summers remained in Elwood until his death in 1998. (Courtesy John Carpenter.)

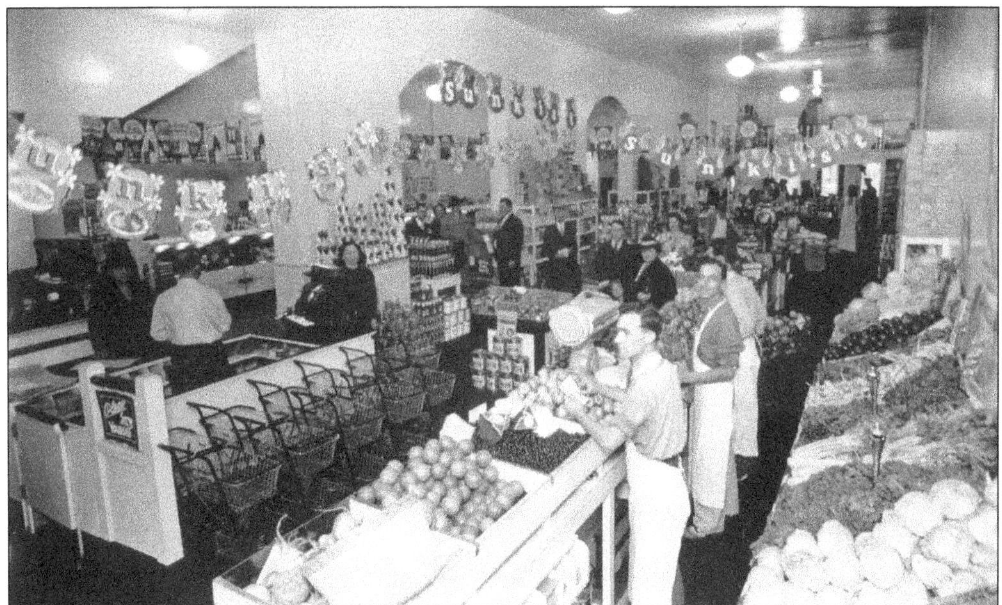

John Creagmile opened a grocery store in 1902 at 120-122 North Anderson Street known for its farm-fresh beef and pork. When Creagmile died in 1933, his innovative son Leo relocated to a larger site at 1518 Main Street and established Indiana's first self-serve supermarket. Although it flourished, Leo sold out in 1956 to a liquidator and bought the Golden Gardens building, where he opened an antique store. (Courtesy John Carpenter.)

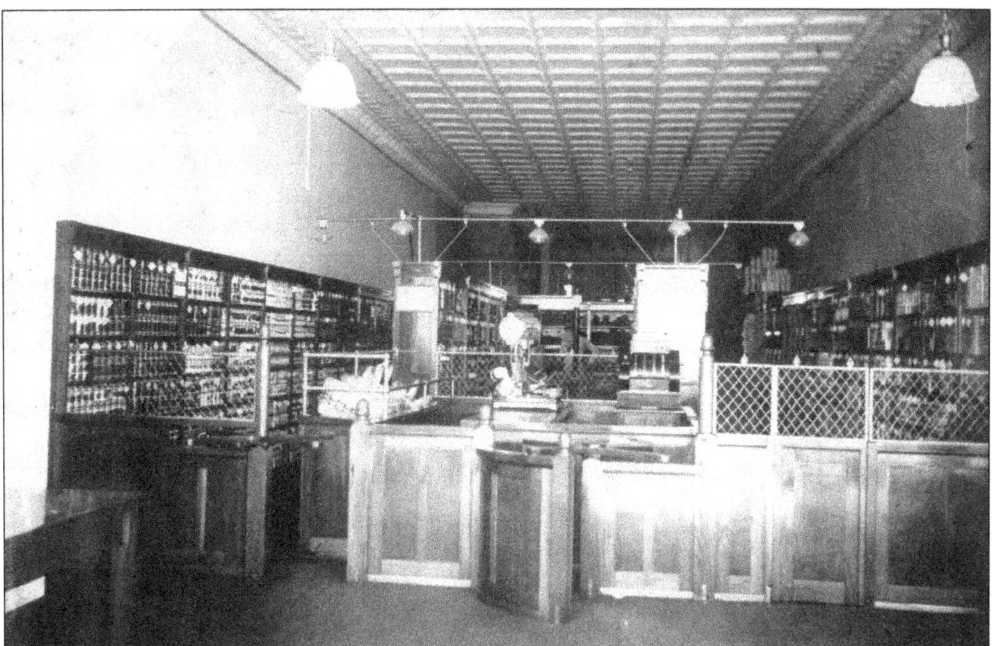

Piggly Wiggly Store No. 9 opened at 208 South Anderson Street on March 27, 1918. For days leading up to the grand opening, the company ran little ads stating only "Piggly Wiggly?" igniting curiosity and causing readers to think a new movie was coming. Piggly Wiggly was a new kind of store, ahead of its time, that introduced a self-serve, lower-priced, cash-and-carry business model.

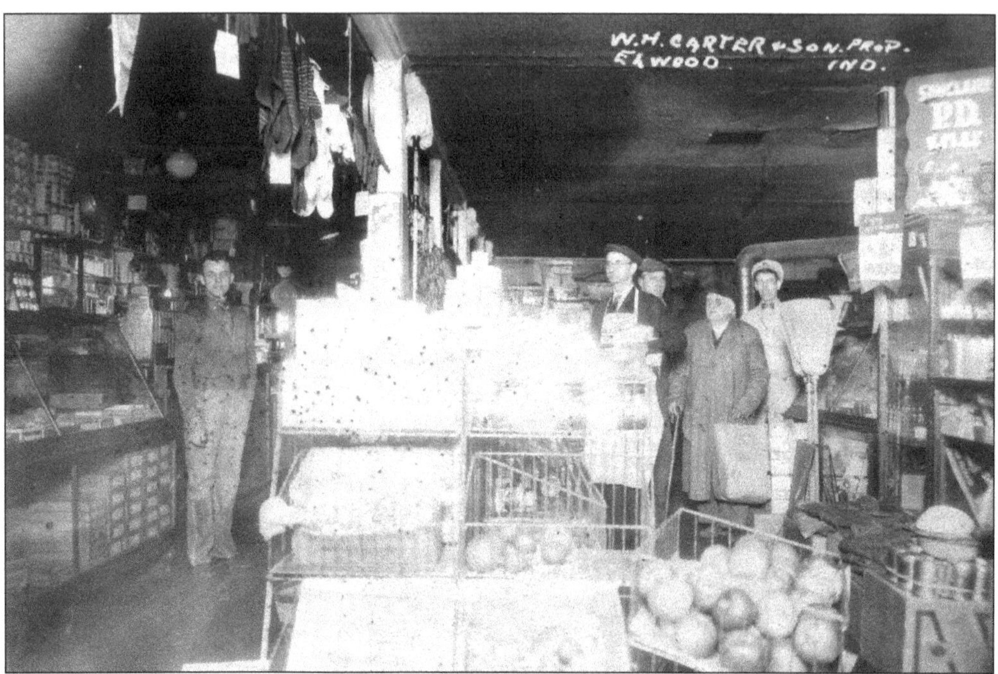

William H. Carter (left) came to Elwood from Fairmount in 1891. In 1909, he opened a store at 1411 South I Street, selling groceries and general merchandise. He sold his store in 1946 to longtime employee Harry Austin, who renamed it Austin & Son Groceries and worked many years with his son, Danny. Harry's grandson Tom became Elwood Community School Corporation superintendent, serving 1994 to 2010. (Courtesy Elwood Heritage Center.)

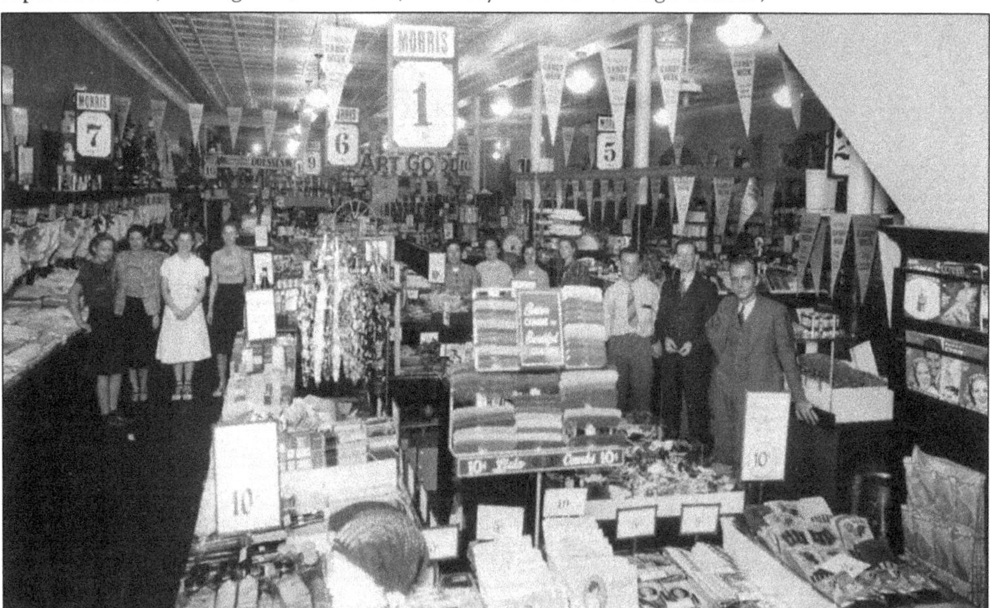

Employees of Morris 5 & 10 pose during its October 1939 Candy Week promotion. Elwood's Morris 5 & 10, one of 62 stores in the Morris chain, opened on South Anderson Street around 1905 and remained an integral part of the city's downtown business for decades. In 1951, G.C. Murphy purchased the chain, and the store was renamed Murphy's 5 & 10.

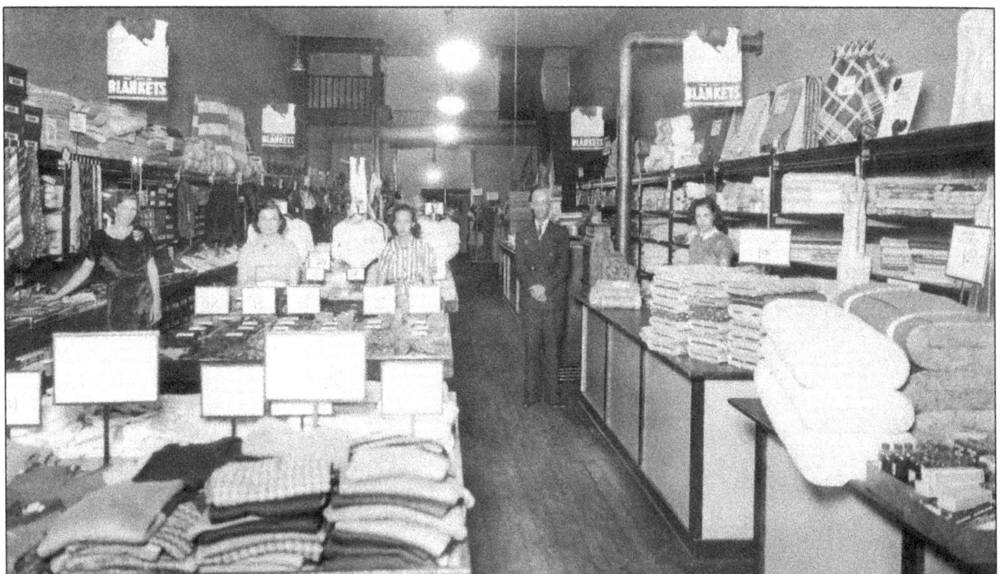

Raymond C. McDaniel Dry Goods and Clothing store opened in August 1935 at 222 South Anderson Street. Four years later, the store relocated to 114 South Anderson Street, where it remained until McDaniel retired in 1967 and closed. Shown in this 1939 photograph, from left to right, are Vonna Wire, Fanny Fernun, Raymond's daughter Ruth, Raymond McDaniel, and his daughter Kathy. Raymond died in 1987 at age 91. (Courtesy Ron Hinshaw.)

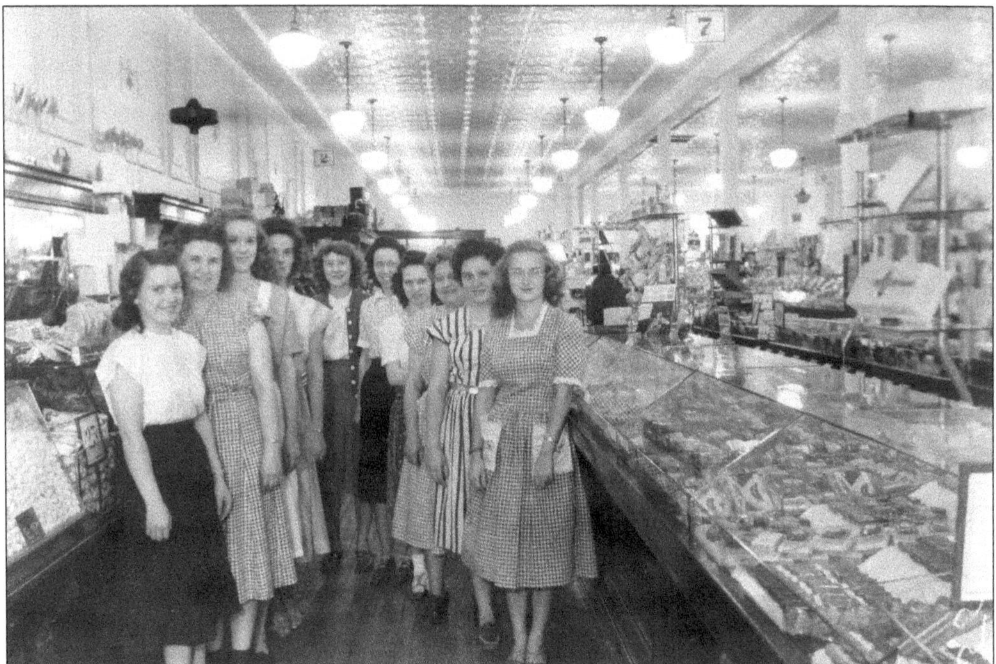

The sales staff at F.W. Woolworth's, located at 208 South Anderson Street, pose for this 1942 photograph. The store opened June 10, 1922, when, as the *Call-Leader* reported, "The store was literally jammed at all times and visitors gave hearty approval." Woolworth's closed its doors for the last time on December 31, 1965. Seventh from left is Mary Call. (Courtesy Steve, Pam, and Mary Savage.)

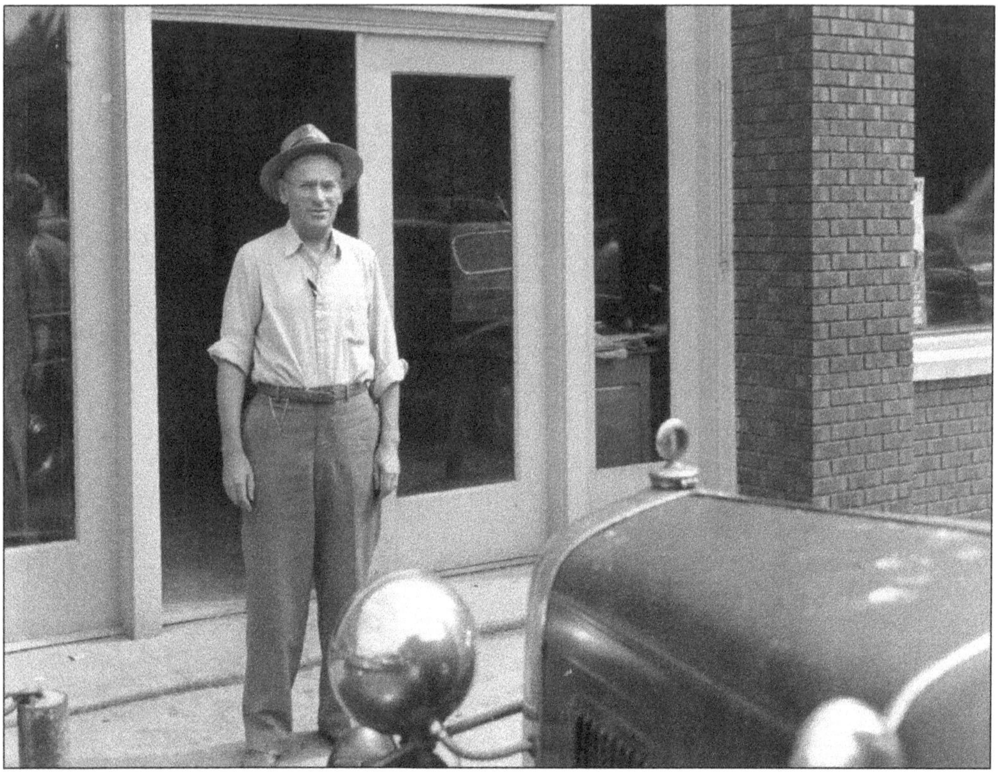

Gail Orbaugh stands outside B&O Motor Sales at the corner of North Anderson and North B Streets. Orbaugh bought the Ford dealership with Lloyd Burkhart in 1934. But after Burkhart was killed two years later, Orbaugh kept the "B" in the name as a tribute to his friend. A lifelong Elwood resident, Orbaugh died in 1966. He was 73. (Courtesy Ann Brewer.)

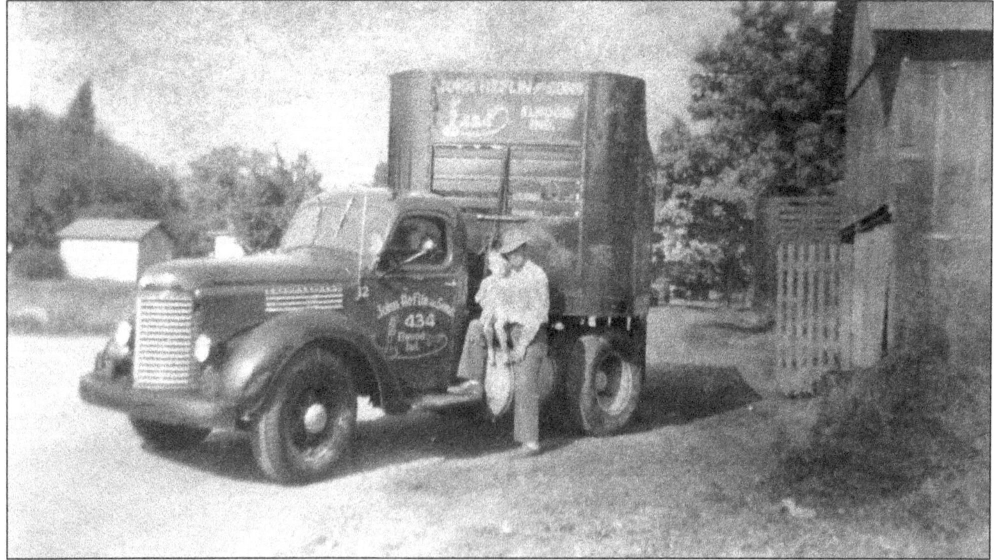

John Heflin poses with his son Chuck around 1950. Heflin ran a sand, crushed stone, and gravel business at the time of this photograph. He was born in 1906 in Tipton and died in 1991 in Elwood, where he lived the last 60 years of his life. (Courtesy David and Linda Heflin.)

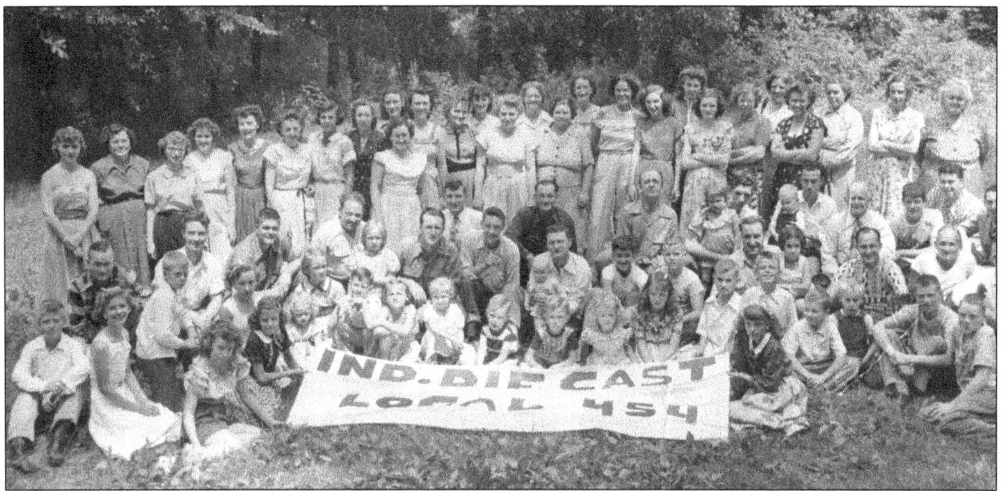

Employees and families of Elwood's Indiana Die Cast gather at their annual picnic on July 23, 1950, at the park in Noblesville. The company opened on South J Street in early 1948, employing 300 workers at the height of its operation. In 1954, however, after it was unable to agree on a new union contract, it closed. The building was taken over by Ex-Cell-O Corporation in 1955. (Courtesy *Elwood Call-Leader*.)

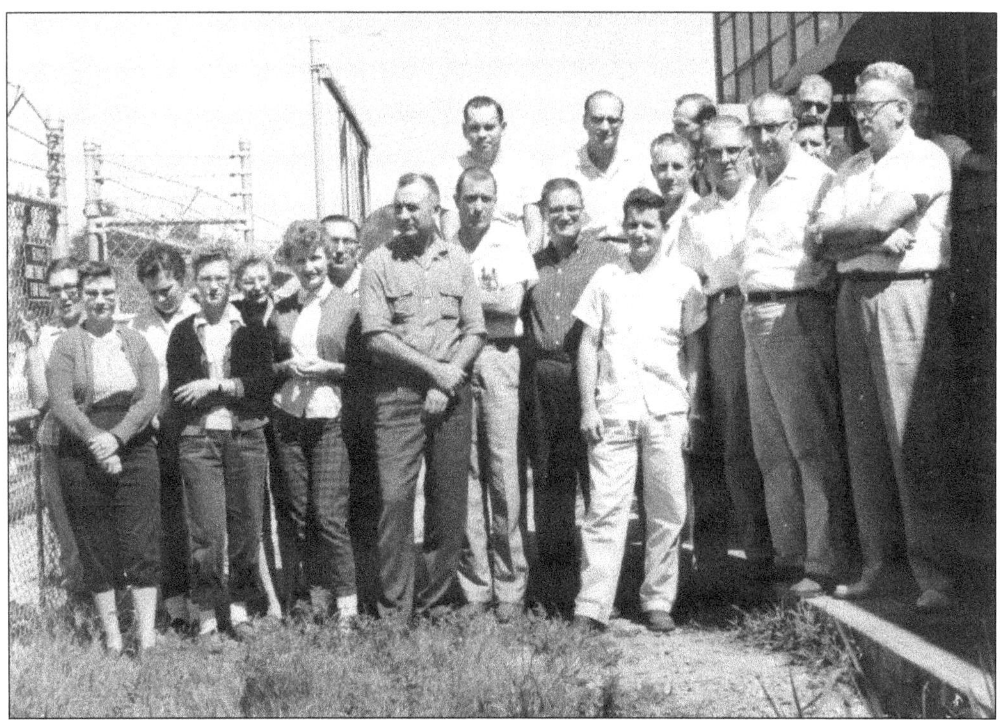

Ex-Cell-O employees pose outside the Elwood plant around 1960. Identified are Marilyn Beeman, third from left; Robert Miller, ninth from left; and David Jones, eleventh from left. Operations began in 1956 at the former Indiana Die Cast plant on South J Street manufacturing compressor blades for jet engines and later missile components. In 1987, Ex-Cell-O was renamed Airfoil Textron and closed in 1991, dislocating some 300 workers. (Courtesy Marjorie Pierce.)

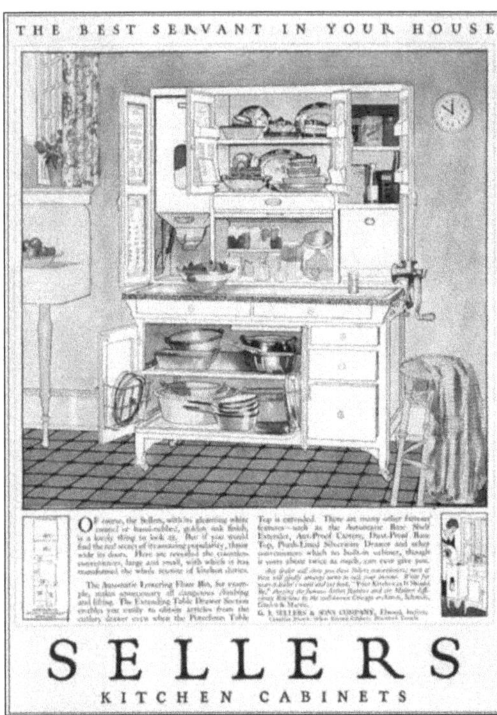

G.I. Sellers Company of Elwood manufactured kitchen cabinets from 1905 through 1950. Alfred Sellers was already a successful, Kokomo-based cabinetmaker when he purchased a furniture factory in Elwood and relocated there in 1905. He renamed the business after one of his sons, and utilizing high-quality production practices and innovative marketing, he grew the business into one of Indiana's largest and best known.

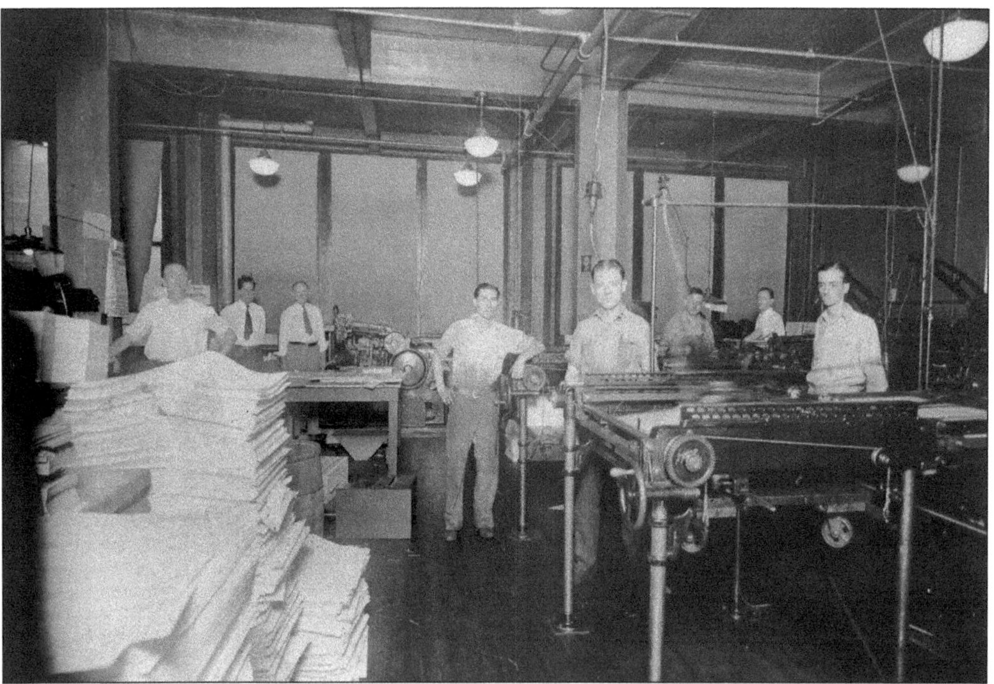

Employees of the *Call-Leader* stopped the press to pose for this c. 1935 photograph. The *Call-Leader*, then located at 1534 Main Street, dates back to 1889, when E.E. Fornshell and C.M. Hane started a weekly newspaper, the *Elwood Leader*. At the same time, Will Spruce was publishing the *Elwood Call*. Three years later, Fornshell bought the *Elwood Call*, and the rest is history. (Courtesy Elwood Public Library.)

Three

Elwood's People

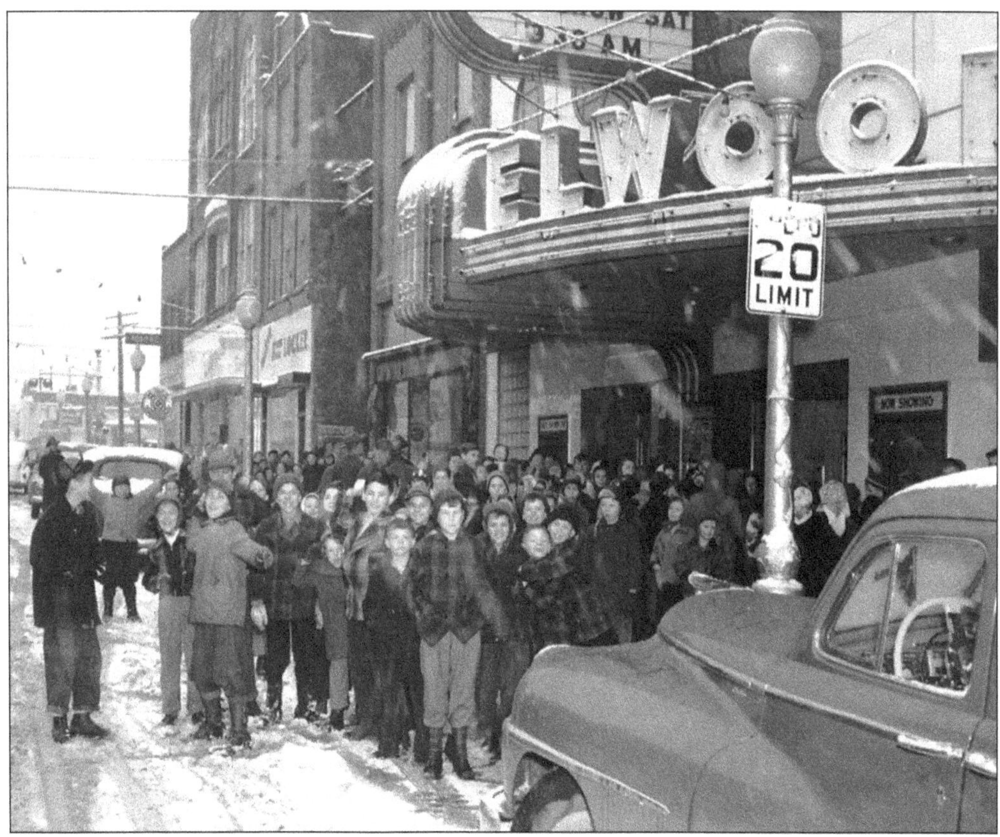

Elwood kids were not deterred by an overnight snowfall as they awaited admission to the Elwood Theater on Saturday, December 17, 1949, for a free showing of two hours of cartoons, sponsored jointly by the theater management and the Elwood Lions Club. Santa also attended as the special guest, and, in typical Claus fashion, presented each child with a special gift. (Courtesy Ginny Noble.)

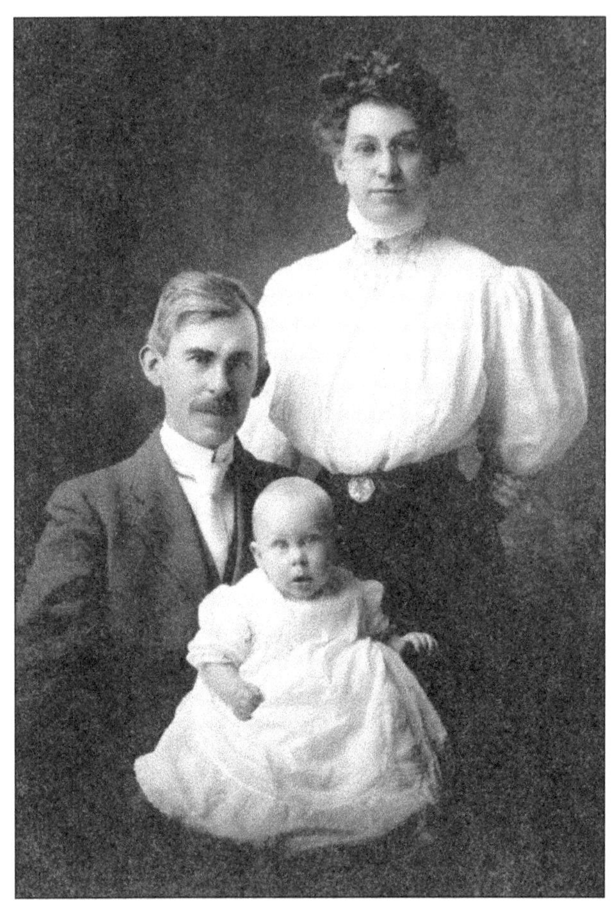

Left, Dr. Carrol C. "C.C." and Stella Cotton are shown with their son Perry. A native of Vevay, Indiana, Dr. Cotton graduated from the University of Louisville in 1891. After practicing medicine in Point Isabel for four years, he moved to Elwood in 1895. He married Stella Everingham, a nurse from New Jersey, in 1906. Dr. Cotton had an affinity for racehorses and owned several, which allowed him to make house calls at record speeds. His favorite, Fox, is shown below hitched to Dr. Cotton's buggy parked on North B Street, outside the Cottons' residence. When Fox died in 1907, the *Call-Leader* honored him with a front-page obituary. Dr. Cotton died in 1926 at age 61. (Courtesy Amy Seright Updike.)

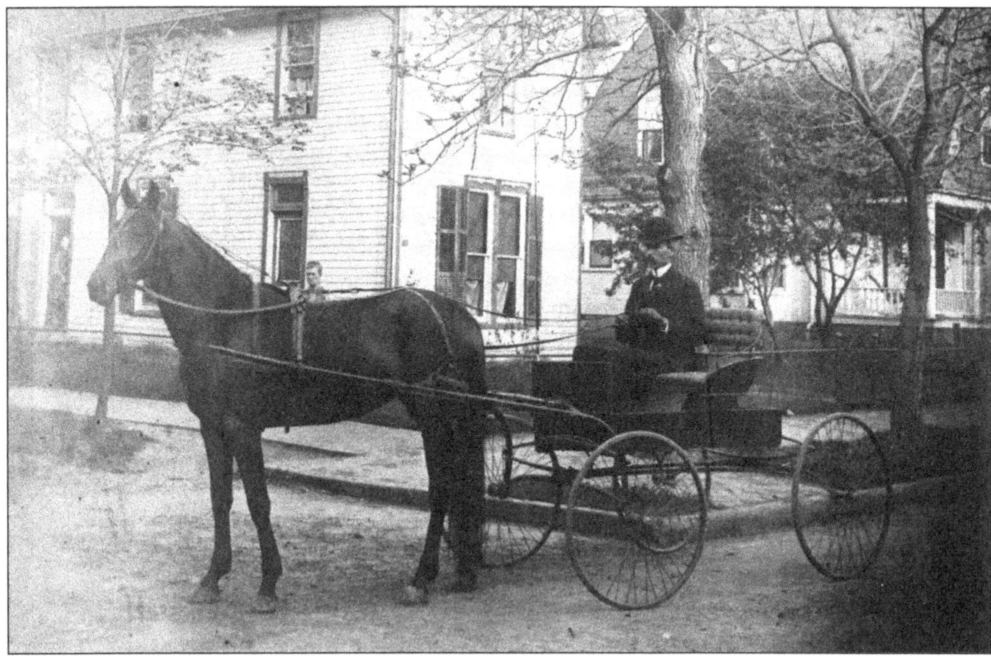

Dr. Perry Cotton graduated from Elwood High School in 1925 and Indiana University School of Medicine in 1934. He and his wife, Evelyn, had seven daughters. He served as chief of staff at Elwood's Mercy Hospital and was a charter member of the Elwood Lion's Club. He died tragically November 29, 1948, in a car-train crash while driving home from a house call in Tipton. He was 40. (Courtesy Amy Seright Updike.)

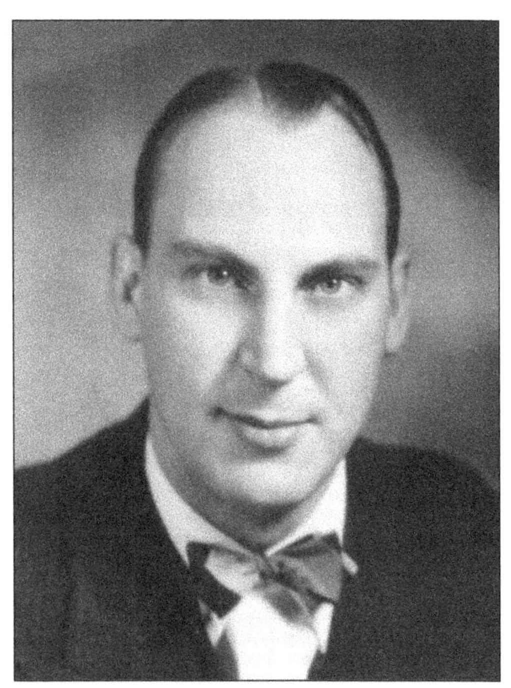

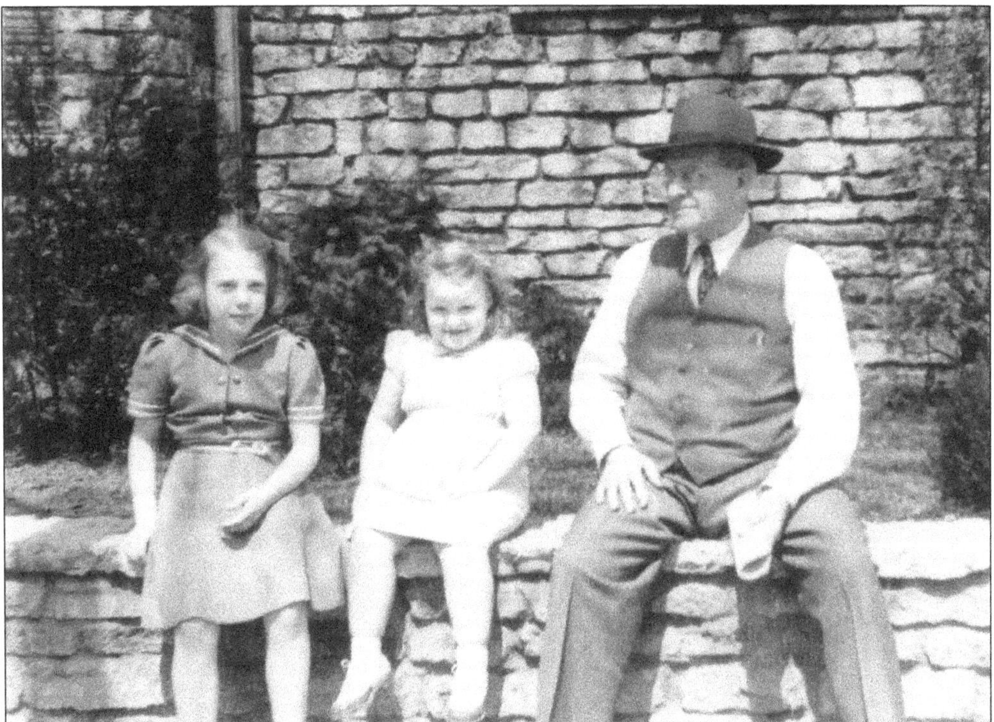

Elwood's first mayor, William DeHority, poses with Carol and Joyce Cotton, daughters of family friend Dr. Perry Cotton, around 1942. Born in the village of Quincy in 1868, DeHority was 22 when he was elected mayor in 1891. During his term, he oversaw many firsts for the city, including the police and fire departments and electric and water systems. DeHority died in 1943. He was 75. (Courtesy Amy Seright Updike.)

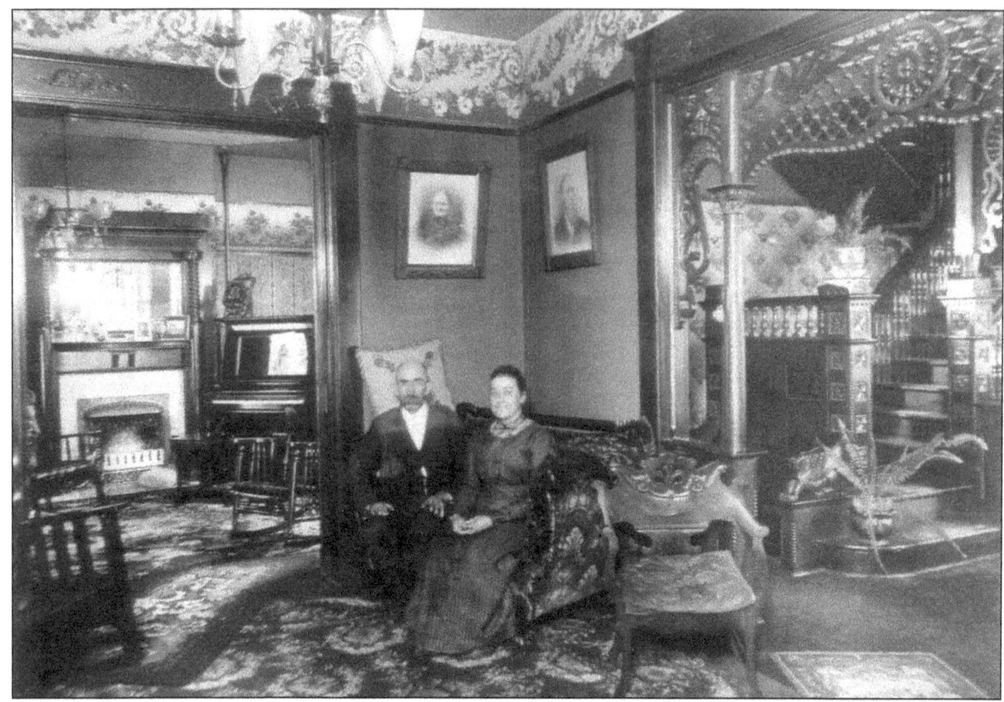

Joseph and Otilda Glass are seated at their 1903 East Main Street home, which they purchased from M.E. Good for $3,425 in 1912. Before moving to Elwood, Joseph built and operated the Windfall Telephone Exchange. They resided in their Elwood home until Otilda died in 1932. Joseph, who was born in 1858, died in 1937. The house was later owned by the Fettig family. (Courtesy Dave and Cathy Case.)

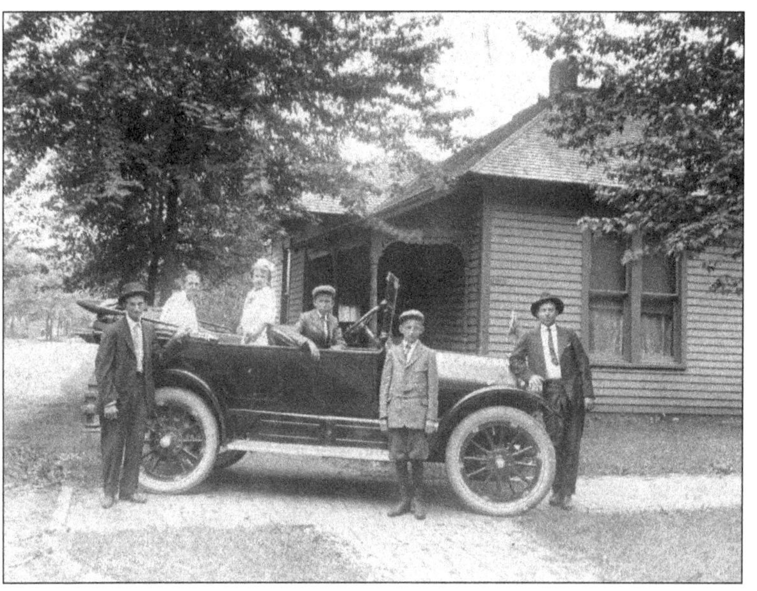

The Erdman family—from left to right, Francis, Ida May, Frances, Floyd (seated), Roy, and unidentified—pose with their new touring car during the summer of 1915 outside their home at 1835 North B Street. At the time of his death in 1967, Floyd still lived in the house. (Courtesy John Carpenter.)

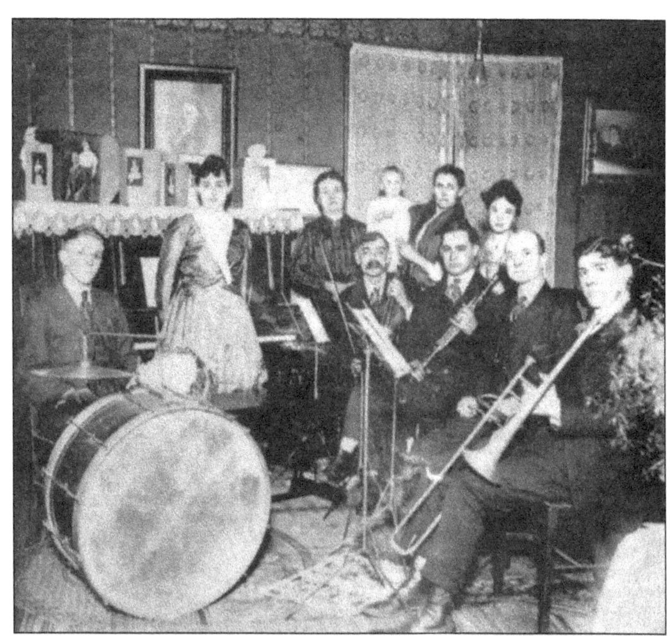

Elwood social, church and school functions, held 1908–1930, frequently included music by the Parrish Family Orchestra. Pictured from left to right are Nolan Watkins, drums; Edna Parrish Watkins, piano; John Parrish, violin; Fred Parrish, clarinet; Lon Maudlin, trumpet; and Earl Smith, trombone; standing behind them, from left to right, are Arabelle Parrish, Wuanita Wright, and Locha Parrish. A 1927 dinner featuring the Parrishes also featured celebrated coach Knute Rockne. (Courtesy Judy Koehler-Newell.)

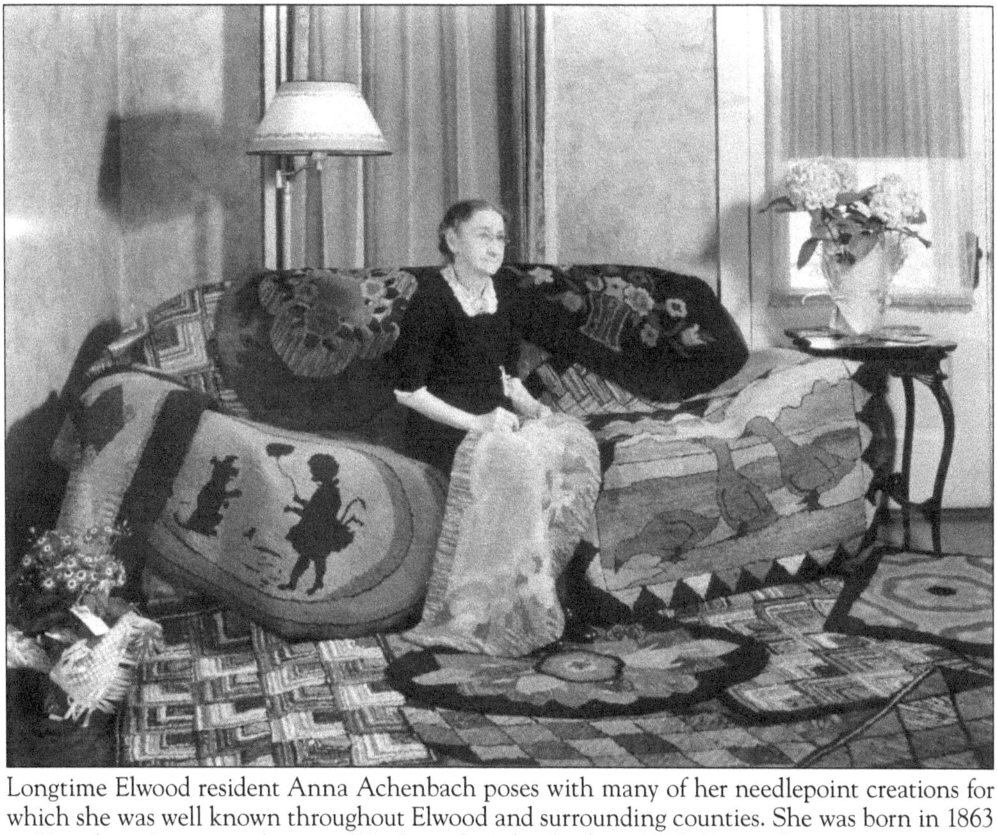

Longtime Elwood resident Anna Achenbach poses with many of her needlepoint creations for which she was well known throughout Elwood and surrounding counties. She was born in 1863 in Hamilton County and married Zephaniah Achenbach in 1885. She made news in May 1947, when her grandson, Don Orbaugh, took her flying for the first time. She was 84. Anna died in February 1954. (Courtesy Ann Brewer.)

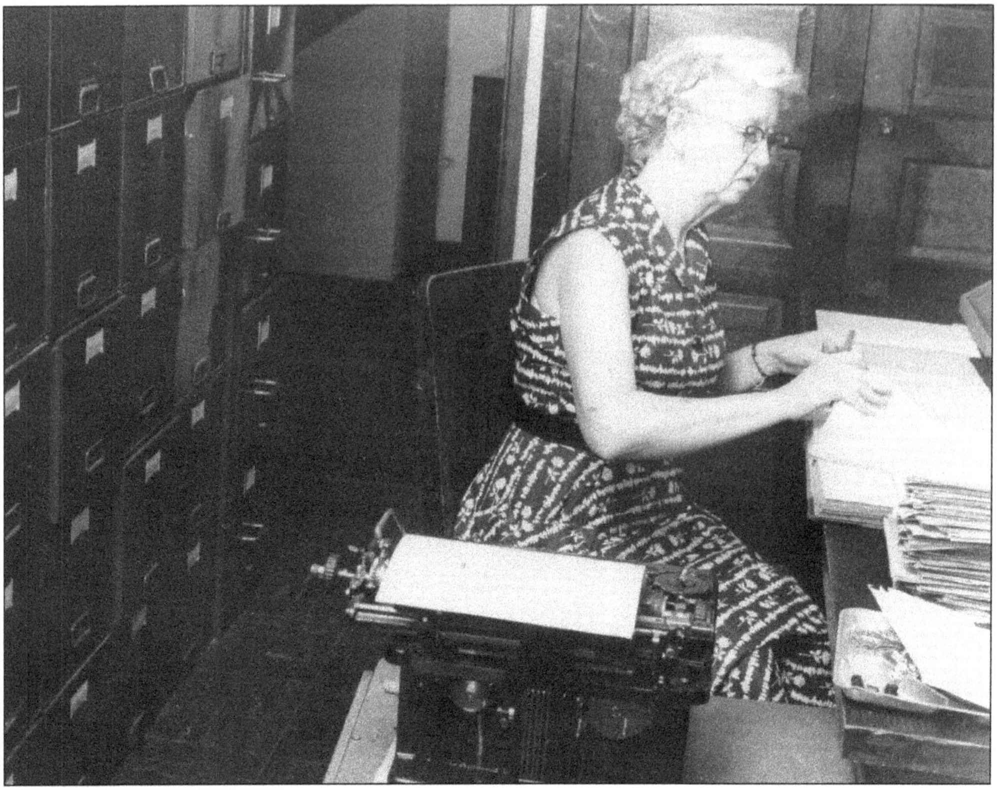

Bernadette Short was a lifelong Elwood resident, who spent her entire professional career as supervisor of the patient records department at Mercy Hospital. Here, she is shown around 1968 at work in her office, surrounded by her files, accounting books, and her vintage manual typewriter. Short died in 1983. She was 80. (Courtesy St. Vincent Mercy Hospital.)

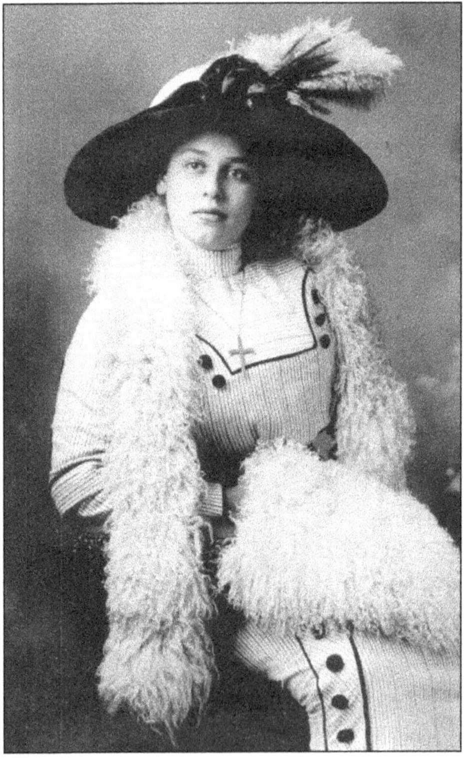

Rose Manghelli Kelich was born in Chicago in 1895. Her father, Sam, and her brothers operated a popular Elwood produce stand, which they grew into a large distribution business. She and John Kelich married in 1913 and had nine children. Rose died in 1959. (Courtesy Rita Kelich.)

Beulah Perkins Smith admires the books donated by Sigma Phi Gamma in memory of her sorority sister, Beatrice Bambrough, to the Elwood Public Library in March 1982. Smith also was an active member of the Elwood Garden Club. She and her husband, Roy, were longtime Elwood residents. She passed away two years after this photograph was taken. (Courtesy Carolyn S. Julius.)

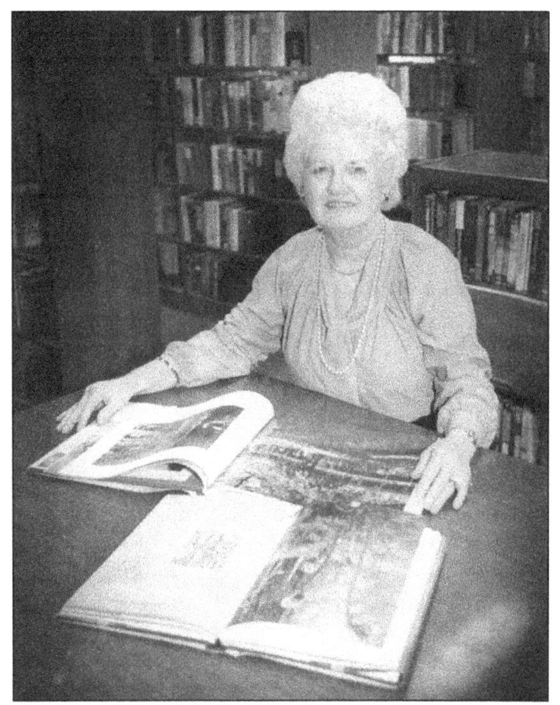

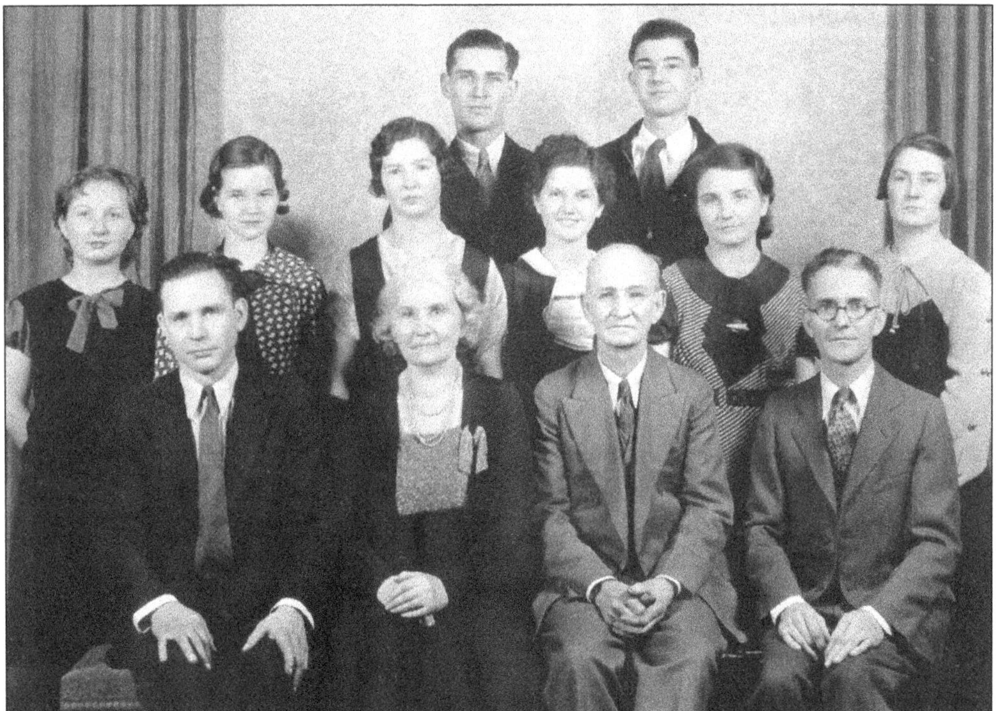

The Perkins family posed for this image in 1935. From left to right are (first row) Roy, Lottie Cole, David, and Ray; (second row) Charlotte Moore, Elizabeth Glotzbach, Mary Schlemmer, Beulah Smith, Carrie Williams, and Connie Rockafellar; (third row) Glenn and Floyd. David, the family patriarch, lived his entire adult life in Elwood. He died in 1956. (Courtesy Carolyn S. Julius.)

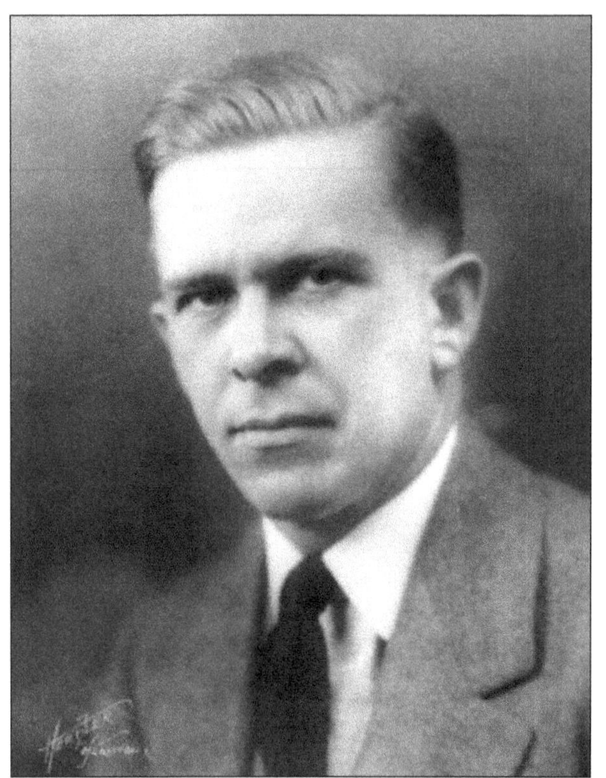

Elwood-born Donald Mellett, son of *Elwood Daily Press* owner Jesse Mellett, worked throughout Indiana and Ohio before joining the *Canton Daily News* as editor. His editorials exposing local corruption sparked death threats, resulting in his assassination in 1926. The next year, honoring Mellett's diligence, the paper received the Pulitzer Prize. Mellett was inducted into the Indiana Journalism Hall of Fame in 1969. (Courtesy Stark County, Ohio, Historical Society.)

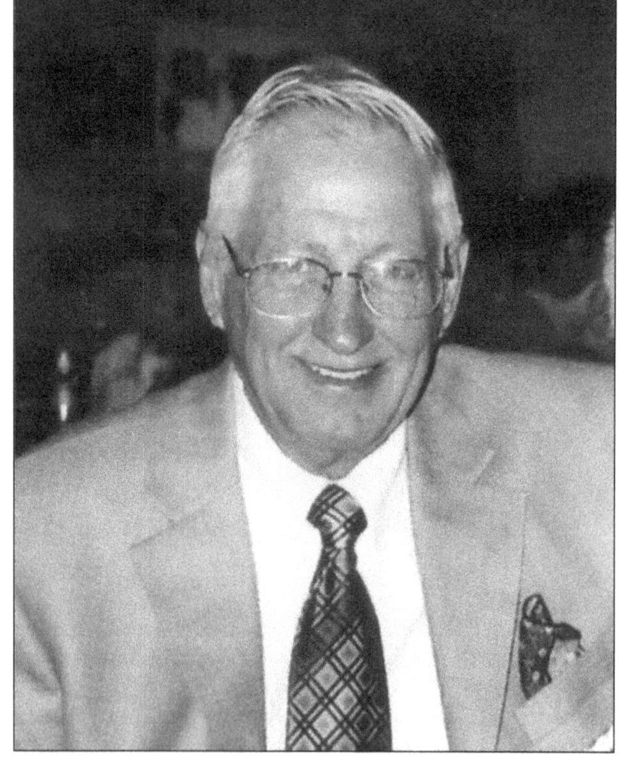

Elwood native Gene Conard became the *Call-Leader*'s sports editor in 1961. After moving on in 1967, he built a prestigious career, covering Indiana sports for the rest of his life. He was frequently honored for his writing and/or coaching, including inductions into the Howard County Sports Hall of Fame, the Indiana Wrestling Coaches Association, and Indiana Semi-Pro Baseball organization. Conard died in 2015. He was 86. (Courtesy Carol Dever.)

Dr. Julia Siegfried served her "lady patients" in Elwood 1905–1911. A trailblazer for women's rights, Siegfried became the first female to land a spot on an Indiana ballot when she ran for circuit court judge on the Socialists of Madison County ticket in 1908, twelve years before women won the right to vote. Although Siegfried lost the election, she earned a place in Indiana history. (Courtesy Elwood Public Library.)

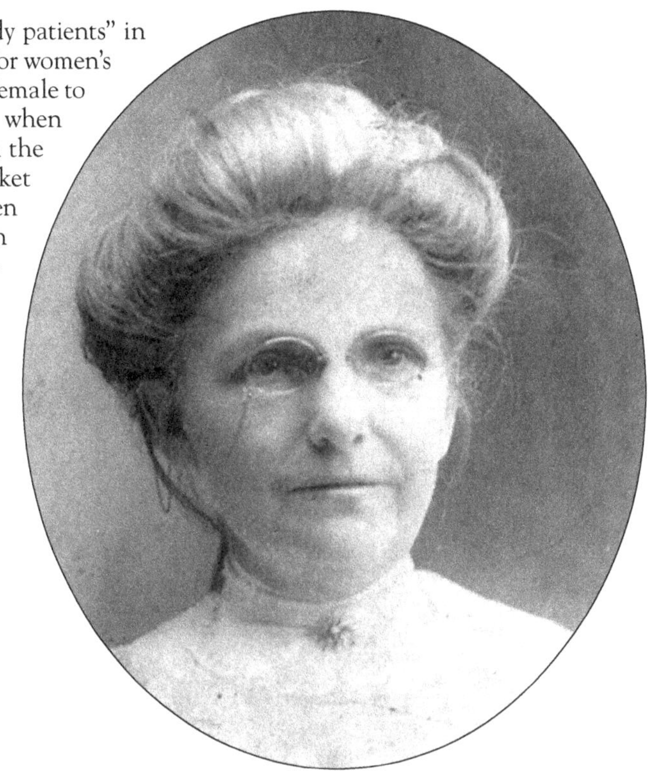

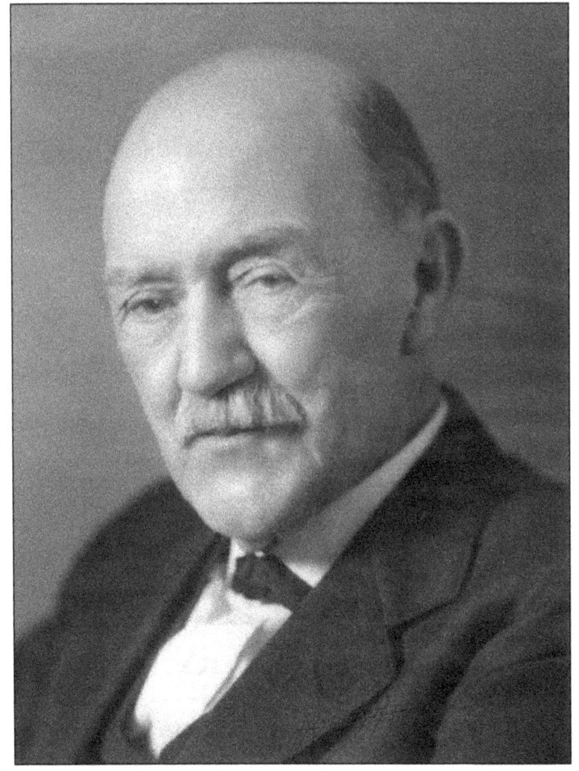

Dr. Daniel Sigler was born in 1843 on a farm southeast of Elwood and graduated Miami (Ohio) Medical College in 1871. He established his Elwood practice the next year, later opening his office at South Anderson and South B Streets. One of the city's true pioneer doctors, Sigler traversed mud streets and country roads on horseback to tend to his patients. He died in 1934. (Courtesy St. Vincent Mercy Hospital.)

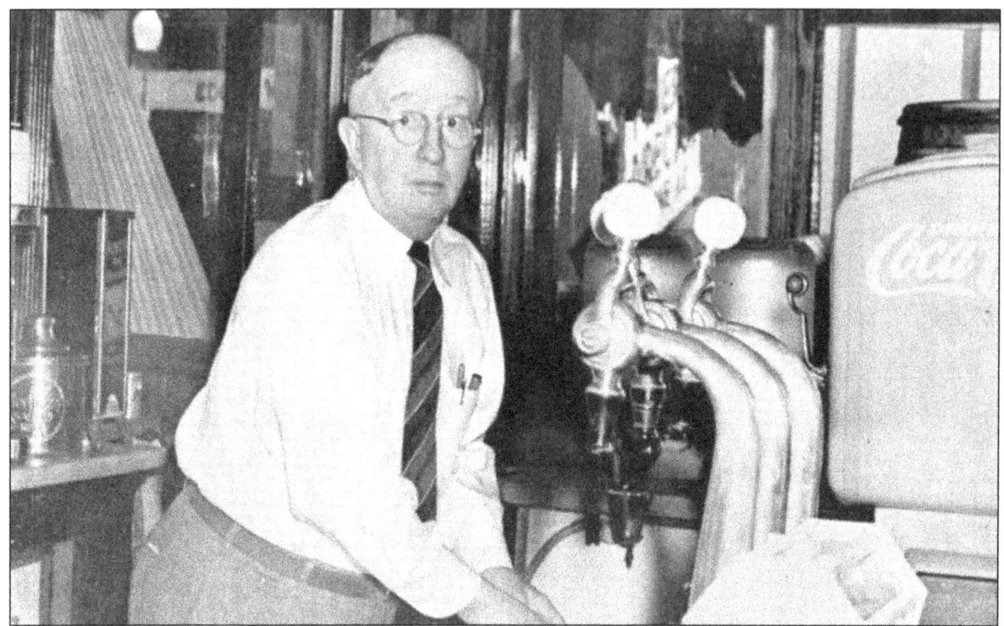

Pharmacist O.D. "Doc" Hinshaw operated Elwood's longest-running drugstore, taking over an already-established pharmacy at 322 South Anderson Street in 1902. Hinshaw loved Elwood and sought ways to enhance its future. He was instrumental in building the city's swimming pool, first president of the Elwood Kiwanis, and a lifelong friend of Wendell Willkie. Hinshaw operated Hinshaw's Drug Store until his death in 1949. He was 74. (Courtesy Dave Berkemeier.)

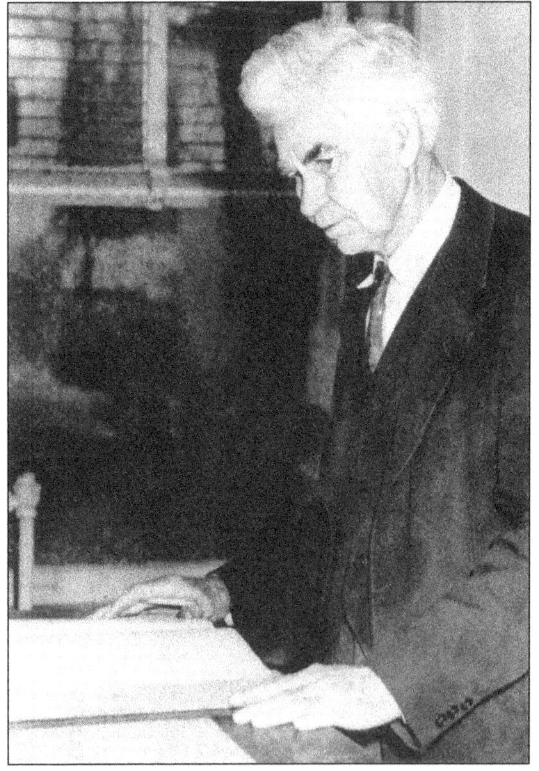

John D. Seright lived most of his life in Elwood. A civil engineer, he was Elwood's city engineer from 1917 until he resigned in 1959. During his tenure, he staked out the park shelter house, put in the park lighting, the sewer system, the baseball diamond, three-quarters of the city sidewalks, and wrote the specifications for the city's streetlights. Seright died in 1970. He was 91. (Courtesy Amy Seright Updike.)

The Invincibles first performed for their high school Christmas program in 1972. After graduation, they traveled the nation, providing backup for several well-known musical artists, such as Marty Robbins and Percy Sledge. In 1976, they performed for Vice Pres. Nelson Rockefeller. From left to right are (seated) Brad Smith and Jeff McDaniel; (standing) Frank Parente, Joe Jordan, Jeff Poe, Randy Moore, and Chris Loepke. (Courtesy Jeff Poe.)

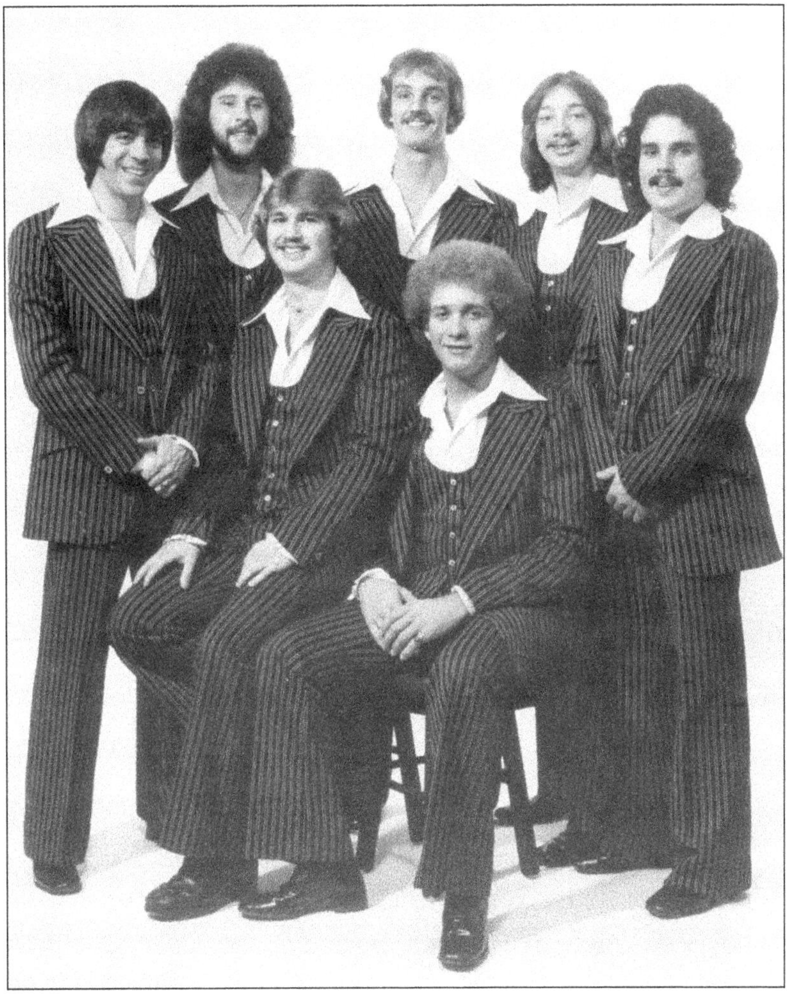

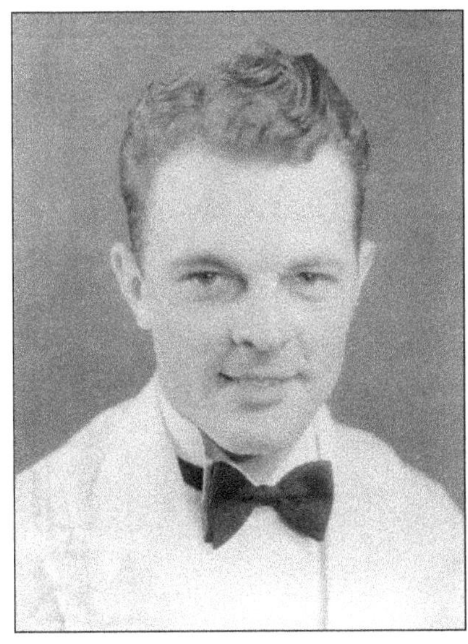

Elwood native Kenneth Sprong was a vocalist who toured the Midwest in the 1930s, often performing at the Indiana Ballroom. Later, touring with the Charlie Agnew Orchestra, he performed in Chicago on WGN Radio and onstage at the Palmer House. In 1937, he gave up his singing career, returned to Elwood, and took up farming. He continued to sing locally until he died in 1964. (Courtesy Ann Brewer.)

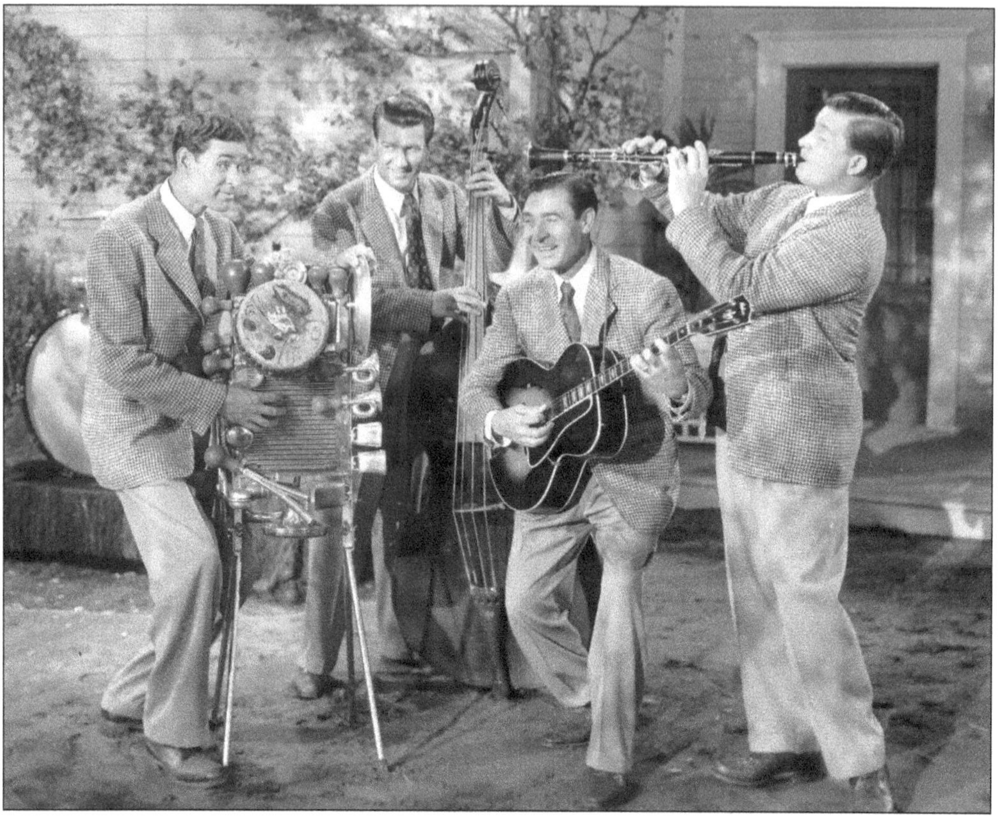

The Hoosier Hot Shots graced America's stages, movie screens, and radio airwaves with their unique, down-home musical antics from the height of the Depression through the 1940s. Besides playing clarinets and guitars, the Hot Shots popularized washboards, bells, whistles, and automobile horns as musical instruments. From left to right are Ken and Paul Trietsch, Gil Taylor, and clarinetist Charles Otto "Gabe" Ward, who grew up in Elwood.

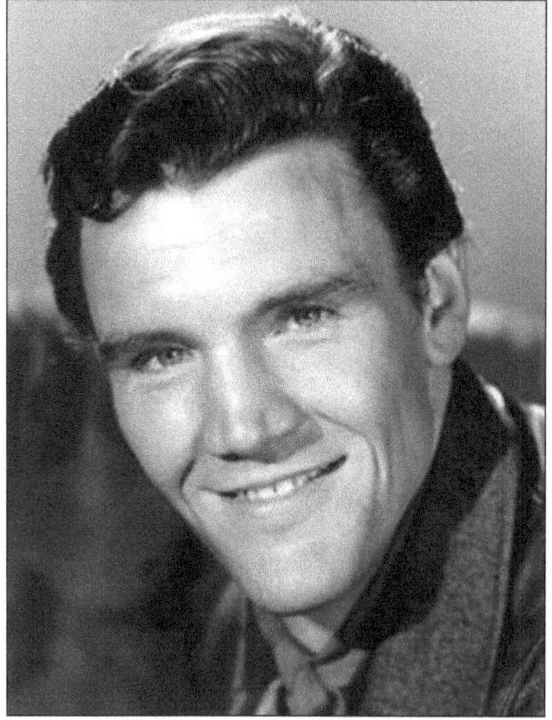

Actor David Canary was born in Elwood in 1938 to Hilary and Lorena Canary. He starred in the TV soap *All My Children* from 1984 through 2011, earning 16 Daytime Emmy nominations and winning five. Although featured in several movies, he was best known for TV, including regular gigs on *Peyton Place* and *Bonanza*. Late in his career, he turned to live theater. Canary died in 2015.

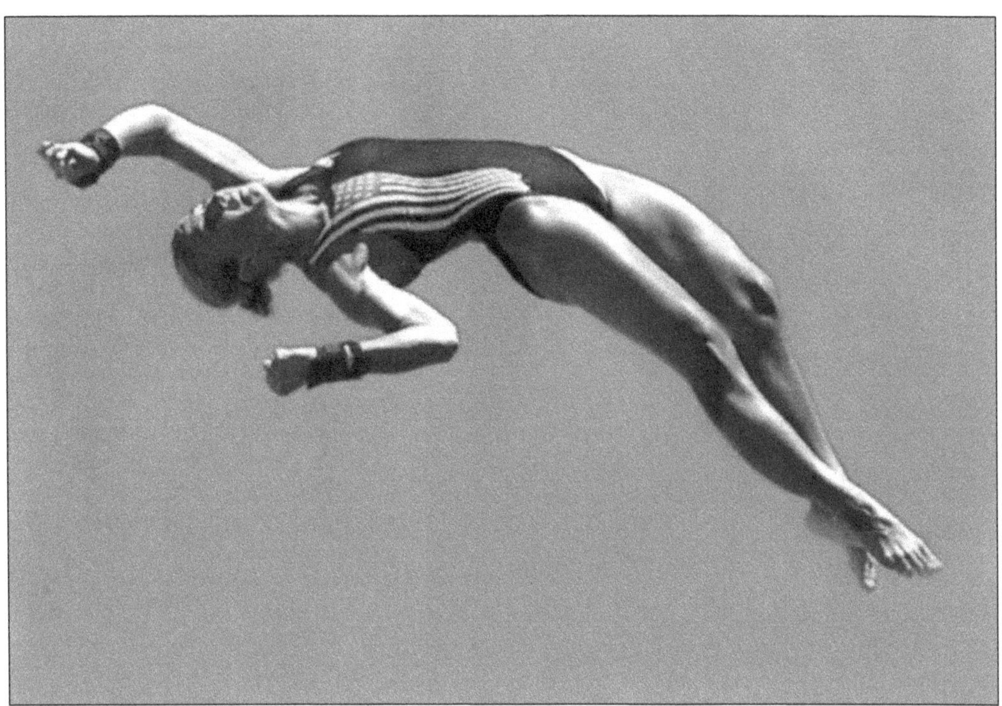

At 15, Elwood's Mary Beth Dunnichay became the 2008 US Olympic diving team's youngest member, placing fifth at Beijing in the synchronized 10-meter platform and second at the 2009 World Championships. As a Purdue University student, Dunnichay excelled in Big Ten and NCAA events, earning All-American status in 2015, the same year shoulder injuries forced her to retire from diving. Elwood's aquatic center bears her name. (Courtesy the Dunnichay family.)

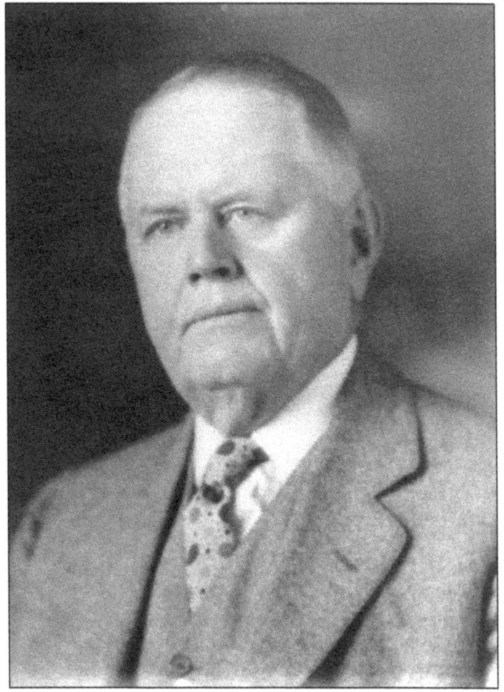

Wayne Leeson was a real Yankee Doodle Dandy, born on the Fourth of July in 1863. He took over the family store, R.L. Leeson's, in 1906 after his father, R.L., died. With sons, King and Lawrence, Wayne grew Leeson's into Indiana's largest and most prestigious department store. Like his father, Wayne was a beloved Elwood figure that generously gave back to his community. He died on December 23, 1937. (Courtesy Matt Leeson.)

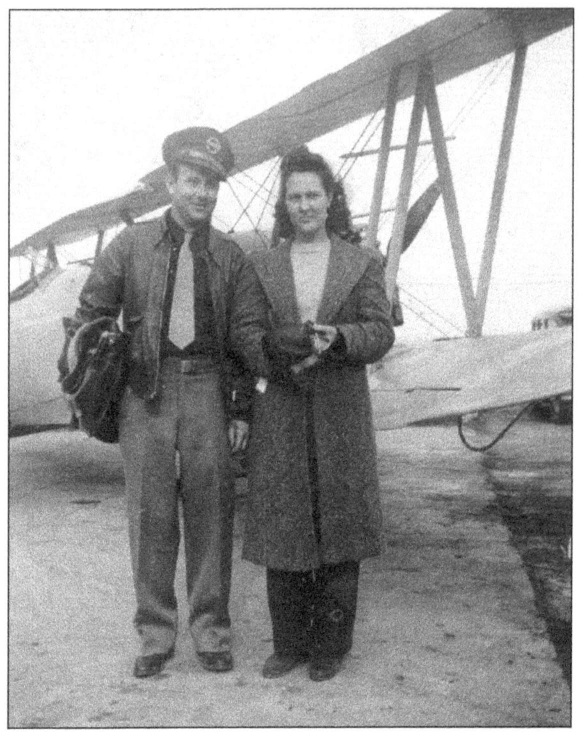

Pilots Don and Georgia Orbaugh pose in 1943 at the Muncie airport, where Don was a flight instructor for Naval ROTC officers. Georgia also was a licensed pilot. Three years later, the Orbaughs built the Elwood Airport (below) near the intersection of State Roads 13 and 37. The grand opening was May 1, 1946. The facility offered flight instruction, a meeting room, an airplane mechanic, flying events, a ground school, and a restaurant. The Orbaughs' daughters, Ann and Donna, spent many hours there as they grew up and regularly gassed and washed the airplanes, mowed the runways and surrounding grounds, and sold pop and candy bars. After Georgia's death in 1993 and Don's in 2000, Ann and Donna managed the operation until 2008, when they reluctantly closed it. (Left, courtesy Ann Brewer.)

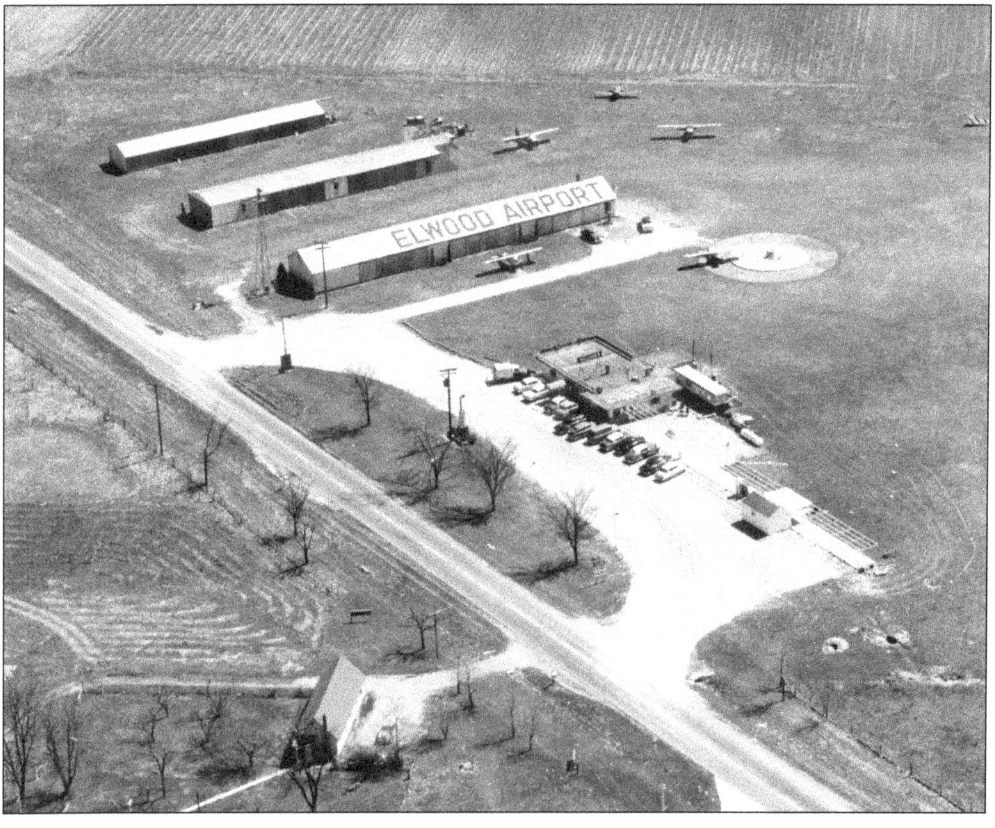

Four

Events and Celebrations

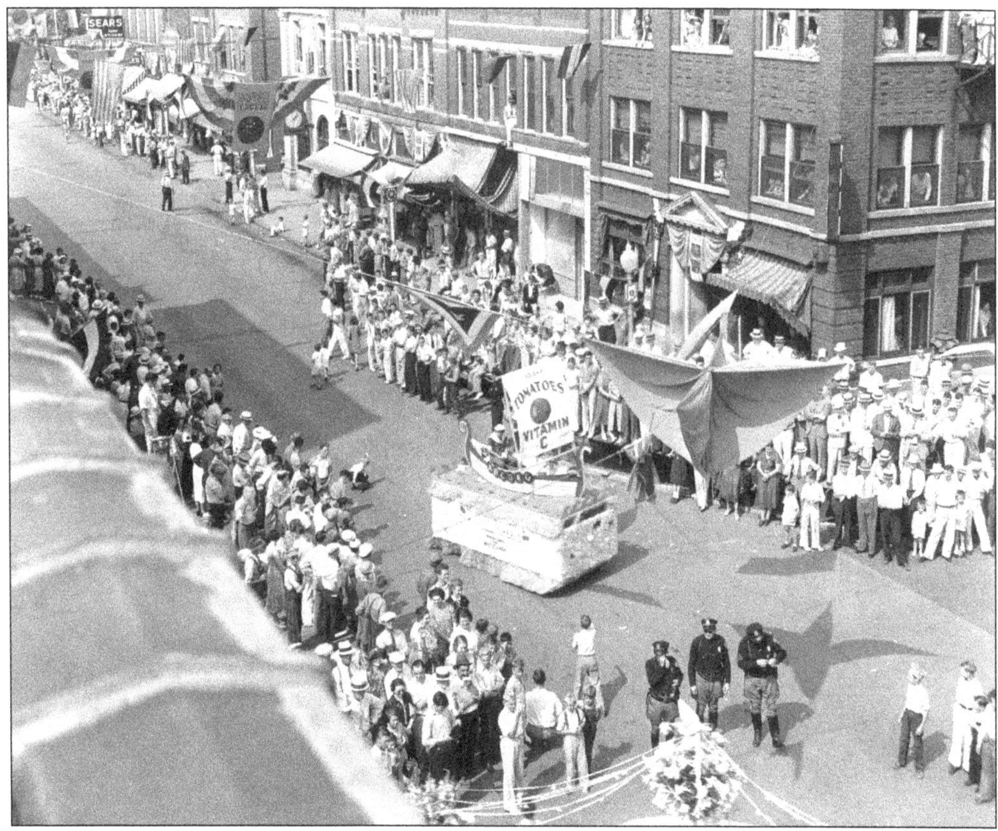

The annual Tomato Festival was Elwood's signature event that celebrated local and state growers from 1937 through 1948. A parade of elaborate, professionally built floats was the event's highlight, featuring a 50-piece, all-state band and attracting crowds reaching 60,000. This undated photograph shows the lead float heading south on Anderson Street while a throng of spectators lines the street on both sides. (Courtesy Elwood Public Library.)

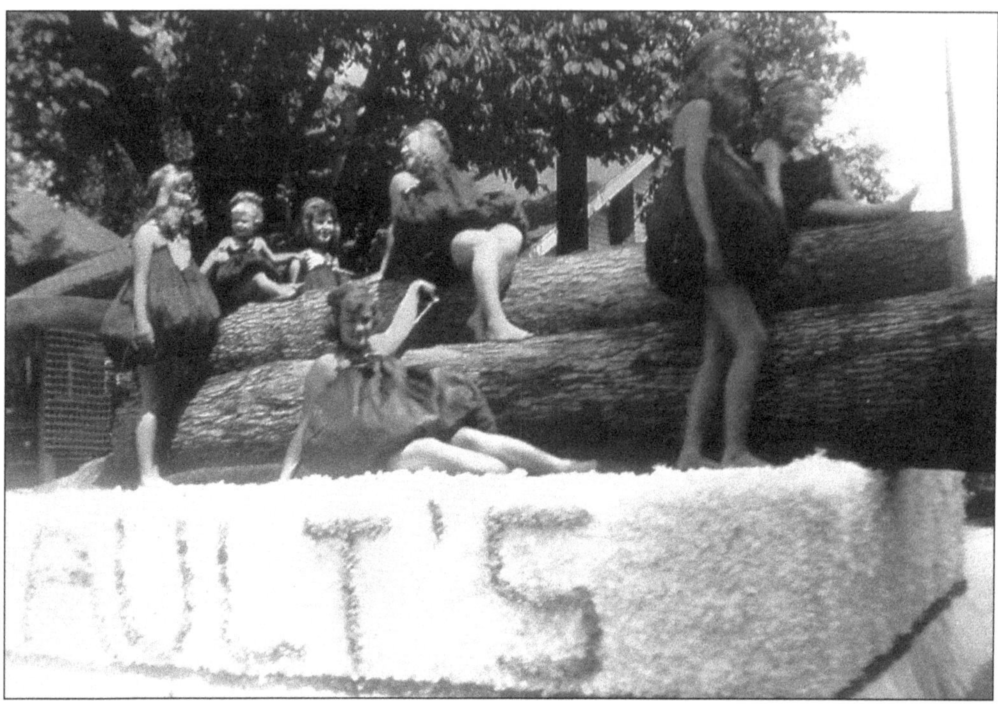

In 1948, the award for best float at the 12th annual, and final, Tomato Festival went to Ault's Saw Mill. The lumber company's entry depicted a horn of plenty with tomatoes tumbling out of it. The float also featured three large logs and several young girls dressed up as tomatoes. The littlest girl seated on the back of the log is Tena Beckley, then age four. (Courtesy Tena Beckley.)

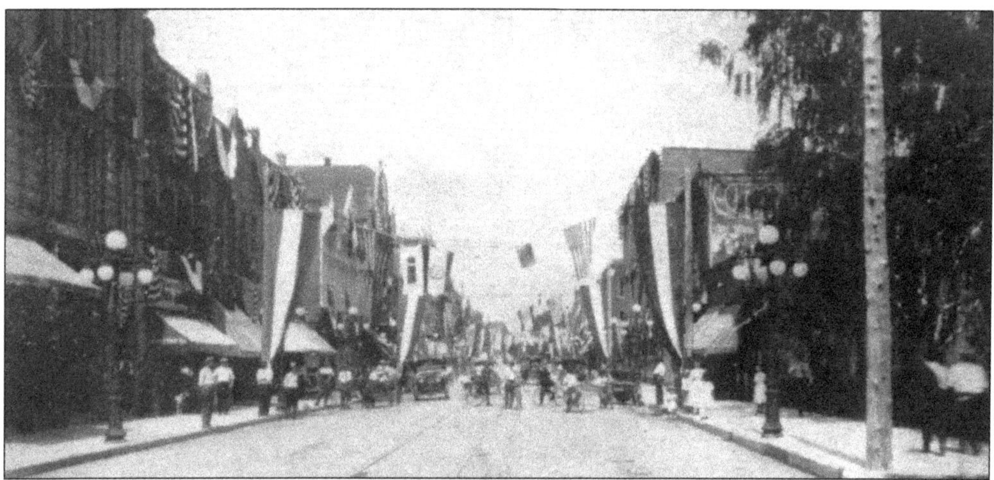

Recapturing the enthusiasm of the original Tin Plate Day of September 13, 1892, the city held a 20th-anniversary celebration for the Tin Plate on September 13, 1912. The city was decorated with colorful flags and bunting, and Indiana governor Thomas Marshall was the special guest. Events included a parade with 200 floats, a band concert, acts by contortionist Elmer Satterly and Daredevil Diver Meyers, and fireworks. (Courtesy Eric Grogan.)

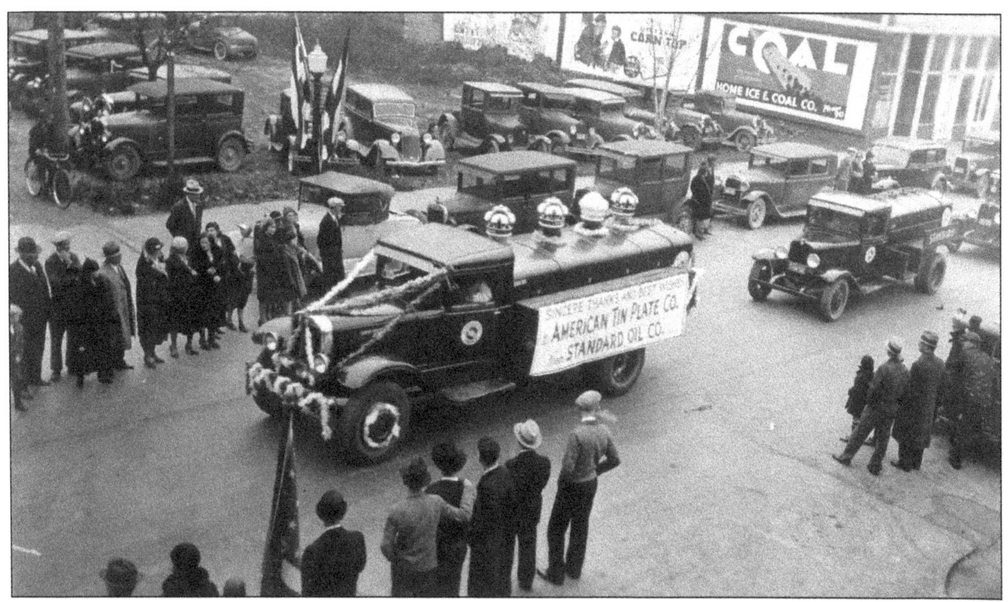

An estimated 30,000 people flooded Elwood on Saturday, December 2, 1933, for Tin Plate Appreciation Day featuring a four-mile-long parade, a barbecue, music, a "mass meeting" at the Armory, and free movies playing at the city's three movie theaters. Heralded as "the greatest celebration ever held in the city," it was sponsored by the Elwood American Sheet and Tin Plate Company's employees to express their appreciation to the company for its "splendid operations." A large delegation of the company's officials, including the vice president, traveled from Pittsburgh as special guests. Store windows displayed tin sheets that read "Hail to the Tin Plate," and the city sparkled with red and green Christmas lights. As the *Call-Leader* put it, "The event surpassed in magnitude the greatest hope of any of its sponsors." (Above, courtesy Elwood Heritage Center; below, courtesy Sue Loser.)

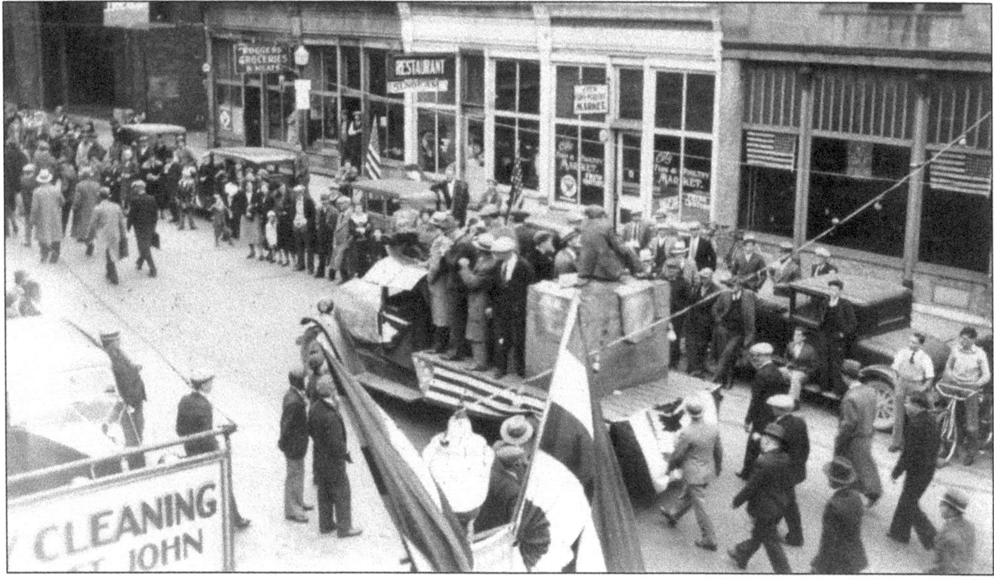

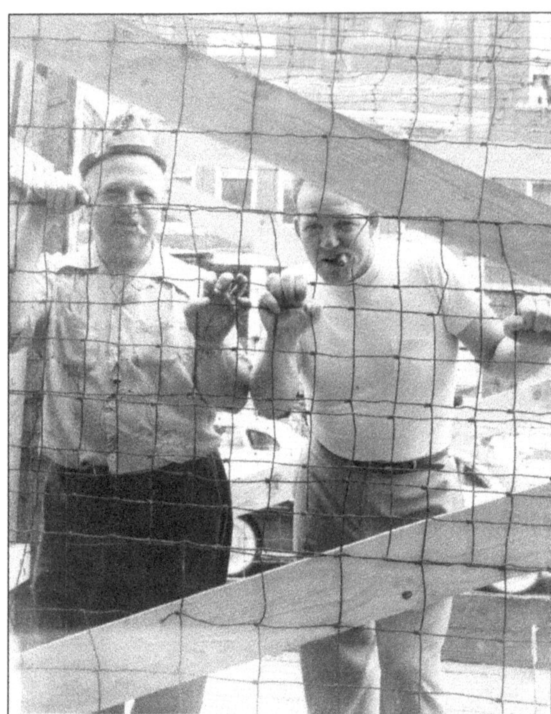

Wayne Jones (left) and Arley "Mac" McQueen were the first men "arrested and jailed" in a downtown stockade on Saturday, May 24, 1952, during the Elwood centennial. The men had violated centennial rules and shaved their beards. They were "tried" in a kangaroo court later that afternoon and required to pay a fine. (Courtesy Terry Jones.)

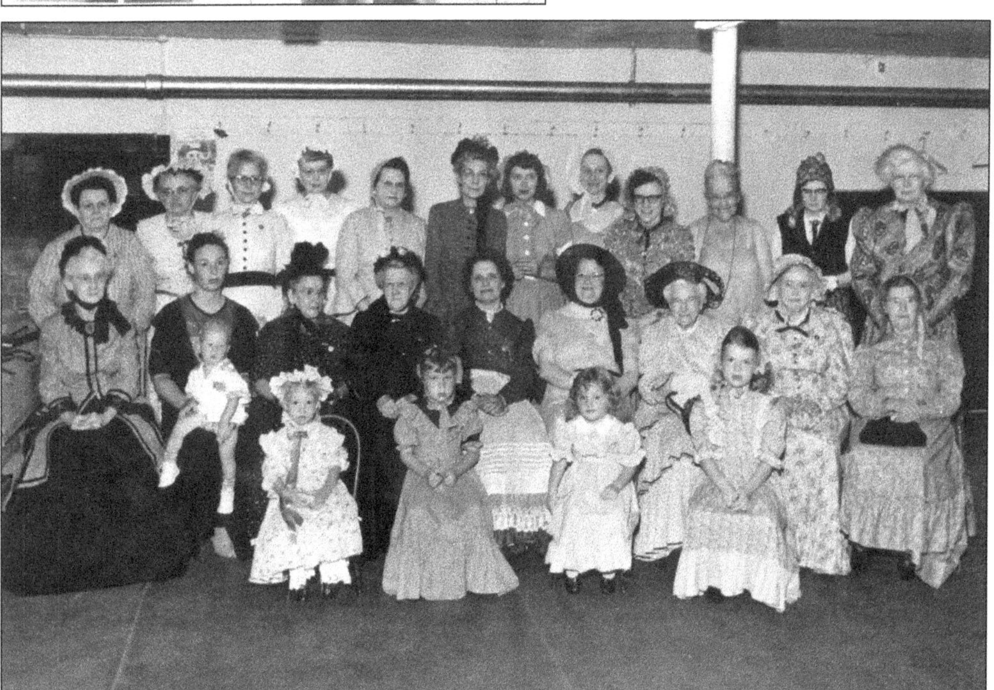

The King's Daughters Class of the East Main Street Christian Church invited their members and guests to dress in typical centennial garb at their June 1952 meeting. That event observed not only the city's 100th anniversary but celebrated the church's as well. Elwood's Christian Church was established shortly after the town of Quincy was laid out in 1852. (Courtesy East Main Street Christian Church.)

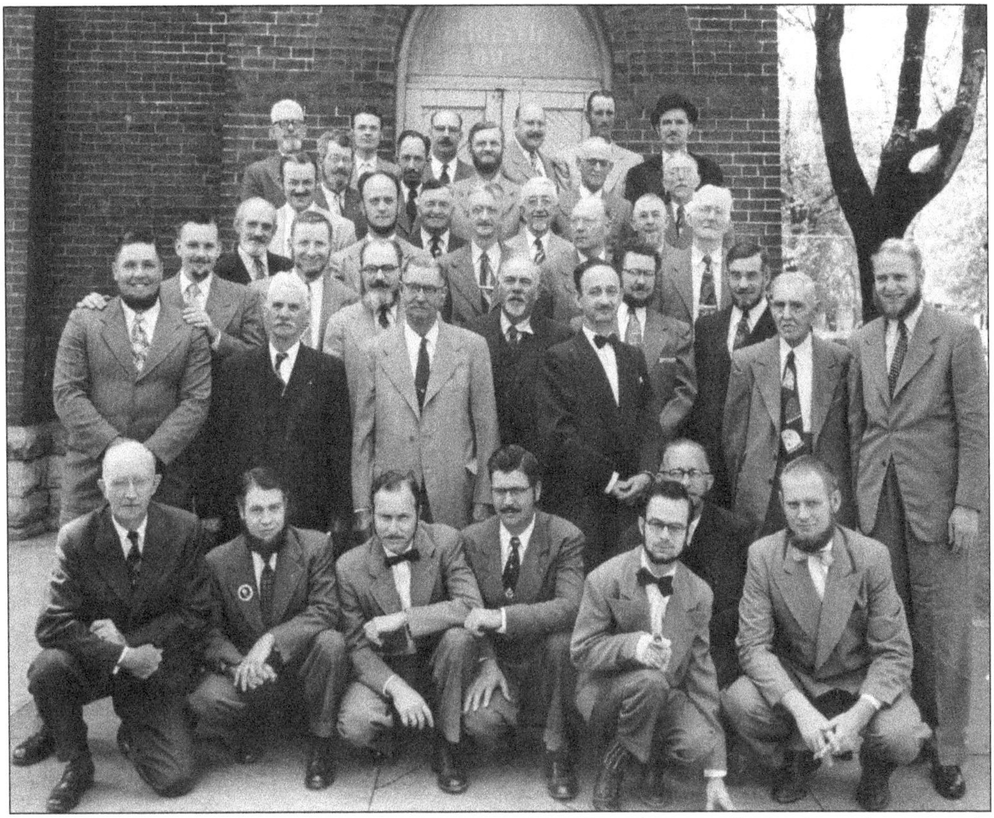

The men of Elwood's East Main Street Christian Church gather outside the front door in early June 1952 to show off the facial hair they sprouted for the city's centennial. On Sunday, June 15, the church held a Father's Day service and dinner, during which a panel of judges awarded prizes to the fathers with beards deemed best looking, longest, fullest, and scratchiest. (Courtesy East Main Street Christian Church.)

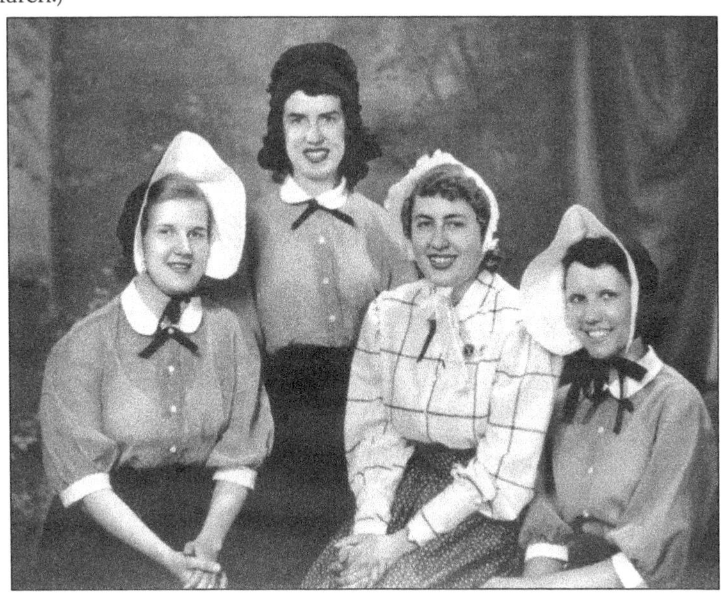

These First Farmers Bank employees pose in period costume for their participation in Elwood's centennial celebration in 1952. From left to right, the ladies are Joan Reid Tyner, Nora Mae Smith Ladd, Margaret Smith Off, and Jeanine Sanders Rittenhouse. (Courtesy John Carpenter.)

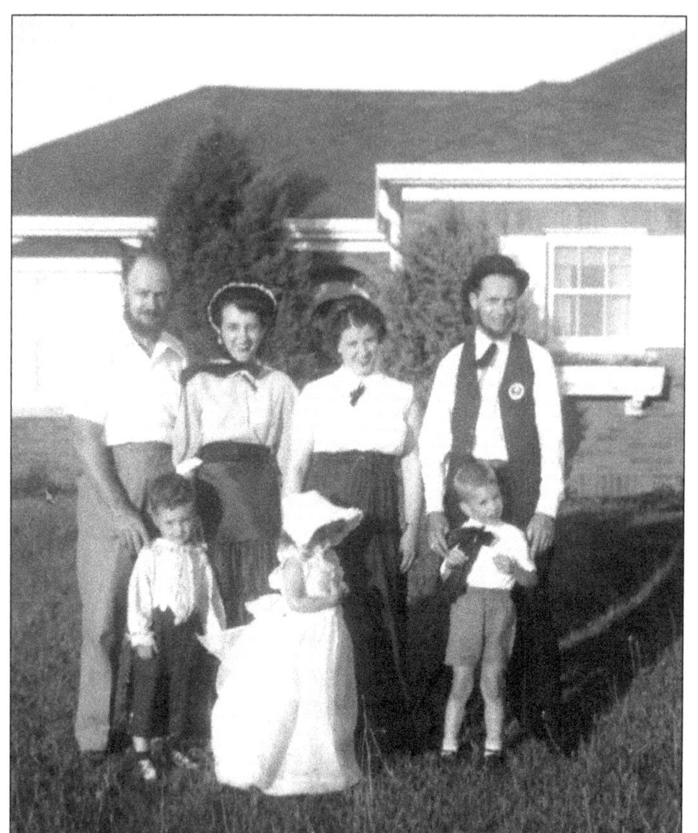

Longtime residents and friends show off their fashionable, early-1900s attire in celebration of Elwood's centennial festivities in 1952. The adults pictured from left are Allen and Lil Trimble and Louise and Mel Moore. The children, from left to right, are Terry Trimble and siblings Linda and Dan Moore. (Courtesy Linda Moore.)

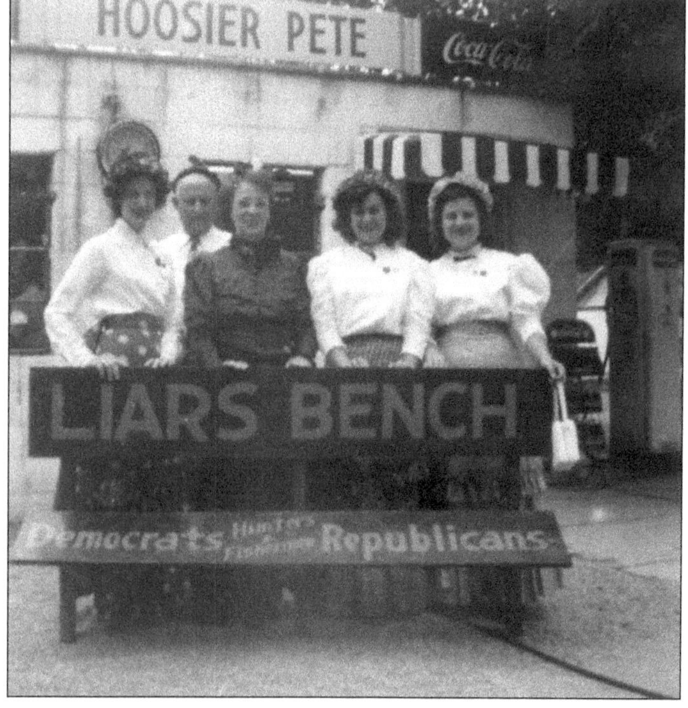

From left to right, Jeanne Padfield Arehart, two unidentified persons, Rose Schimmel, and Jayne Padfield pose behind the "Liars Bench" outside the Hoosier Pete gas station at the corner of Anderson and North J Streets. The friends are dressed in their period costumes for Elwood's June 1952 centennial celebration. (Courtesy Jeanne Arehart.)

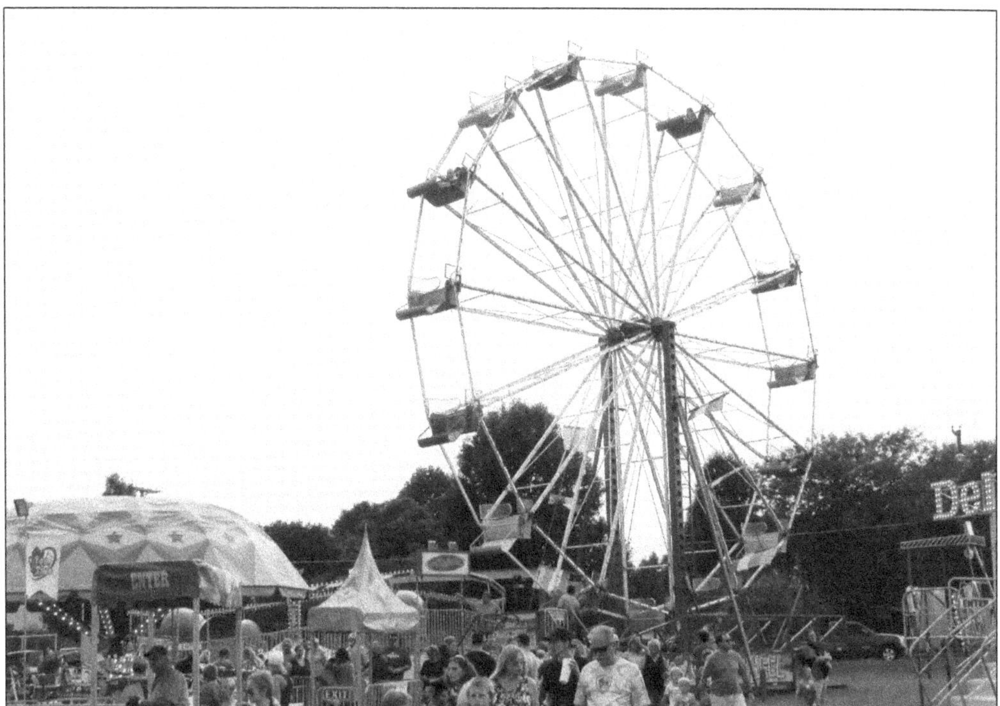

Elwood's annual Glass Festival originated in 1972 as a tribute to the city's rich heritage of locally produced, hand-blown art-glass. Organized by the Elwood Chamber of Commerce, the three-day festival takes place in Elwood's Calloway Park the third weekend of August and includes a parade, vendors, food, carnival rides, exhibits, demonstrations, entertainment, and contests.

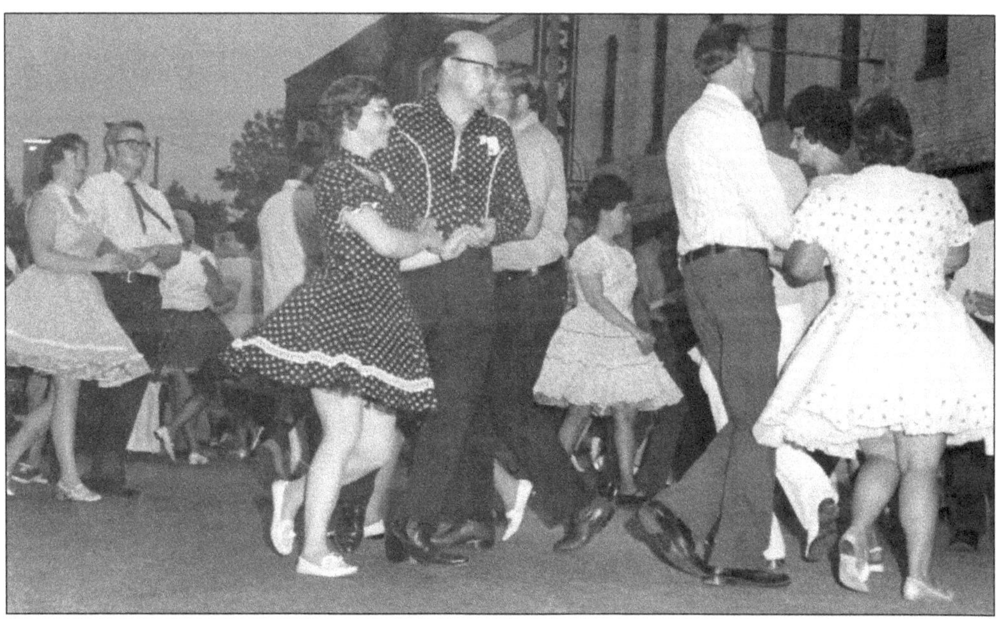

Members of the local square-dance club kick up their heels at the corner of South B and Anderson Streets on June 22, 1972. The hoedown was one of many events featured at the second annual Elwood Glass Festival. (Courtesy Matt Boyland.)

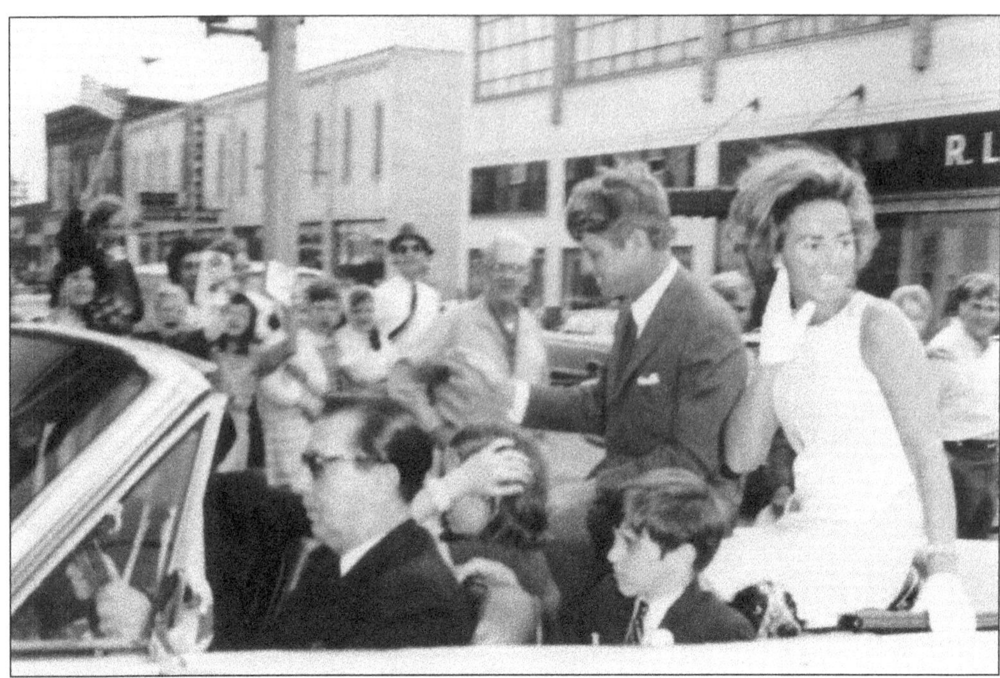

Robert Kennedy's campaign for US president brought him to Elwood the morning of Tuesday, April 24, 1968. His wife, Ethel, and three of their children—Michael, David, and Courtney—and their dog Freckles accompanied him. Elwood was Kennedy's first stop on the second day of his three-day tour through Indiana. Hundreds of supporters greeted him for a coffee and doughnut reception at Mangas Cafeteria, where Kennedy told them he was bringing his message directly to Indiana's voters because winning the state's primary was key for any presidential hopeful. During his remarks, he vowed to move the country away from the welfare system and toward jobs. "Welfare is no substitute for employment," he said. He also noted the shortage of doctors, increasing medical costs, inflation, and the startling rise in crime. (Both, courtesy Rita Kelich.)

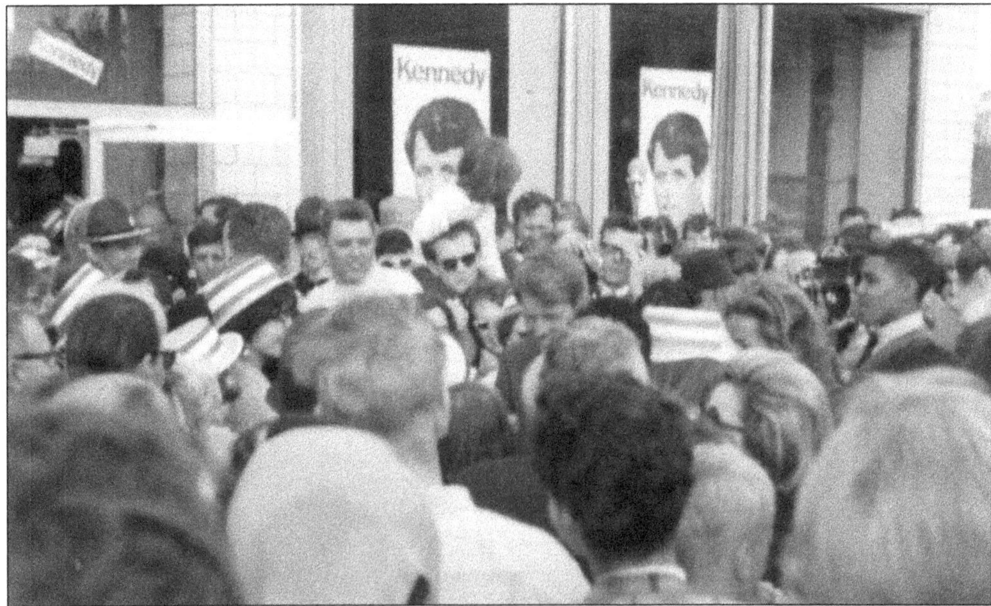

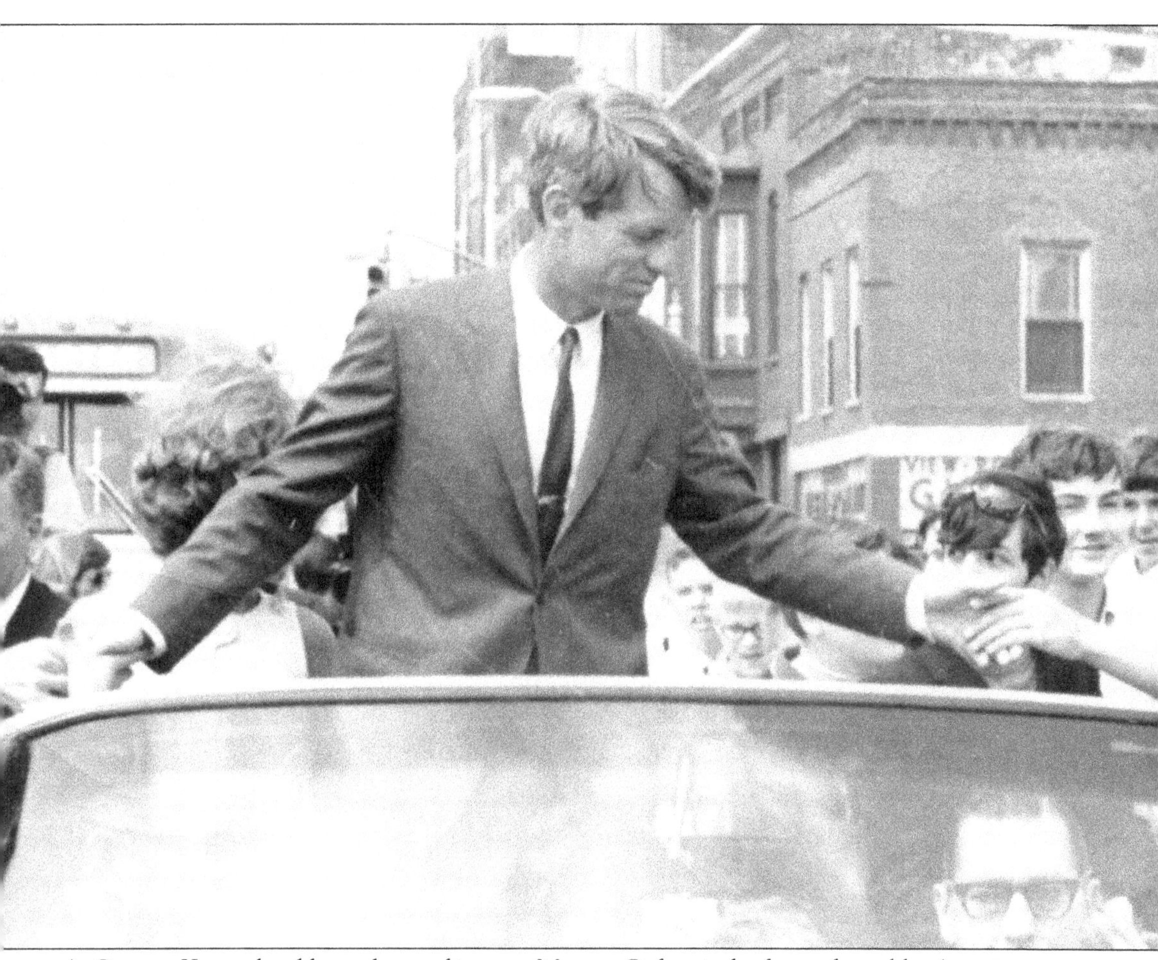

As Senator Kennedy addressed an audience at Mangas Cafeteria, he focused on older Americans, calling them "the rock upon which we built this nation." Departing Mangas, Senator and Mrs. Kennedy shook hands with supporters and signed autographs. He continued shaking hands from the backseat of his convertible as the car rolled eastward along Main Street. Approaching Willkie High School, his caravan slowed for a thousand-plus waiting students. From Elwood, the senator's party continued to Fort Wayne. Kennedy's April 24, 1968, Elwood stop was day two of his second campaign swing through Indiana. His first had been April 4. That day, when Kennedy arrived in Indianapolis, he learned of Martin Luther King's assassination. Amid mounting threats of violence, Kennedy climbed onto a flatbed trailer in a predominantly African American neighborhood and delivered what historians praise as one of the most gripping speeches in US political history. Consequently, while riots broke out across America that night, no rioting occurred in Indianapolis. Forty-two days after the senator's tour through Elwood, Kennedy himself was assassinated. (Courtesy Rita Kelich.)

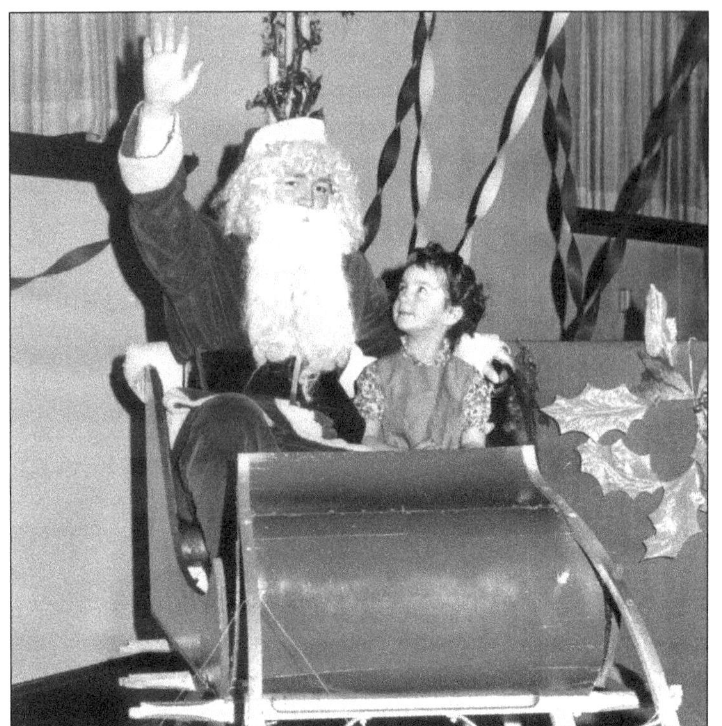

Santa Claus visits with Mary Lou Sheedy, five years old, on November 29, 1963, at his faux North Pole headquarters, located in the old Federal Building at 115 South Anderson Street. Santa made his Elwood arrival official the next day during the annual Christmas parade. (Courtesy Elwood Chamber.)

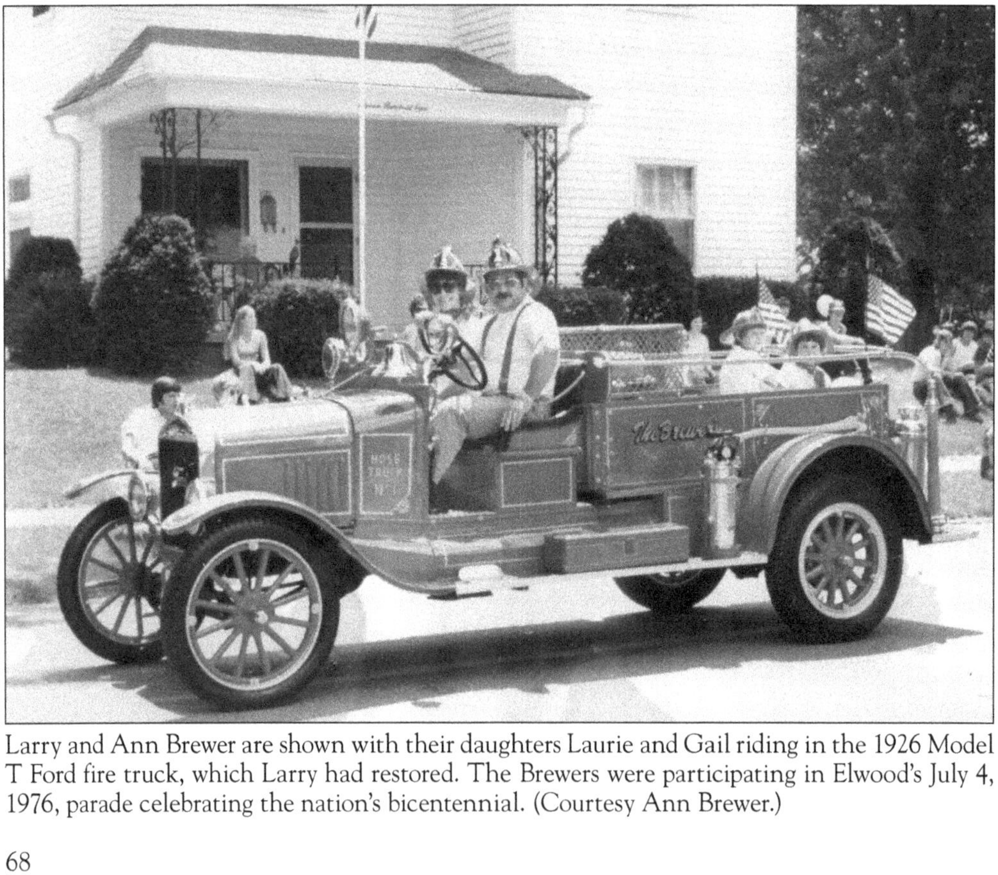

Larry and Ann Brewer are shown with their daughters Laurie and Gail riding in the 1926 Model T Ford fire truck, which Larry had restored. The Brewers were participating in Elwood's July 4, 1976, parade celebrating the nation's bicentennial. (Courtesy Ann Brewer.)

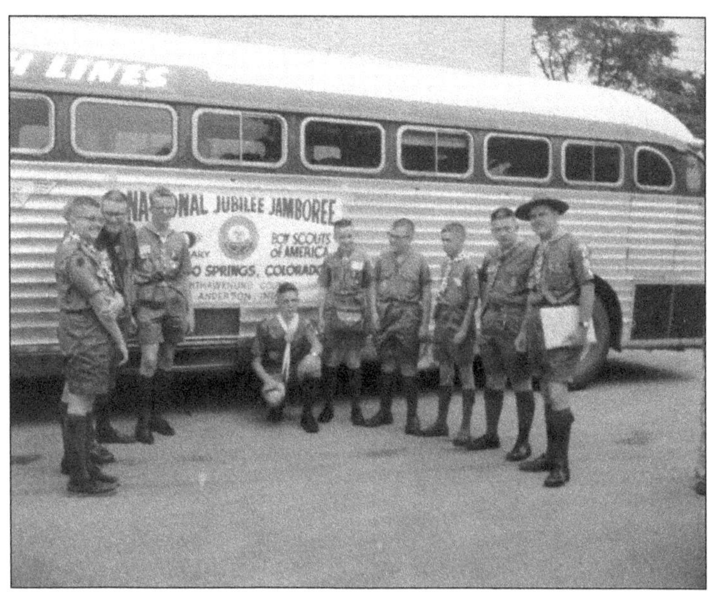

Members of Elwood Boy Scout Troop 84 prepare to board their bus headed for Camp Kikthawenund in Colorado Springs, Colorado, where they will take part in the 1960 National Scout Jubilee Jamboree. From left to right, the boys are Bill Fitzpatrick, Tim Orbaugh, Mike Lewellen, Greg Tunis, Dave Klummp, Jeff Coffin, Larry Hinshaw, and Jack Armstrong, standing next to Scoutmaster Robert Hinshaw. (Courtesy Ron Hinshaw.)

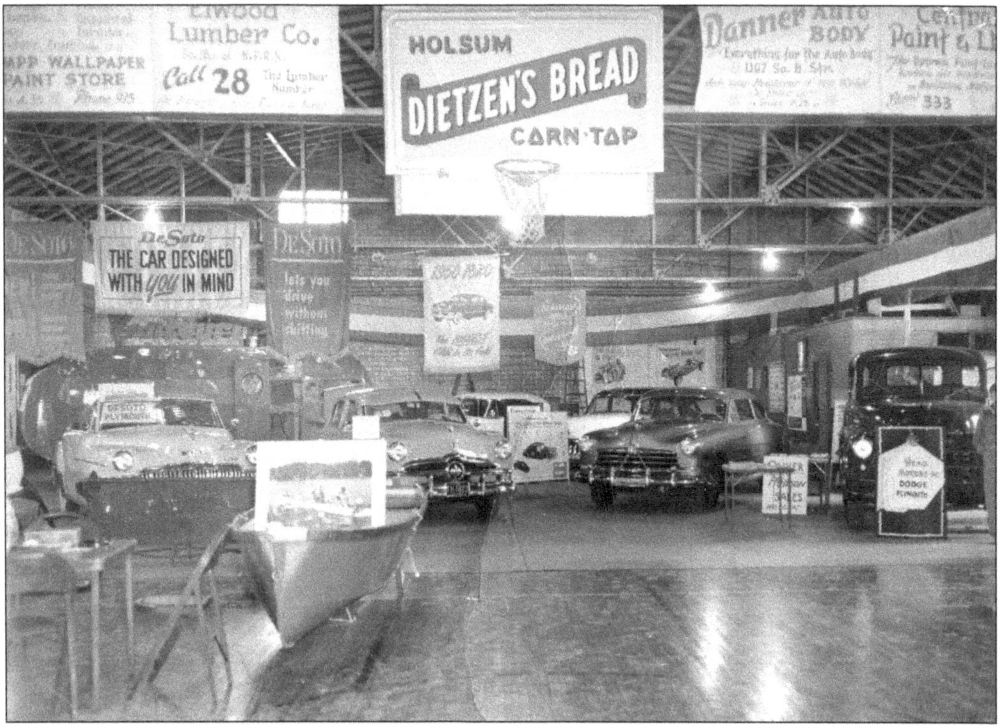

The Elwood Conservation Club sponsored its first Sportsman Show in April 1950 at the National Guard Armory, then located at South B and 16th Streets. Area businesses displayed the latest sporting goods, from fishing rods to automobiles. The *Call-Leader* asserted hope that the club "deems the show of sufficient success to make it an annual affair." The show did become an annual event but only through its 1957 event. (Courtesy Al Mottweiler.)

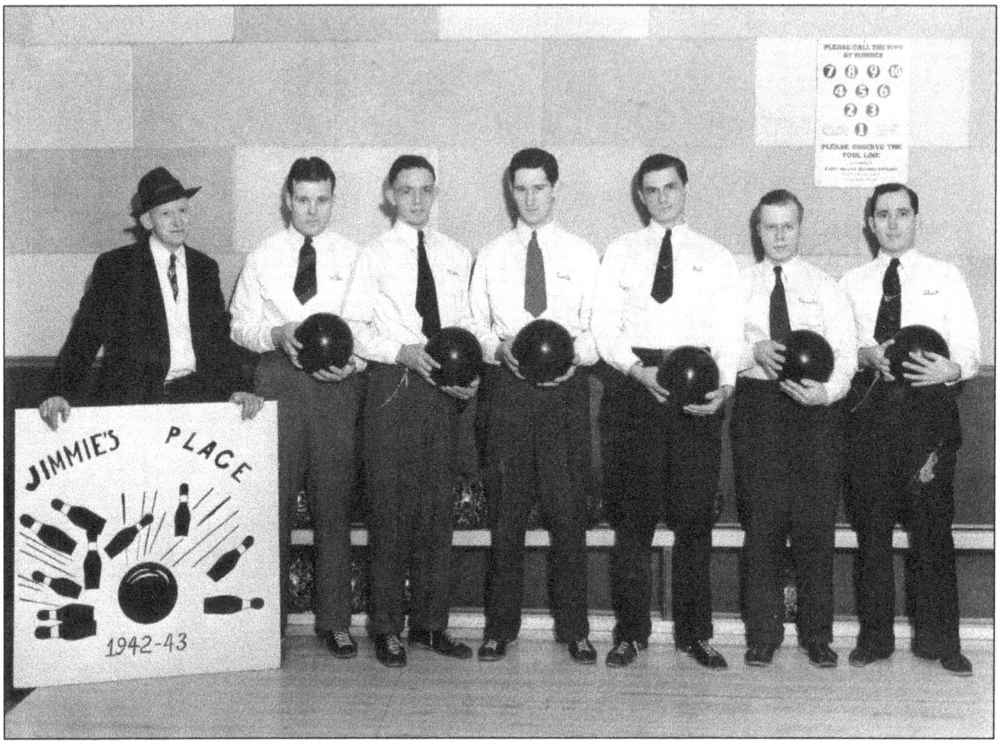

The Jimmie's Place team finished the 1942–1943 city bowling league season at Ballard Bowl deadlocked with Elmore's for the first-place title. Each team had racked up 33 wins and 21 losses. Pictured from left to right are Jimmie's Place owner Jimmie Peel, Mike Kilgore, Max Kleinbub, Louie Linsmeyer, Russell "Rut" Harrell, Marvin Call, and Ehrmal "Shorty" Odom. Jimmie's Place was a pool hall located at 1514 South A Street. (Courtesy Cathy Ogden.)

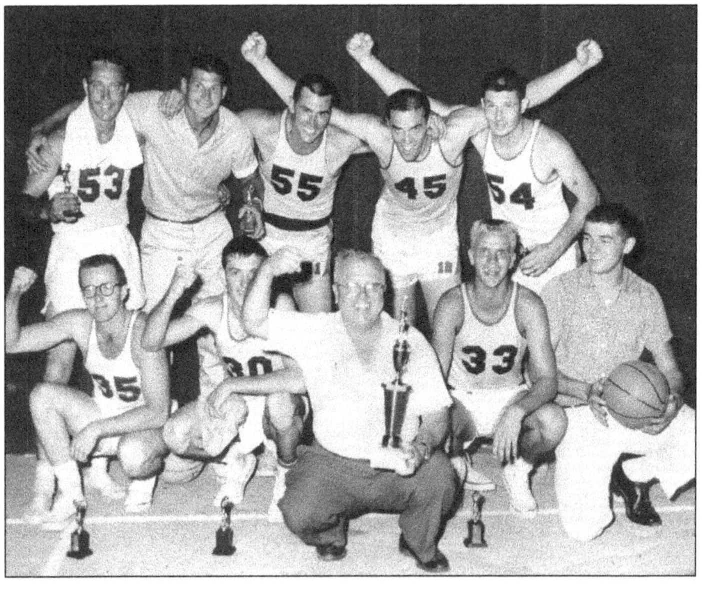

The Jones' Firestone team whoops it up after clinching the 1959 Lions Club Summertime Outdoor Basketball Championship by a nail-biting 53-51 at the Callaway Park court. From left to right are (first row) Fred Jones, Bruce Yeagy, Wayne Jones (sponsor), Tom Phillips, and Dick Mitchell; (second row) Jim Stone, Darrell McQuitty, Carl McNulty, Dave Jones, and Bill McQuitty. (Courtesy Terry Jones.)

Five

Disasters

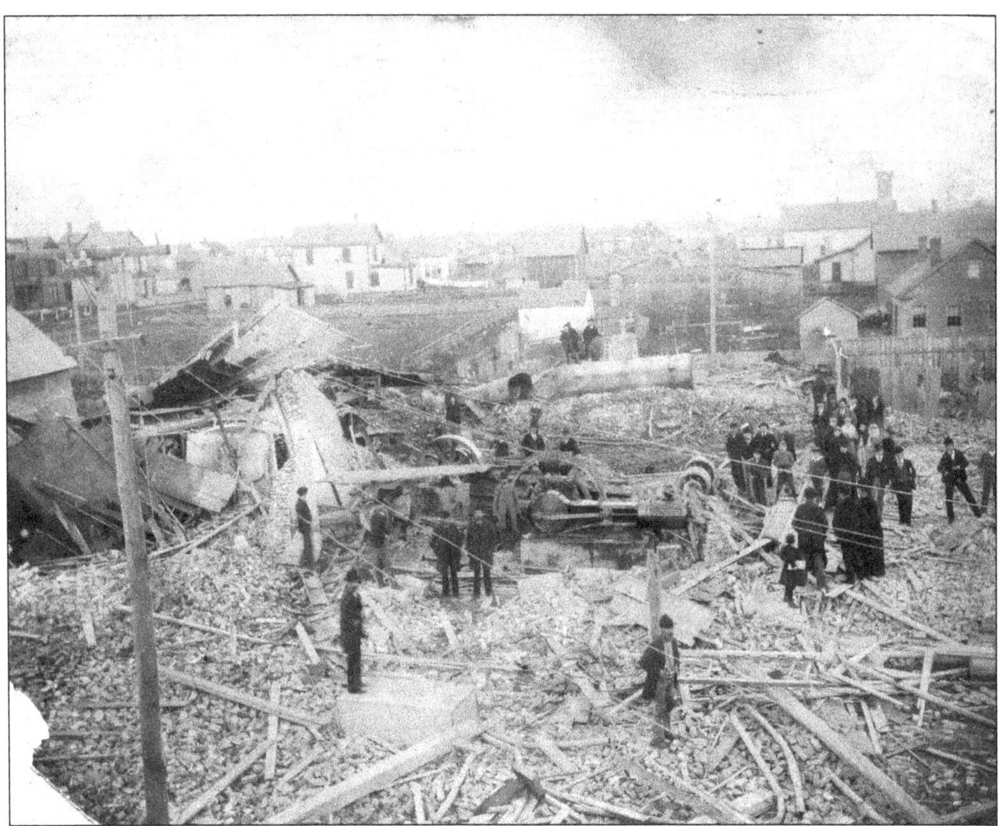

At 4:20 p.m. on November 29, 1893, Elwood's Electric Light and Street Railway plant exploded, blowing off its roof, leveling its brick walls, scattering debris for blocks, and leaving the city in darkness. Miraculously, no one died. Investigators blamed the blast on a spark that ignited a gas leak under the plant's floor. Replacement of the building and equipment was roughly $2,500, a hefty amount in 1893. (Courtesy Elwood Public Library.)

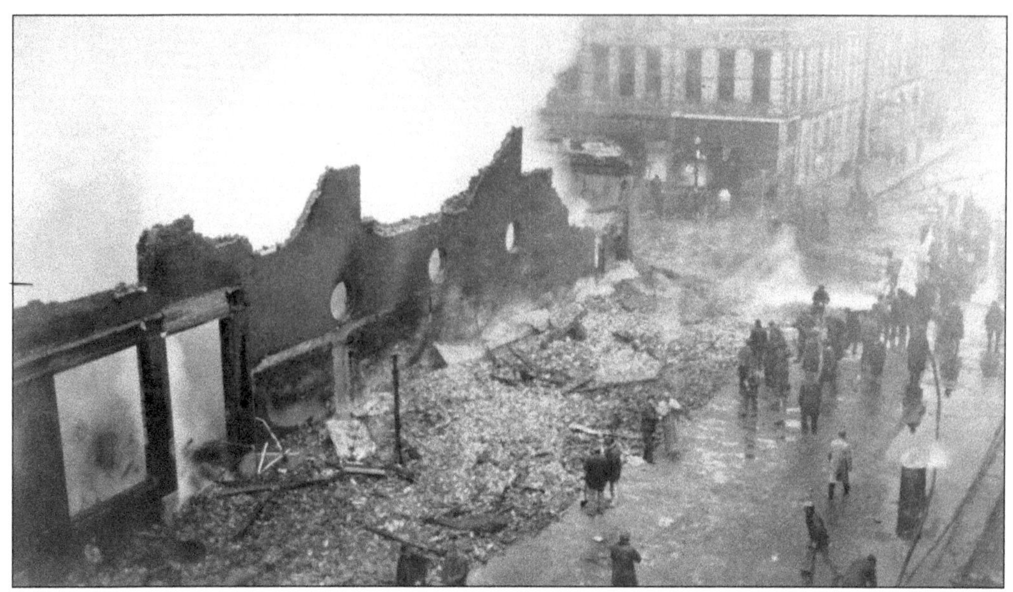

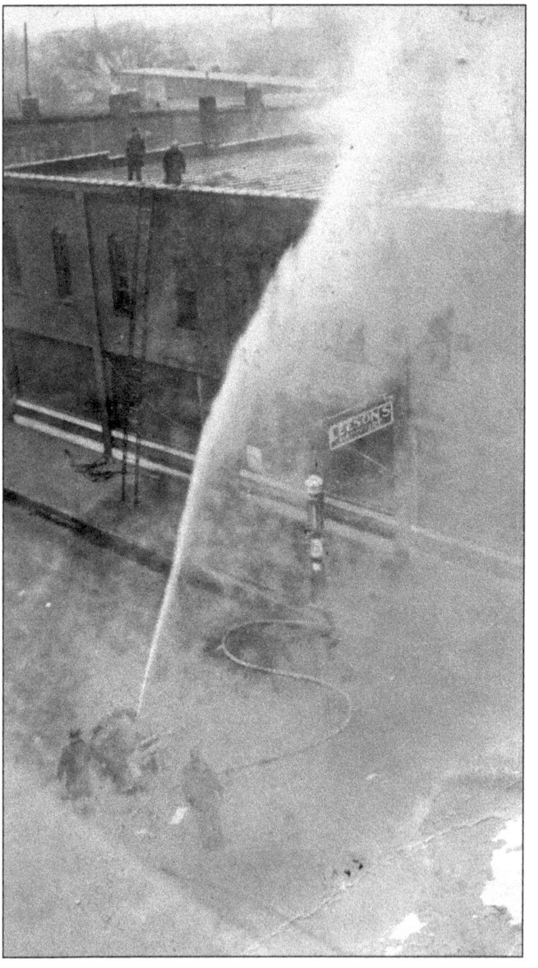

Fire erupted early in the morning in the Leeson's building at South Anderson and A Streets, and burned it to the ground on Tuesday, January 2, 1934. The flames damaged several nearby buildings, causing an estimated total loss of $600,000. Firefighters from Tipton, Alexandria, and Anderson assisted the Elwood department, while police roped off the streets to prevent hundreds of curiosity seekers from entering the danger zone. The fire started in the store's basement and turned into an inferno by 5:30 a.m. when it was discovered. Flames leapt across Anderson and South A Streets, and quick-thinking firefighters aimed their water hoses at the neighboring buildings, keeping serious damage at bay. The Hotel Sidwell on South A and Leeson's Hardware Store, however, did not fare as well. Both suffered excessive fire and water damage. (Both, courtesy Sue Loser.)

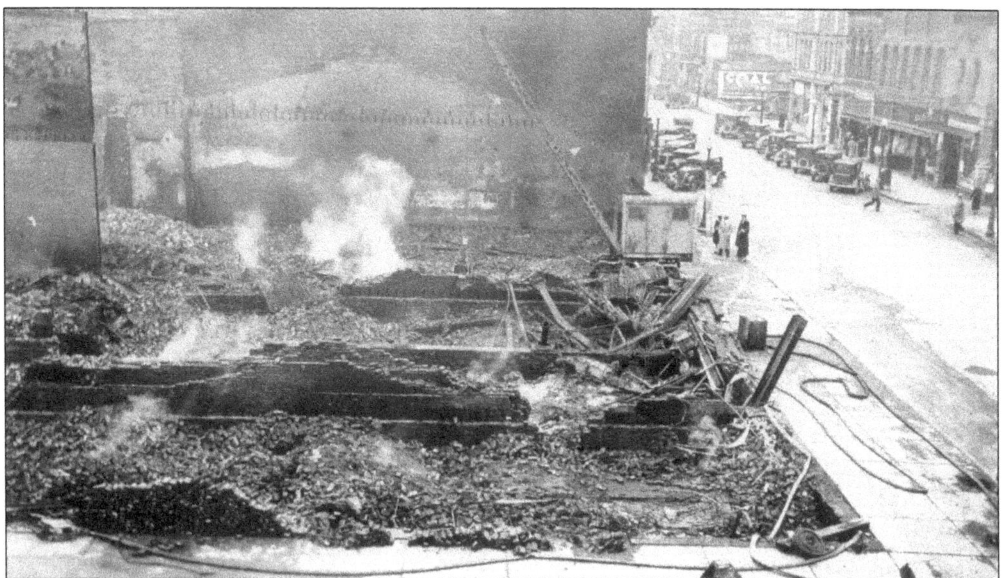

Walls that did not crumble during the fire were knocked down by the fire department as a precaution. Once the flames were doused, Mayor Bonham donned a raincoat and boots and directed city employees, who removed bricks and other debris from the streets. The *Call-Leader* reported the disaster as one of the most devastating conflagrations in the city's history. Fortunately, only one minor injury occurred. (Courtesy Sue Loser.)

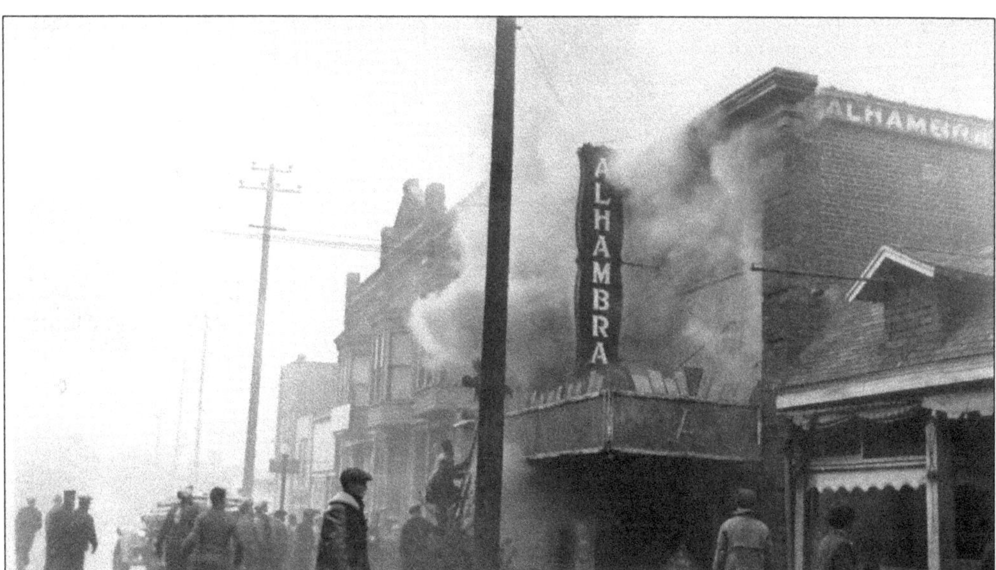

The afternoon of the day of the Leeson's fire, a spark from the generator at the Alhambra Theater on Main Street ignited the movie screen, causing considerable damage and quickly filling the auditorium with smoke. The feature film was the Marx Brothers' *Duck Soup*. Damage was estimated at $5,500. The theater reopened in February. (Courtesy Sue Loser.)

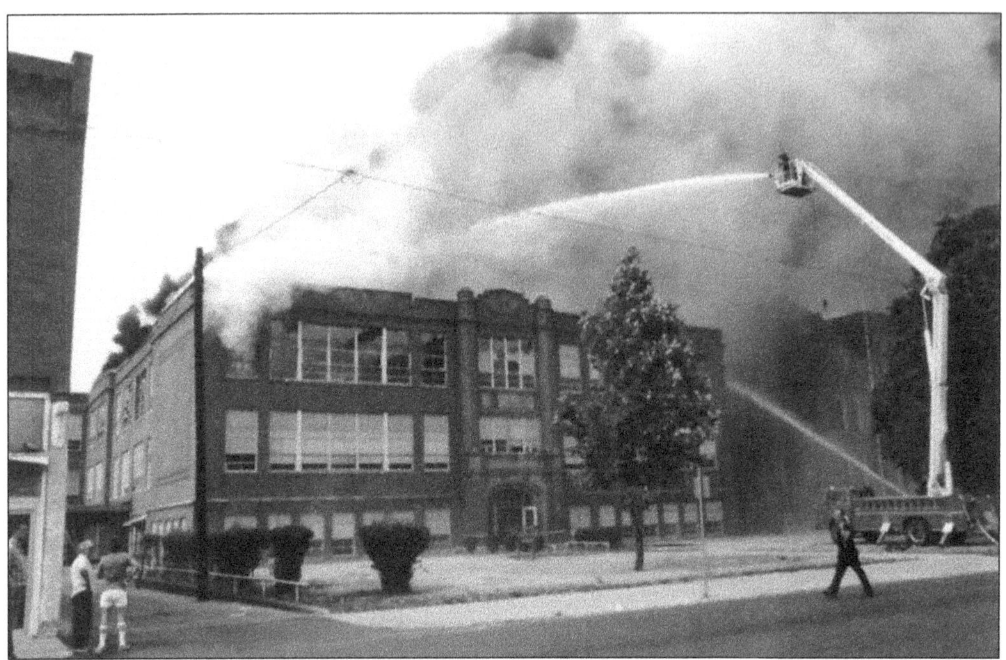

After the 1972–1973 school year, the old high school was maintained for seventh and eighth graders until June 22, 1988, when fire erupted in the auditorium. More than 100 firefighters from Elwood and surrounding communities battled the flames, while members of the community moved sports equipment, sewing machines, woodworking cabinets, and more from the school to the library's front lawn. As the battle wore on, local merchants supported firefighters with food and cold drinks. Despite everyone's heroic efforts, however, the high winds and near 100-degree heat hindered progress. The beloved school was gutted. The loss was deemed the city's largest and most sentimental tragedy. (Above, courtesy Ginny Noble; below, courtesy Elwood Public Library.)

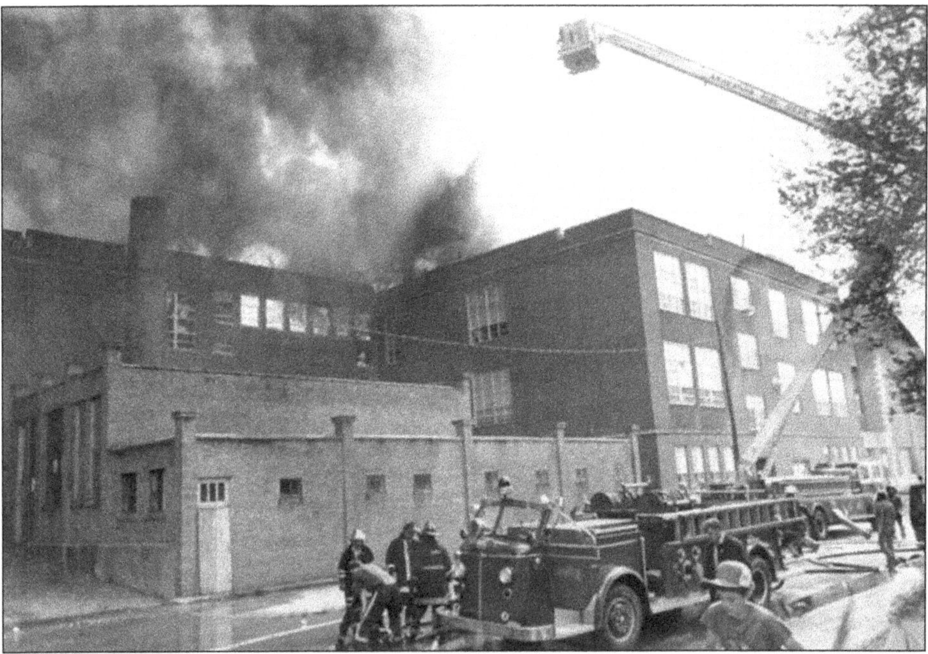

The worst flood in Elwood's history occurred in March 1913, when heavy rains pelted the Midwest for days. Power outages left Elwood residents shivering in the dark and forced many businesses and factories to close. The West Main Street Bridge, pictured, survived the flood and was a godsend to people seeking higher ground. Although hundreds in Elwood suffered loss of property, no lives were lost. (Courtesy Eric Grogan.)

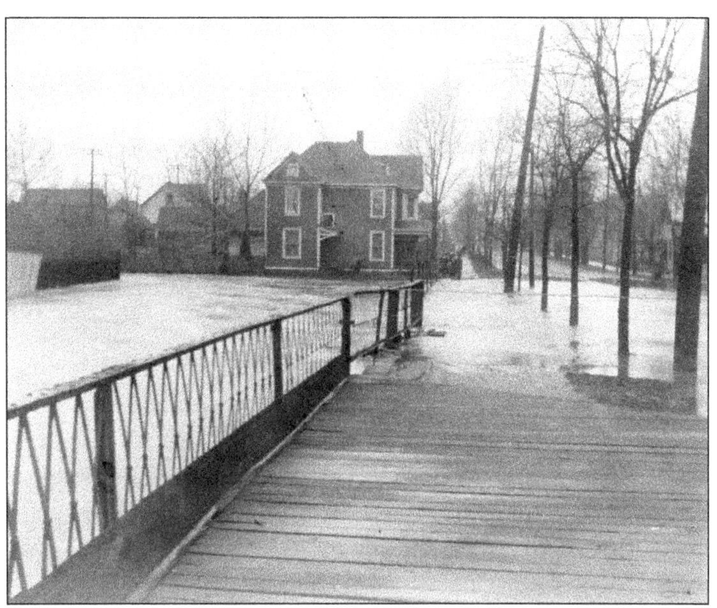

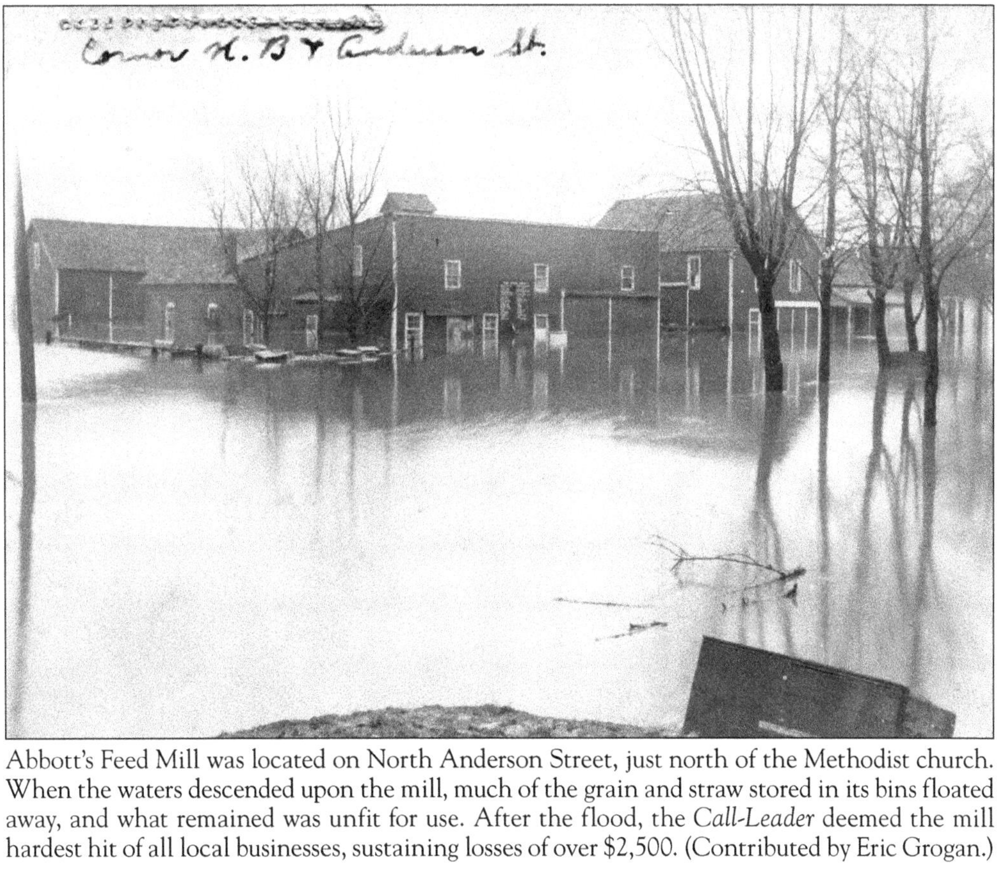

Abbott's Feed Mill was located on North Anderson Street, just north of the Methodist church. When the waters descended upon the mill, much of the grain and straw stored in its bins floated away, and what remained was unfit for use. After the flood, the *Call-Leader* deemed the mill hardest hit of all local businesses, sustaining losses of over $2,500. (Contributed by Eric Grogan.)

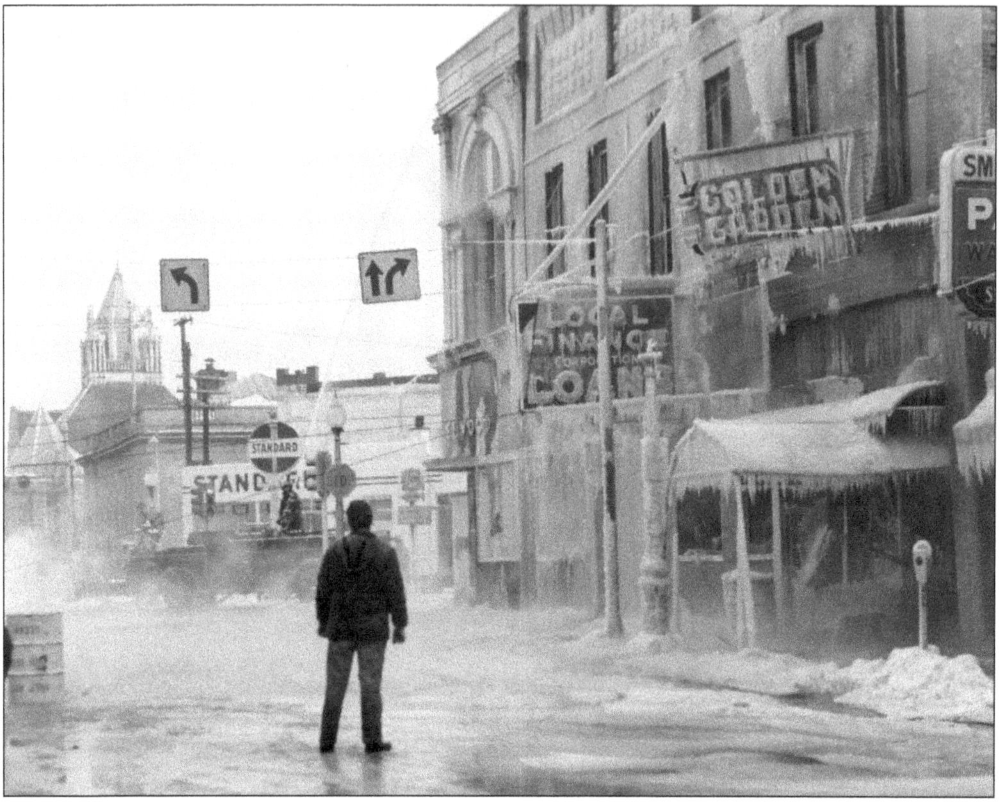

Above, the Elwood Fire Department battles a blaze on February 29, 1960, at the southeast corner of Main and Anderson Streets. The fire consumed a quarter block of Elwood's downtown area while destroying Elwood Federal Savings & Loan, Local Finance, the Golden Gardens, and Smith-Alsop Paint and Wallpaper. Nearly 100 firefighters from surrounding communities helped. Except for suffering near-frozen hands and feet, no one was hurt, and no one was inside the buildings when the fire broke out. Below, the next morning, hundreds of area residents were drawn to the site of the ice-encrusted, but still-smoldering, aftermath. Historians considered the tragedy the most disastrous fire in Elwood in 20 years. (Courtesy Matt Boyland.)

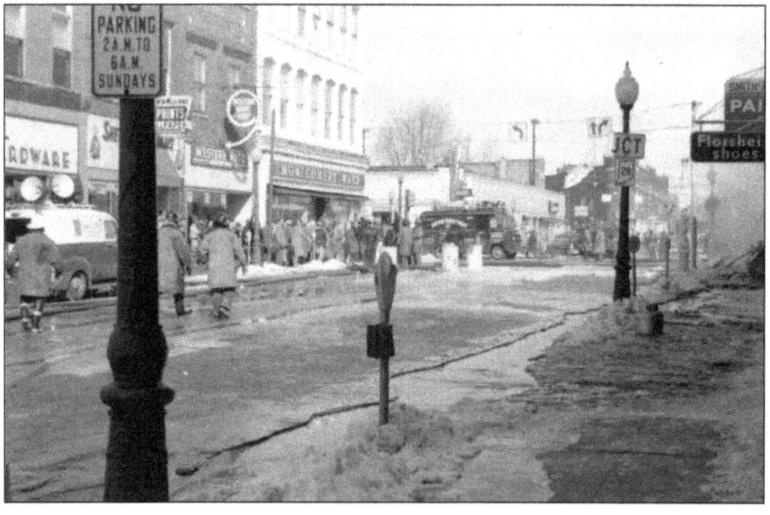

Six

SCHOOLS AND CHURCHES

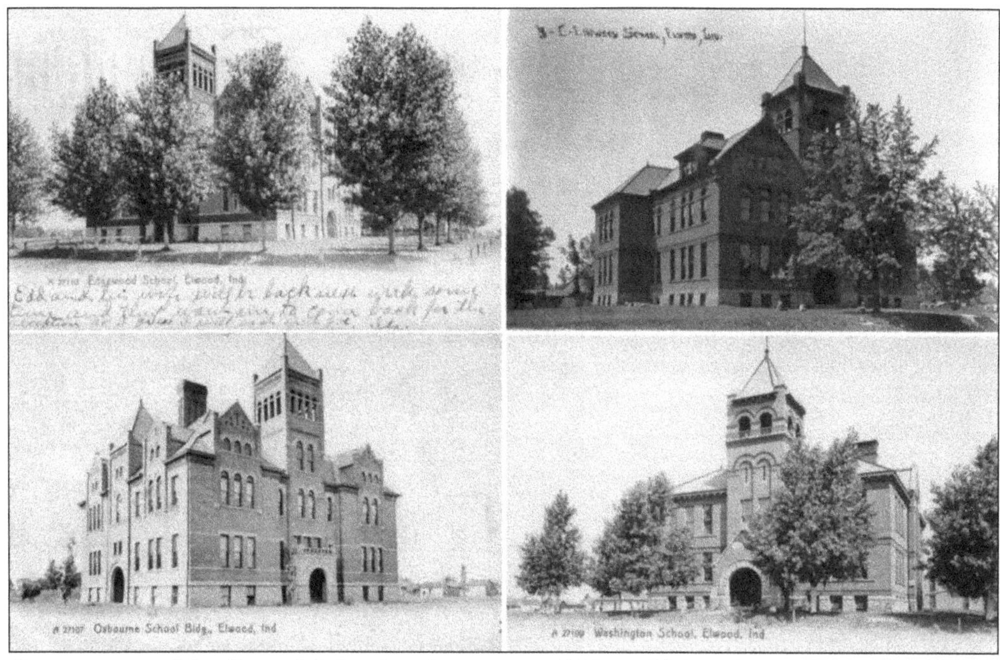

Construction of the Central School at the corner of 18th and Main Streets was undertaken in 1897 and considered one of the nation's finest education facilities. That project was followed by four more schools: Edgewood at the corner of J and North 6th Streets; Linwood at Nineteenth and South L Streets; Osborn at South G and 12th Streets; and Washington at 7th and North A Streets. (Courtesy Eric Grogan.)

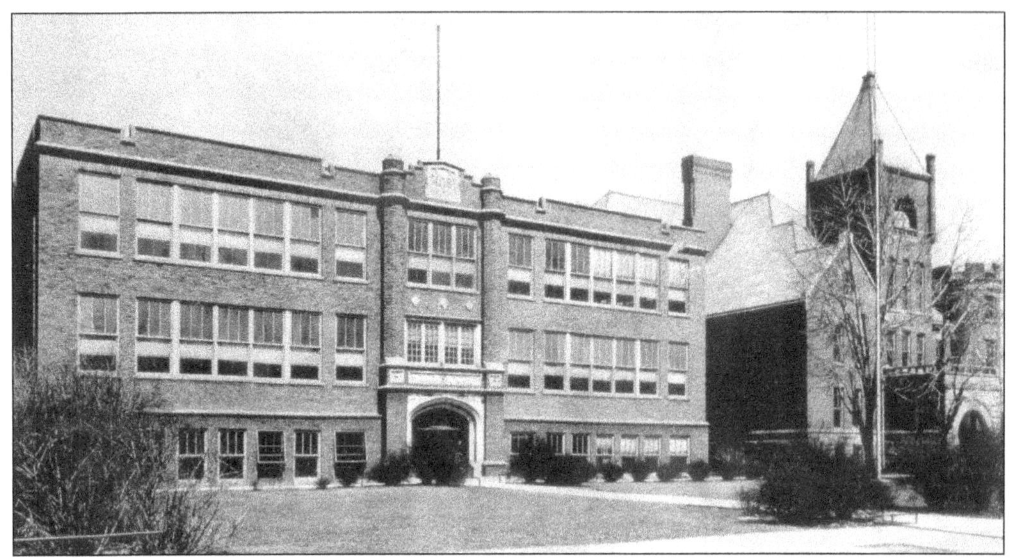

Elwood's original high school building was erected in 1897 at the corner of Main and 18th Streets. It was named Wendell L. Willkie High School in 1944. After a sprawling, modern high school was built north of the city in 1973, the old building was maintained exclusively for seventh and eighth grades.

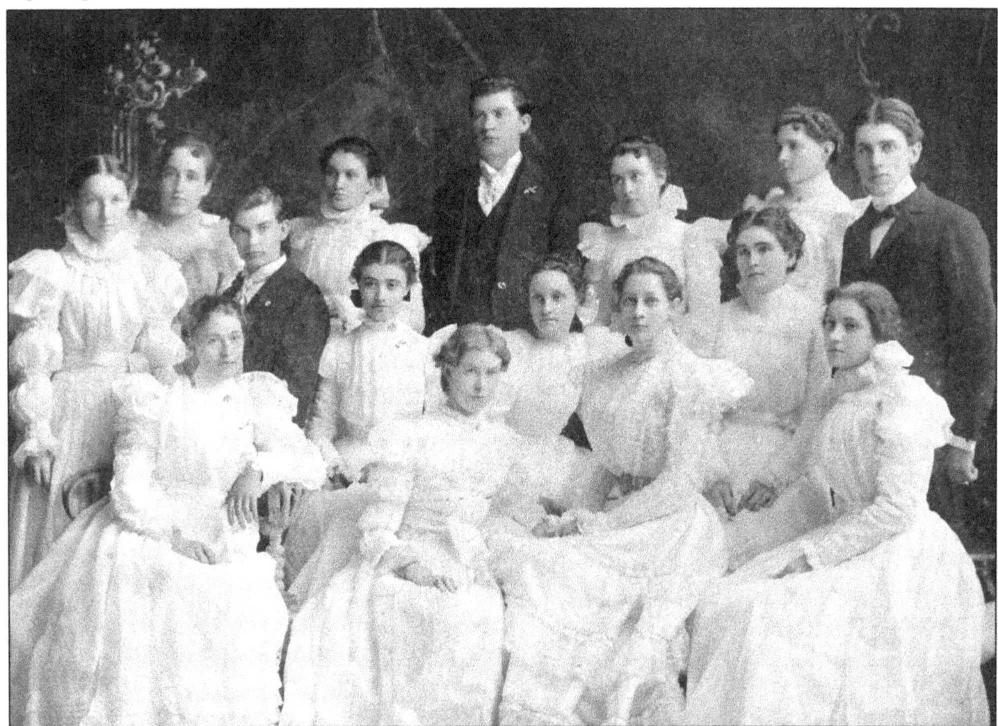

The Elwood High School Class of 1898 was, at that time, the largest in the school's seven-year history. Girls in the class, named in no particular order, were Rowena Canaday, Blanche Minnick, Pearl Burns, Mabel Casner, Maude Gifford, Blanche Hancher, Lenore Uetz, Bessie Clymer, Nellie Heck, Mildred Yelvington, Leona Hillis, and Mary Peed. The boys were John Seright (left), George Seright (right), and Herbert Taylor (center). (Courtesy Amy Seright Updike.)

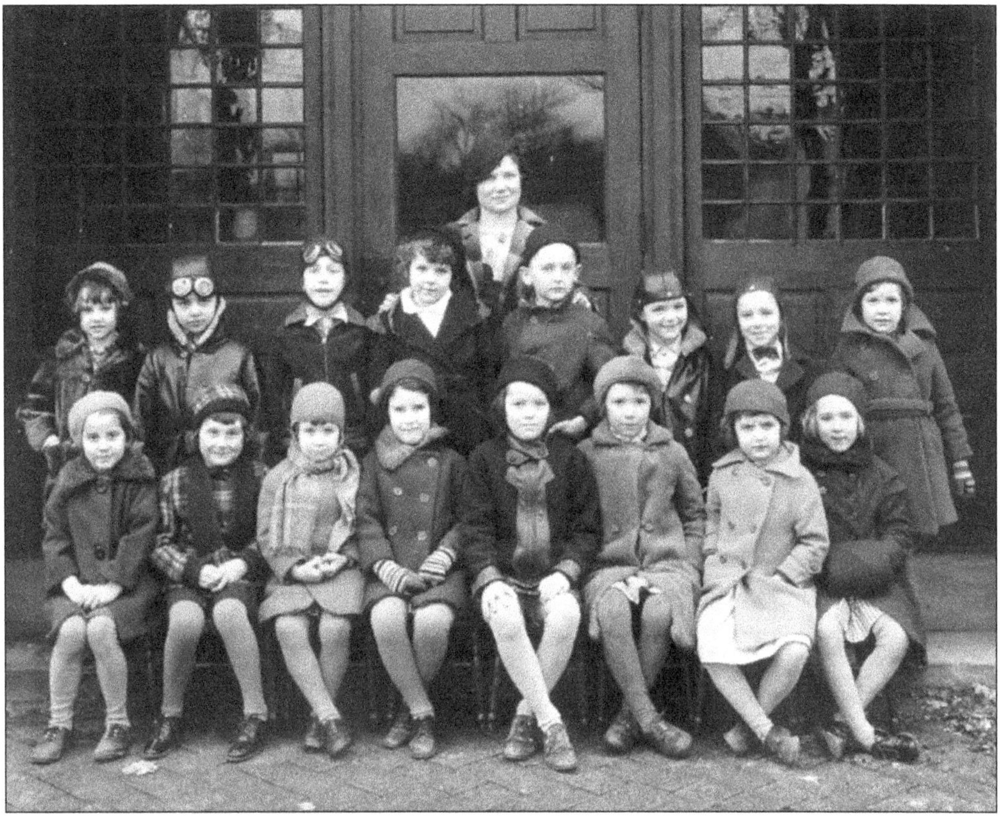

First- and second-graders at Osborn School pose with their teacher, Beatrice Riser (later Bambraugh), in the fall of 1935. The students pictured from left to right are (seated) Lila Ellis, Benjamin Farr, Richard Ott, Katherine Fetz, Roy Erdman, Jack Coston, Bobby Harrison, and Jane Ann Ring; (standing) Madonna Ewing, Kathryn Leeson, Doreen Jones, Rebecca Orbaugh, Carol Leeson, Verna Jean Adair, Betty Ritter, and Jean Parril. (Courtesy Elwood Public Library.)

Teacher Lepha McCurdy poses with her first-grade class in January 1923 outside the entrance of the Osborn School. Students pictured from left to right are Richard Collins, Austin Clary, Paul Glenn, Billy Bryan, Francis Patchett, Kennith Laughbauer, Marcil Borst, Dale Taylor, Waunita Watkins, Rebecca Noland, Jean Robinson, and Vivian Leeson. (Courtesy Elwood Public Library.)

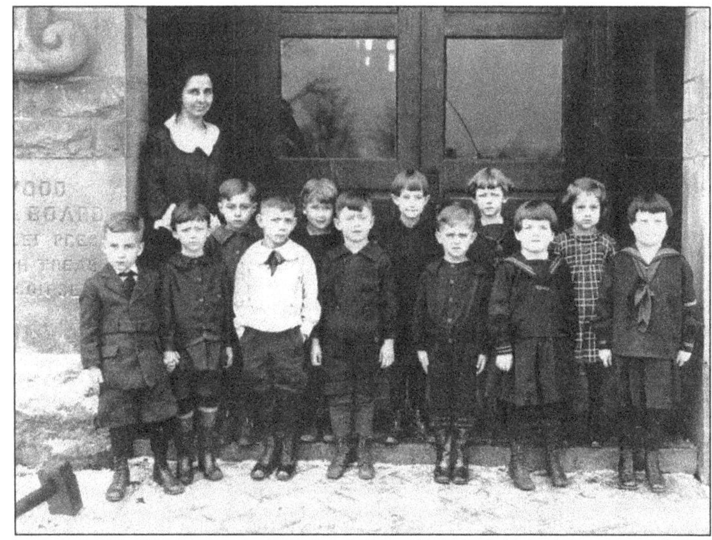

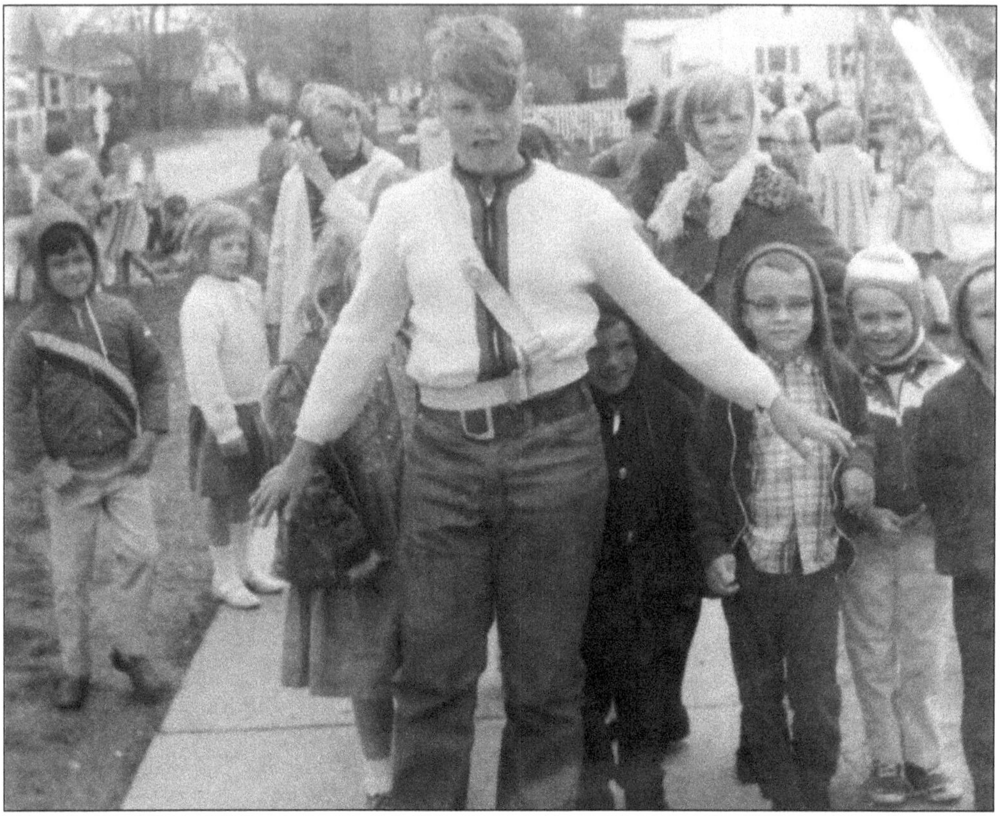

Washington Elementary School's sixth-grade safety patrolman Mike Majors performs his duties and sets a good example as he helps the school's younger children safely cross the street at the end of a school day in 1967. Each elementary school in Elwood participated in the safety patrol program, a national organization established by the American Automobile Association in 1920. (Courtesy Elwood Chamber.)

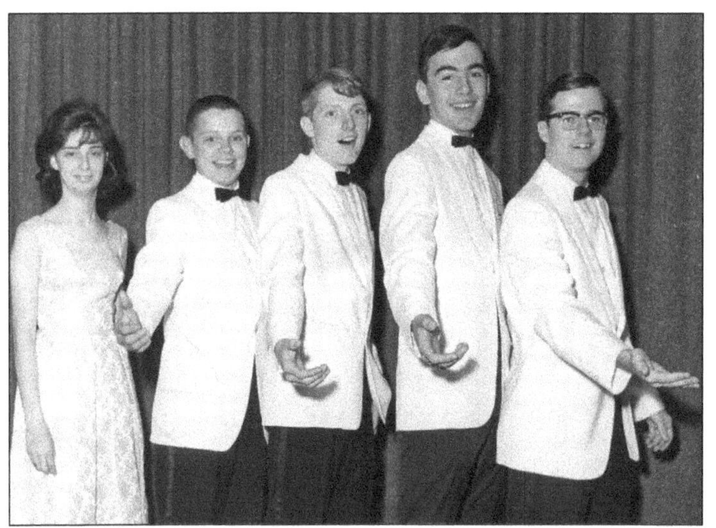

Among Wendell Willkie High School's talented vocal ensembles that performed at various school and civic events throughout the school year was the boys' quartet. Pictured with the 1965–1966 quartet is Alleta Davenport, accompanist, on the left. The group, from left to right, was composed of Steve Wilhoit, Lynn Murray, Jeff Hoffman, and Ken Jones. (Courtesy Terry Jones.)

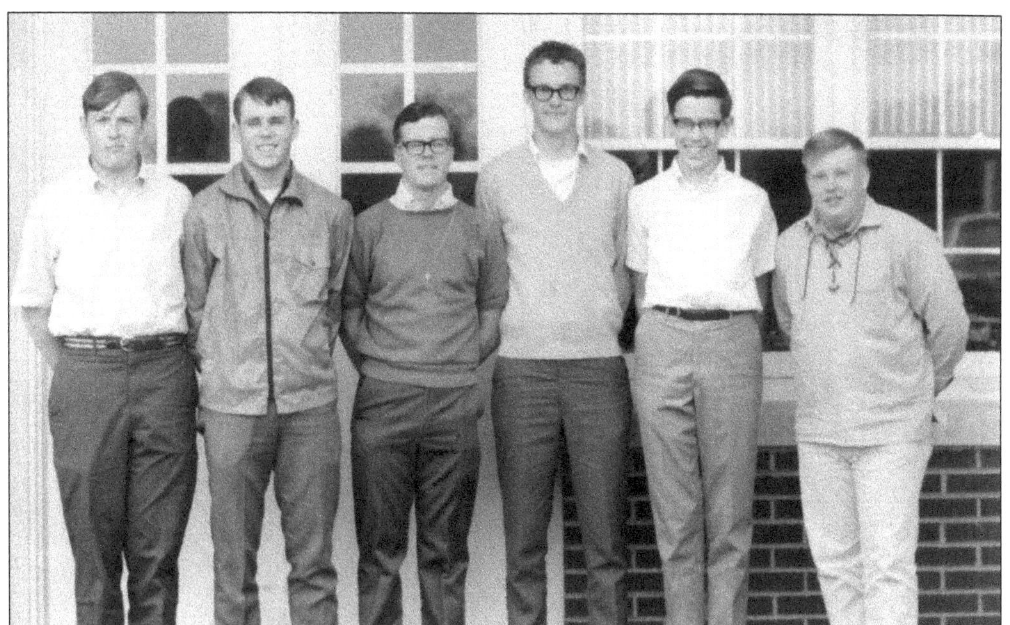

The 1968 Panther Golfers showed their skill on the green, finishing with an impressive 11 and 3 seasonal mark. According to the Wendell Willkie High School yearbook, Crescent, the team finished in a "very high second place" in the Central Indiana Conference. Pictured from left to right are Joe Scott, Tom Austin, Kenny Jones, Kim Hohle, Steve Mayfield, and Jim Saint. (Courtesy Terry Jones.)

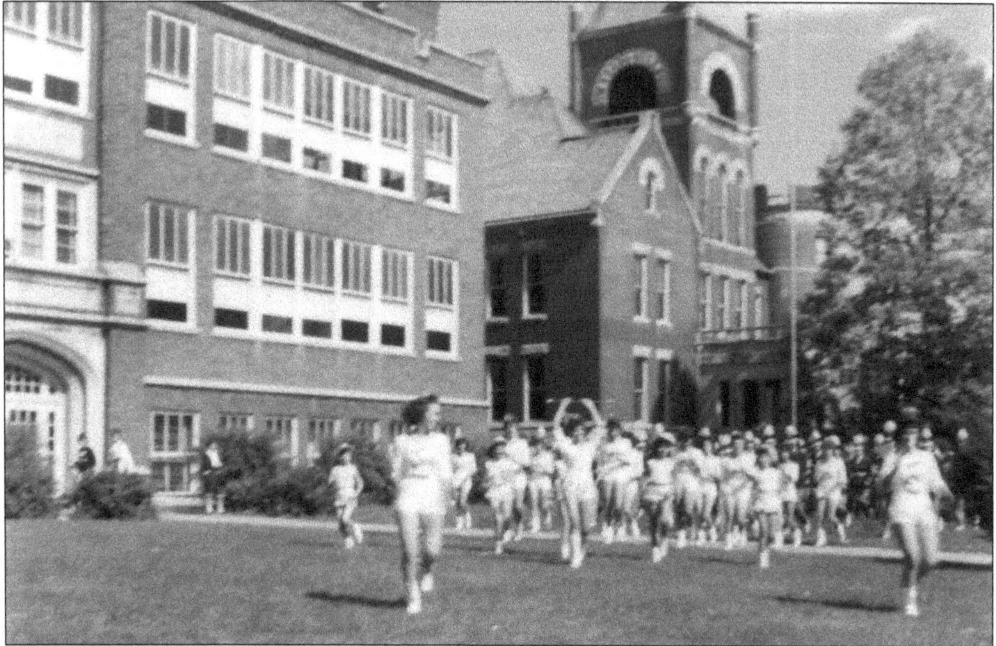

Wendell Willkie High School's Panther Band and the majorettes run across the school grounds, eager to take their places for the 1963 homecoming parade. That year, the band was under the direction of Clifford Brugger and Rex Jenkins. Head majorette was Donna Orbaugh. (Courtesy Ann Brewer.)

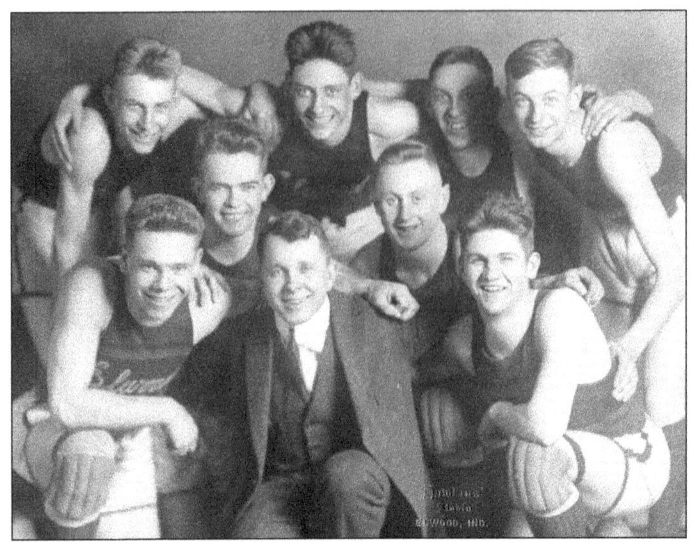

After a winning season of 16-1, Elwood High School's 1918–1919 "Fighting Five" suffered bitter defeat in the first game of the state tournament. Team members pictured from left to right are (first row) Cloyd Hershey, Coach Hugh Miller, and Roy Mitchell; (second row) Ray Gray and Howard Mosiman; (third row) Morris DeHority, Clyde States, William Austill, and Dave Konald. (Courtesy Elwood Public Library.)

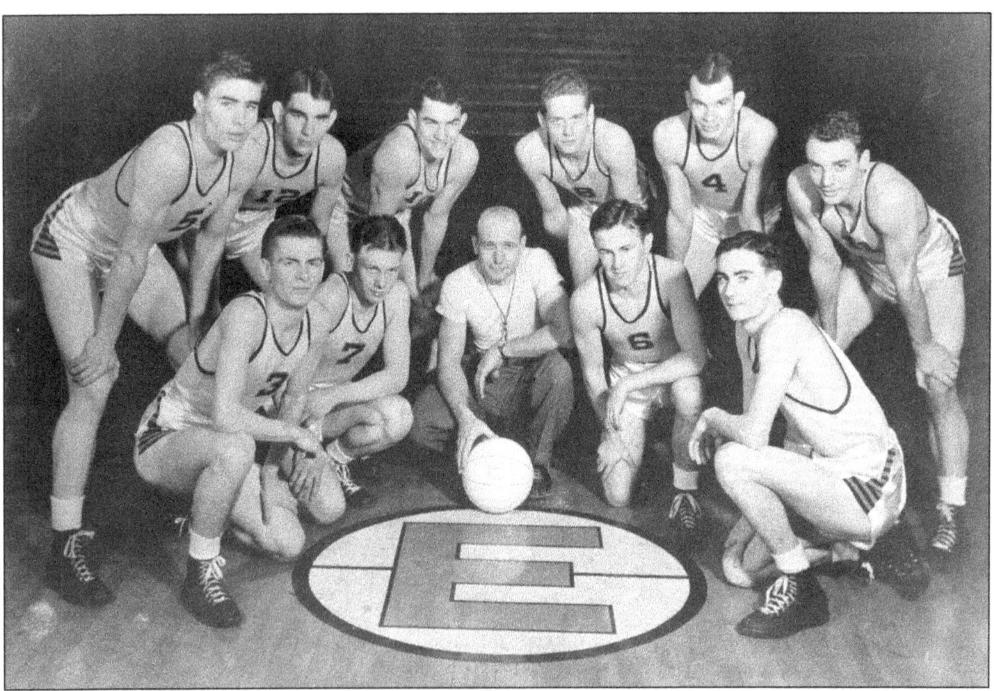

Elwood High's 1938–1939 basketball team endured a tough season. After facing several high-caliber teams, Elwood ended its season in the red, 10-12. From left to right are (kneeling) Paul Davis, George Justice, Coach J.P. Francis, Mickey Carmody, and Maurice Miller; (standing) Harold Dickey, Tom Hartzler, Mulford Davis, Harold Morehead, James Fouch, and Robert Brown. (Courtesy Elwood Library.)

Fullback Jack Coston led his Panthers football team to its first Central Indiana Conference championship when they defeated Peru 37-6 on Friday, October 29, 1948. That year, the Panthers won all six of their conference games. Coston graduated from Wendell Willkie High School in 1949, the same year he married his sweetheart, Dixie Collins. He maintained his love for her and sports until he died in 2015. (Courtesy Dorcas Floyd.)

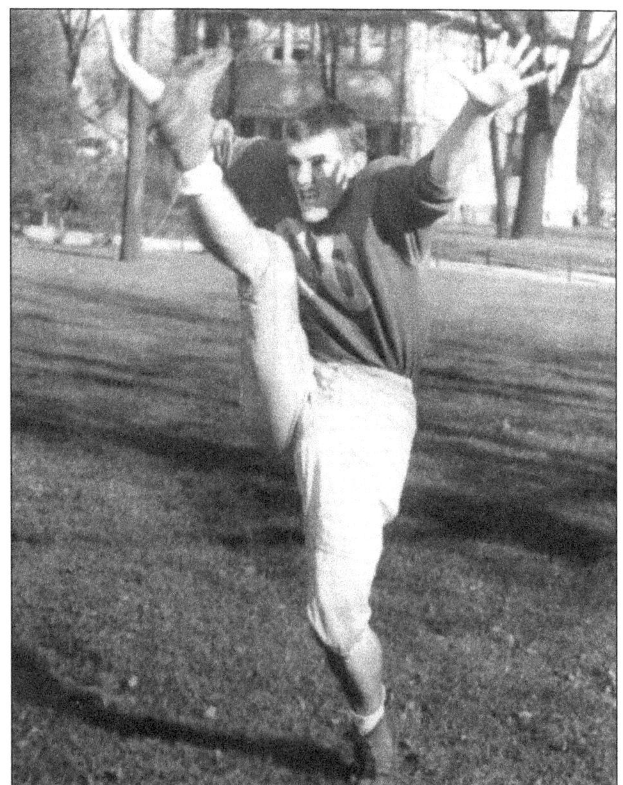

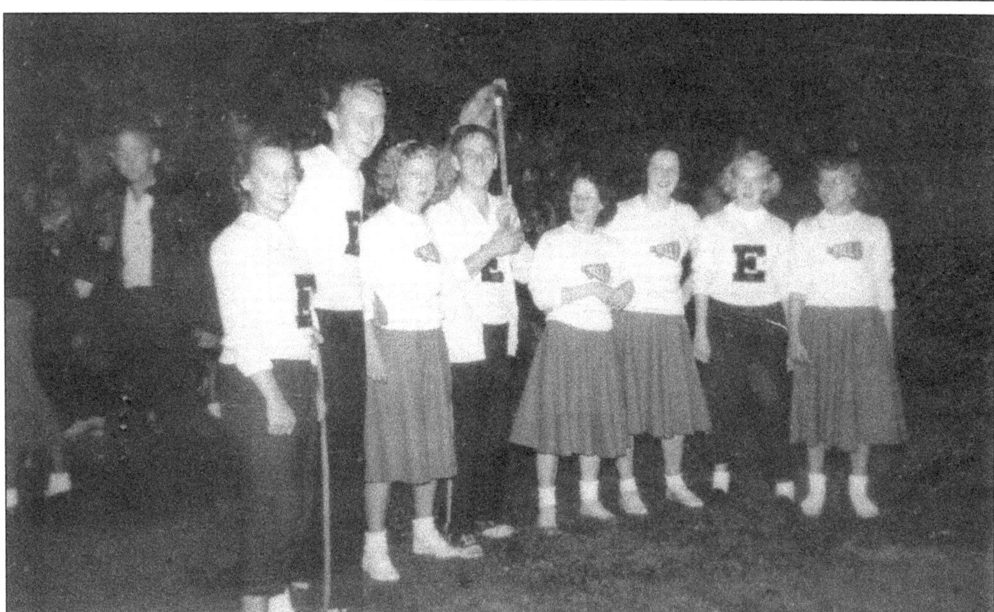

The Elwood Panthers handed the Tipton Blue Devils their first defeat of the 1948 high school football season, 46-6, on Friday, September 24. Despite the outcome, cheer squads for both teams lined up for a friendly photograph. Elwood's cheerleaders, first and second from left, are Kay Gibbons and Johnny Carroll, respectively; third from left, Bill Dever; and seventh from left, Joan Lewis. (Courtesy Carol Dever.)

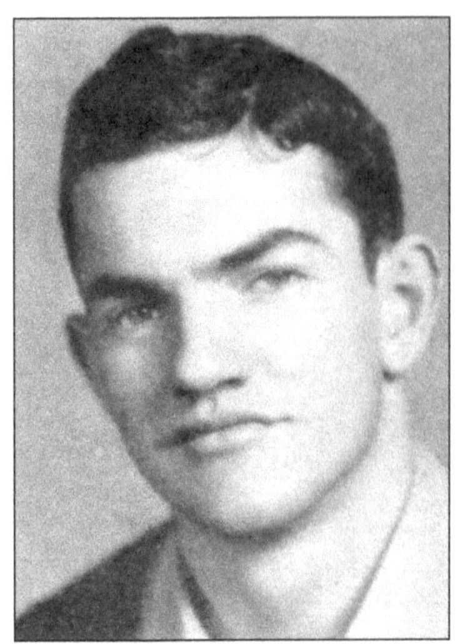

Mulford "Muff" Davis, a 1941 graduate of Wendell Willkie High School, was Elwood's leading scorer for four years and its first Indiana All-Star. Davis went on to play for the University of Kentucky and coached basketball at Frankton High School for 15 years. He was inducted into the Indiana High School Basketball Hall of Fame in 1989. (Courtesy Elwood Public Library.)

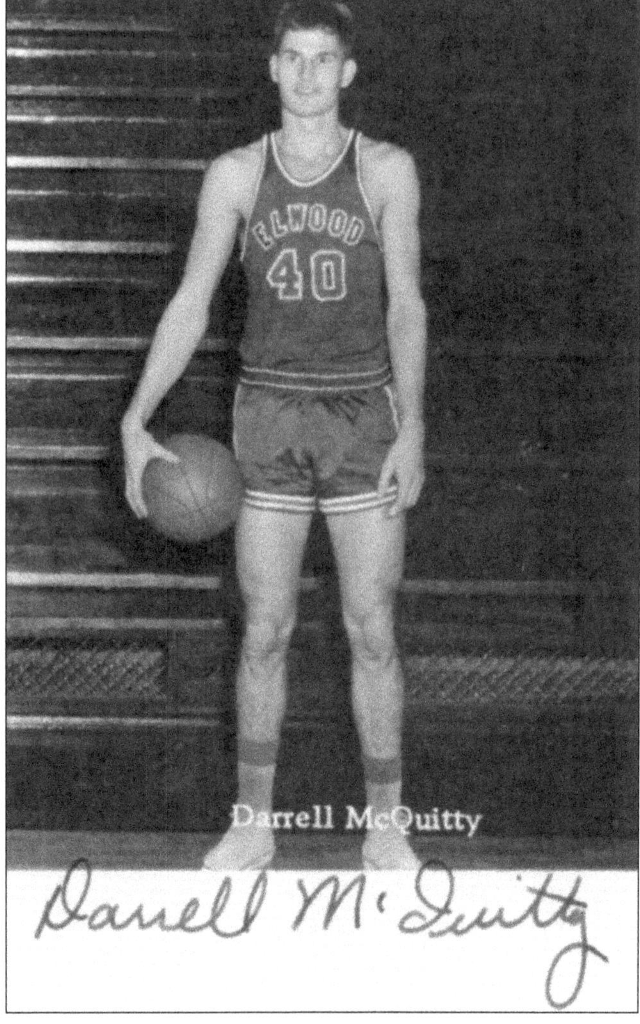

Darrell McQuitty led Elwood to its first sectional title in 1957. A 1958 Indiana All-Star, he was a four-year starter for Wendell Willkie High School, scoring 1,262 points during his high school career. McQuitty coached Elwood varsity basketball for seven years before becoming athletic director in 1983. Retiring in 1995, he was inducted into the Indiana Basketball Hall of Fame in 1999. He died in 2005. (Courtesy Elwood Public Library.)

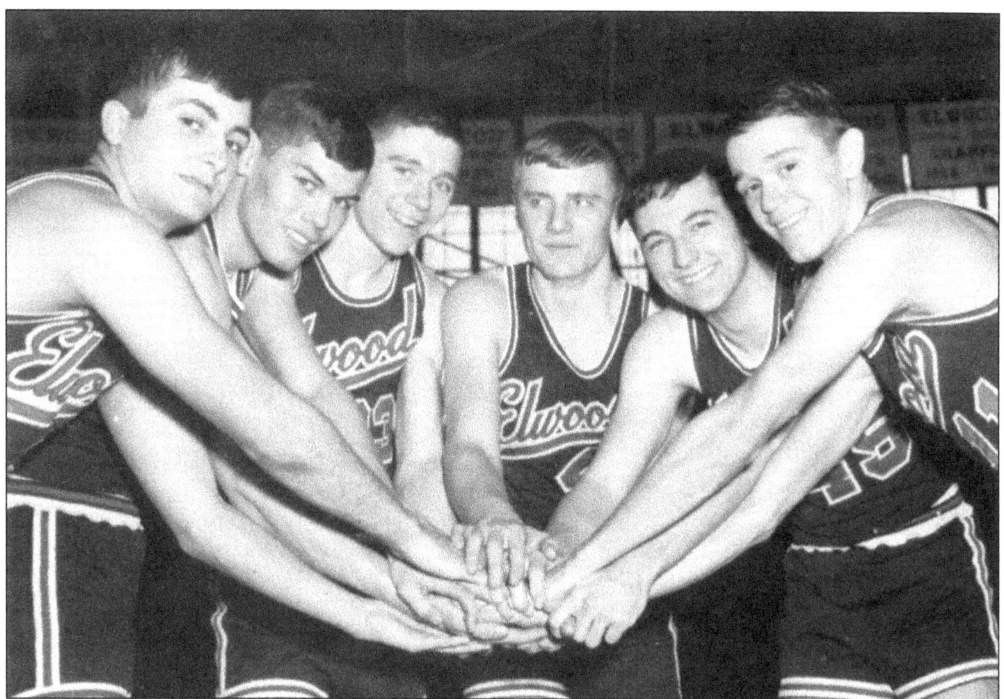

Elwood's John Mengelt is a 1997 Indiana Basketball Hall of Fame inductee. A 1967 Wendell Willkie High School graduate and Indiana All-Star, Mengelt went on to a record-breaking career at Auburn University and 10 years with the NBA. Mengelt is shown here, fourth from left, with his 1966–1967 Elwood teammates. From left to right are Mark Richwine, Jeff Bourff, Bob Drake, Mengelt, Paul Swinford, and Butch Stage. (Courtesy Elwood Public Library.)

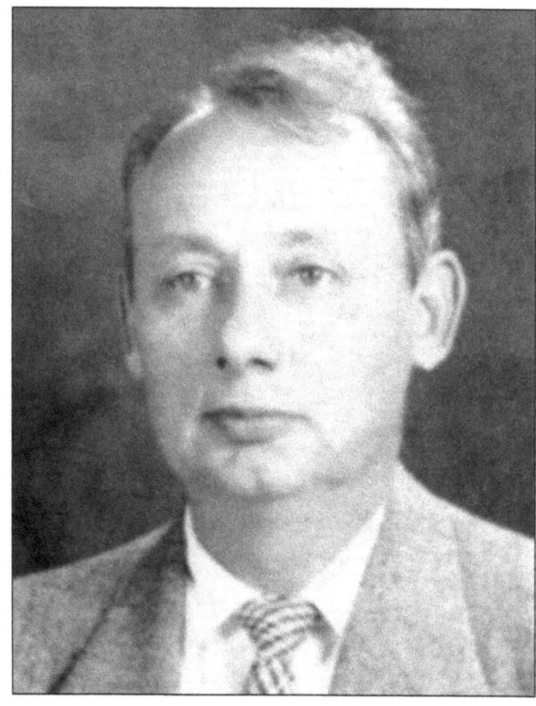

John Ward coached Elwood basketball from 1944 to 1953, compiling a record number of wins. Previously, coaching at Tipton for 15 seasons, he led his teams to 11 sectional wins, two regional titles, and three championships in Central Indiana Athletic Conference, which he founded. He retired as Elwood's athletic director in 1970, the same year he was inducted into the Indiana Basketball Hall of Fame. He died in 1988. (Courtesy Elwood Public Library.)

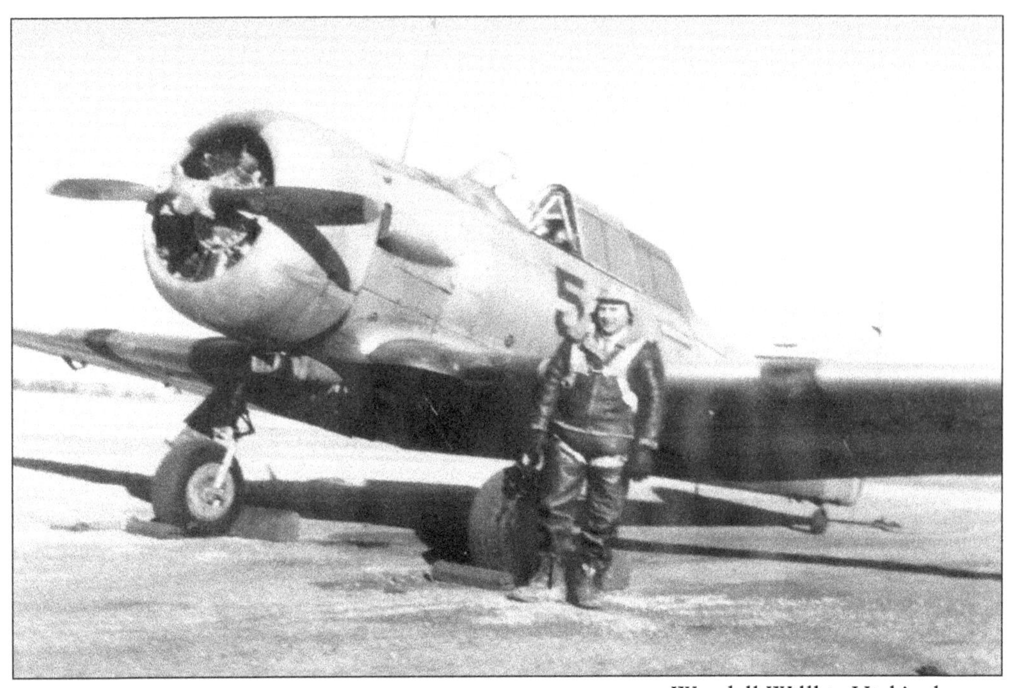

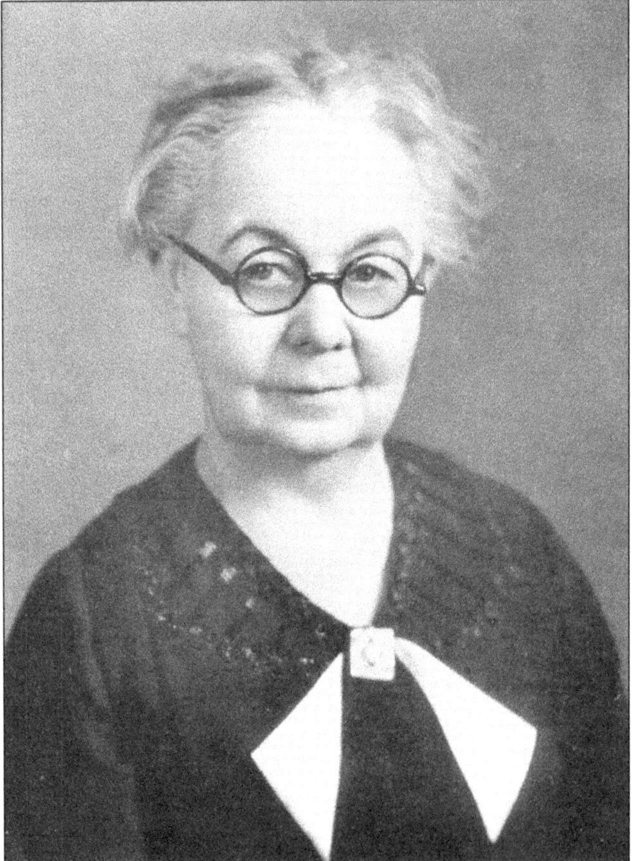

Wendell Willkie High's class of 1947 bought their school an unusual gift—an AT-6 aircraft, used for training purposes during World War II. Local pilot Don Orbaugh traveled to Oklahoma to accept delivery on behalf of the class and flew the plane home. Never again airborne, the plane remained parked at Elwood's airfield and became a hands-on tool for teaching future mechanics. (Courtesy Ann Brewer.)

Mary Elizabeth "Granny" Cox was a beloved Elwood teacher for 53 years, retiring in 1942. She often stated that she was proud to have taught Wendell Willkie the basic facts of economics, civics, and federal government. Born in rural Elwood in 1869, she was a member of Elwood High School's first graduating class (1886) and went on to Indiana University. She died in 1944. (Courtesy Elwood Public Library.)

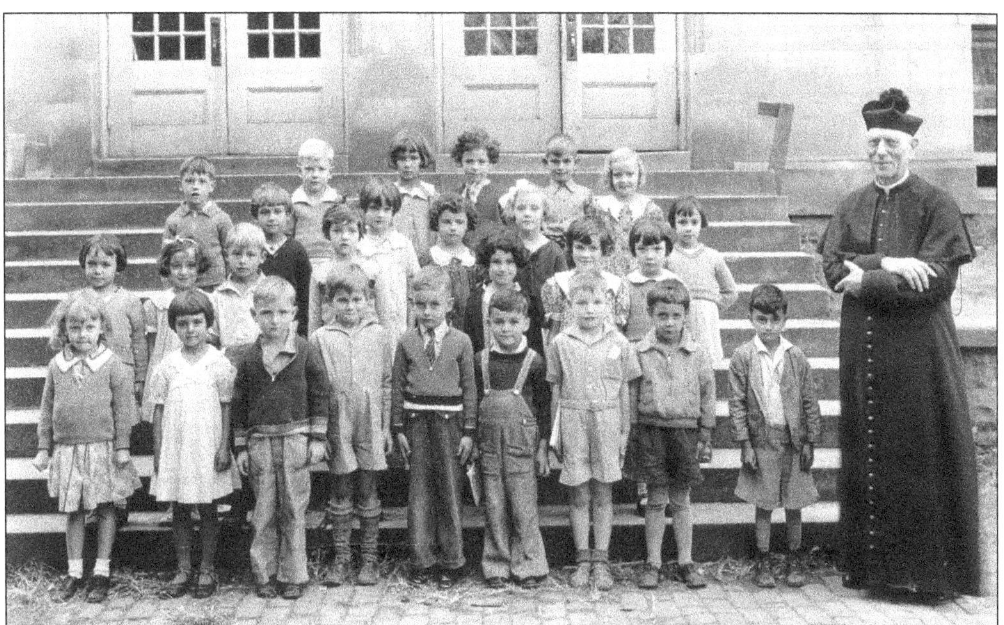

Fr. Balthazer Biegel poses on the steps of St. Joseph's School in 1934 with the class of first graders. The school, dedicated in 1913, operated through 1970, when it was closed. The building was replaced in 1977 with a multipurpose hall. Father Biegel died on August 12, 1935. (Courtesy Elwood Public Library.)

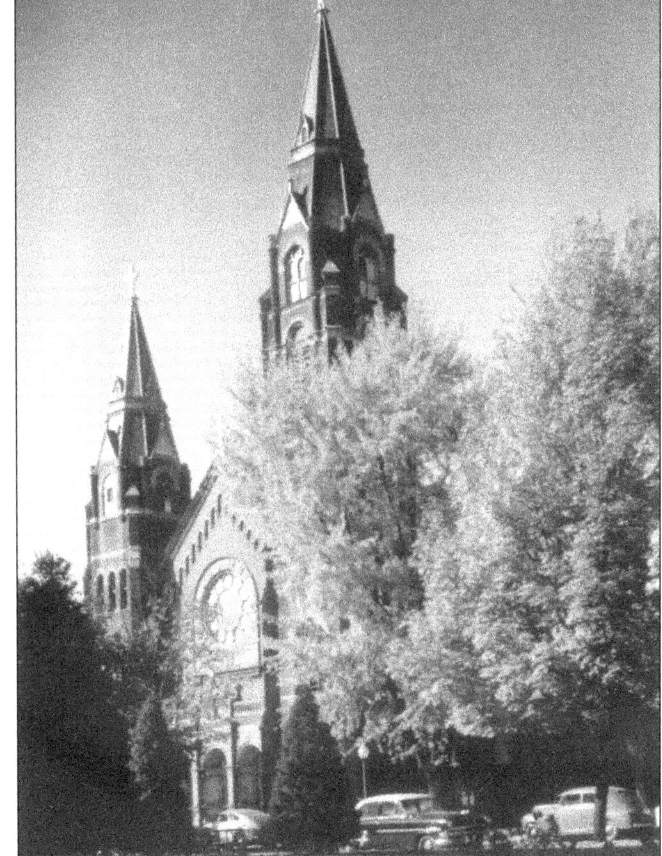

The roots of St. Joseph's Catholic Church extend back to Elwood's earliest "gas boom" days. The cathedral was dedicated in July 1901. Father Biegel was assigned to the parish in 1889 and led it for 46 years. (Courtesy Elwood Public Library.)

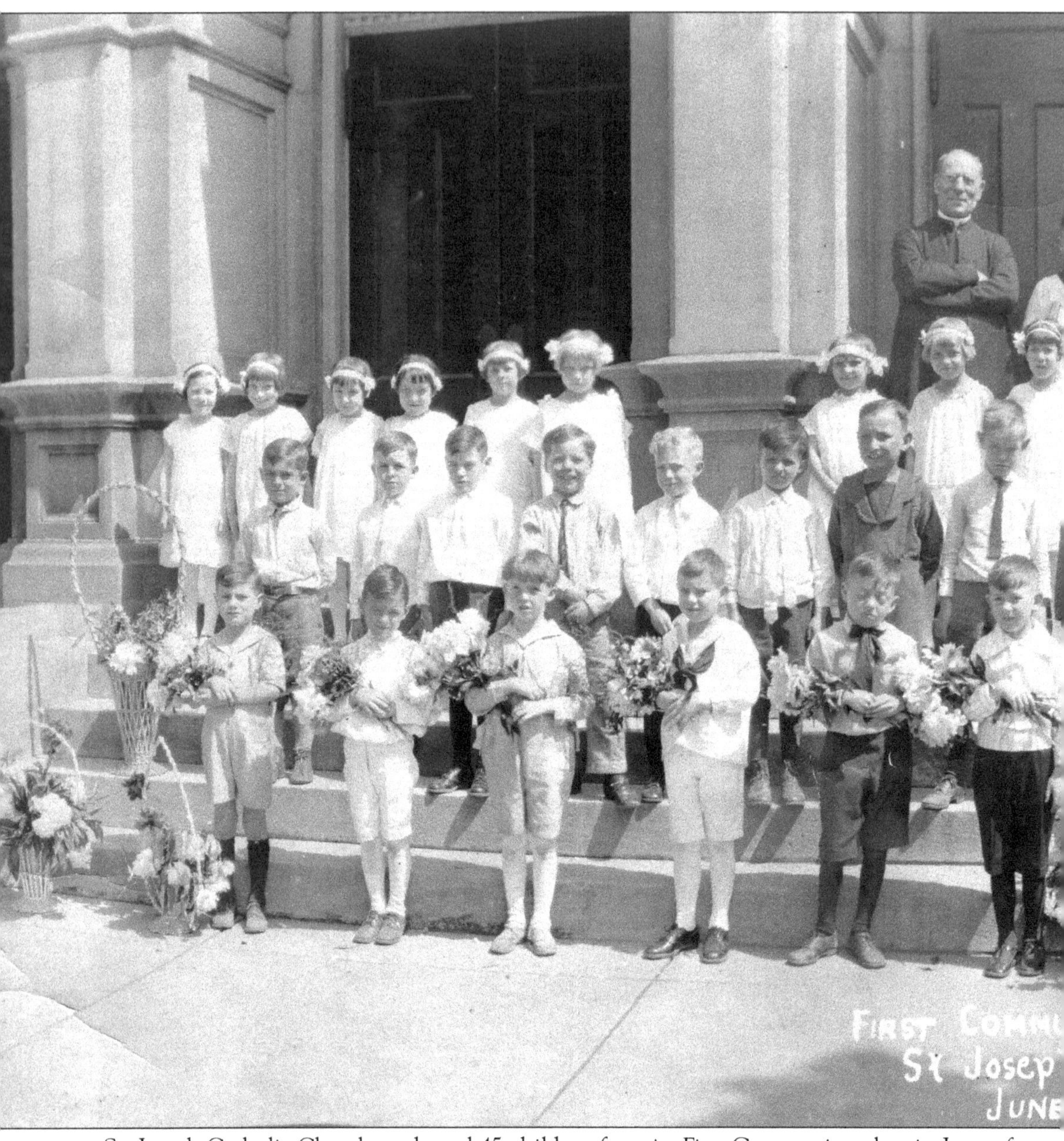

St. Joseph Catholic Church graduated 45 children from its First Communion class in June of 1926. Fr. B.B. Biegel is shown with his students, who include, from left to right, Eugene Blubaugh, unidentified, Patrick Ormsby, William Manghelli, Joseph Deeley, six unidentified persons, and Dorothy Dyer; (second row) Eugene Leever, Joseph Davis, Bob Grosenstraw, Robert McKenzie, unidentified, Orville Bucci, Henry Schrenker, ? Jung, unidentified, Anthony Bonito, Patrick Stine, Frank Moore, unidentified, Maurice Manghelli, Woodrow Wilson, and unidentified; (third row)

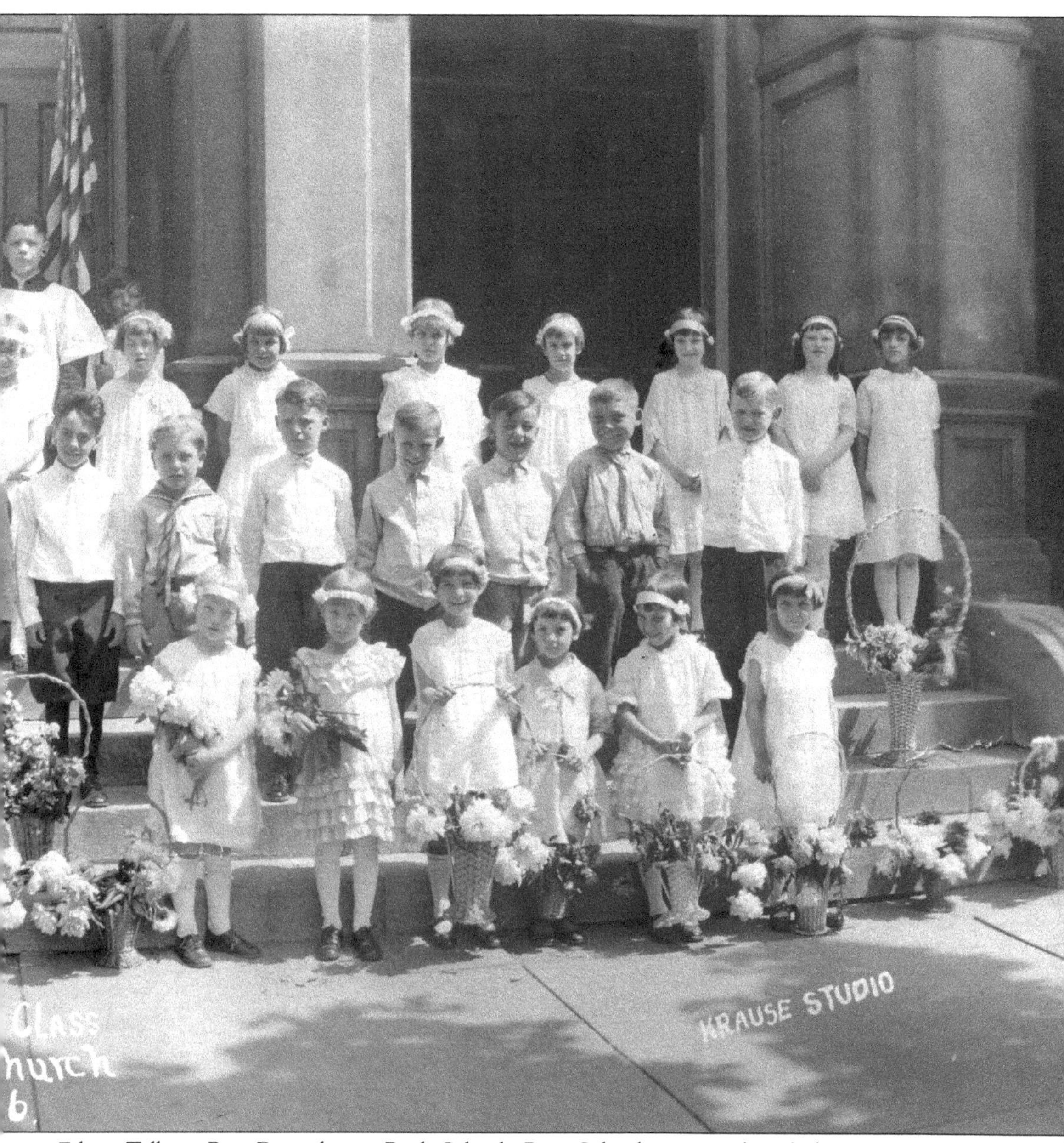

Eileen Talbert, Rita Dauenhauer, Ruth Schuck, Rose Schuck, two unidentified persons, Helen Glotzbach, Roberta Lehr, Virginia Gavin, Lenora Miller, unidentified, Mary Idlewine, Hazel Frazee, Clara Redenbaugh, unidentified, Mary Louise Short, and Julia DePaolo. Altar boys in the fourth row, from left to right, are Lawrence Hershinger John Gavin, and unidentified. (Courtesy Elwood Heritage Center.)

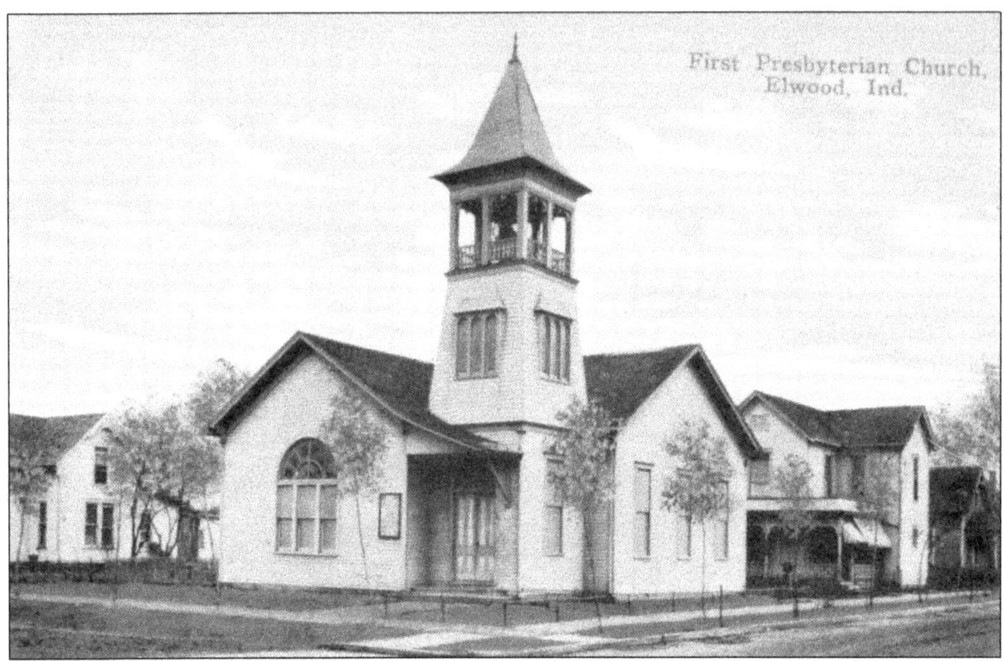

Elwood's First Presbyterian Church organized in 1880 and erected its first building in 1892 at South A and 18th Streets. While the building was expanded as necessary to accommodate its growing congregation, by 1922, it was no longer serviceable. At that time, the congregation moved temporarily into the Elks' while a new building could be constructed. Its current West Main Street location was built in 1992. (Courtesy Eric Grogan.)

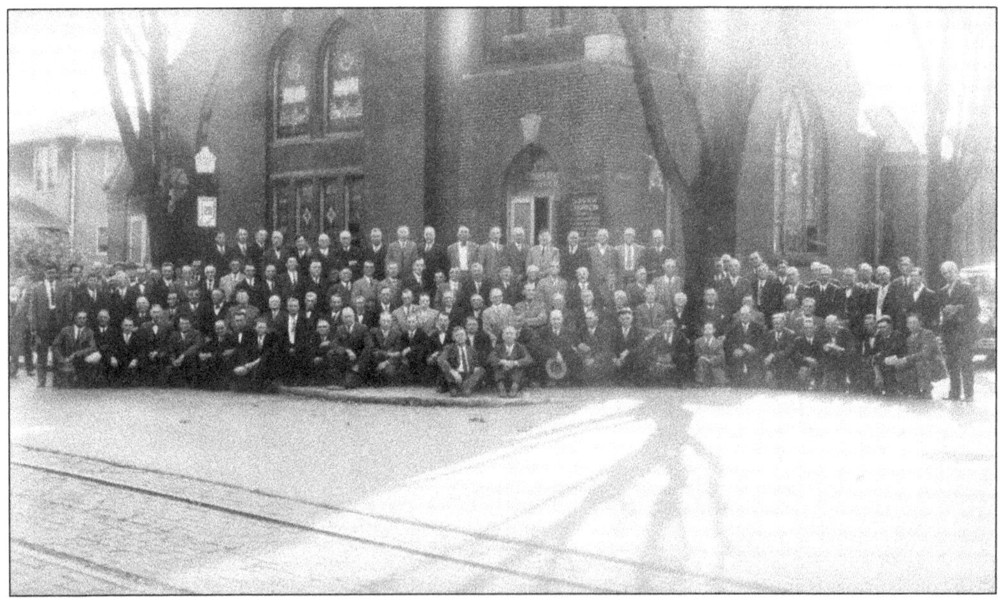

The men of Elwood's East Main Street Christian Church gather for a c. 1935 photograph in the early spring. The church organized in 1852 with 18 charter members. They built a meeting house on Big Duck Creek in 1854, but by 1899, they required a much larger church, which was erected on the corner of 18th and Main Streets, where it still resides today. (Courtesy Eric Grogan.)

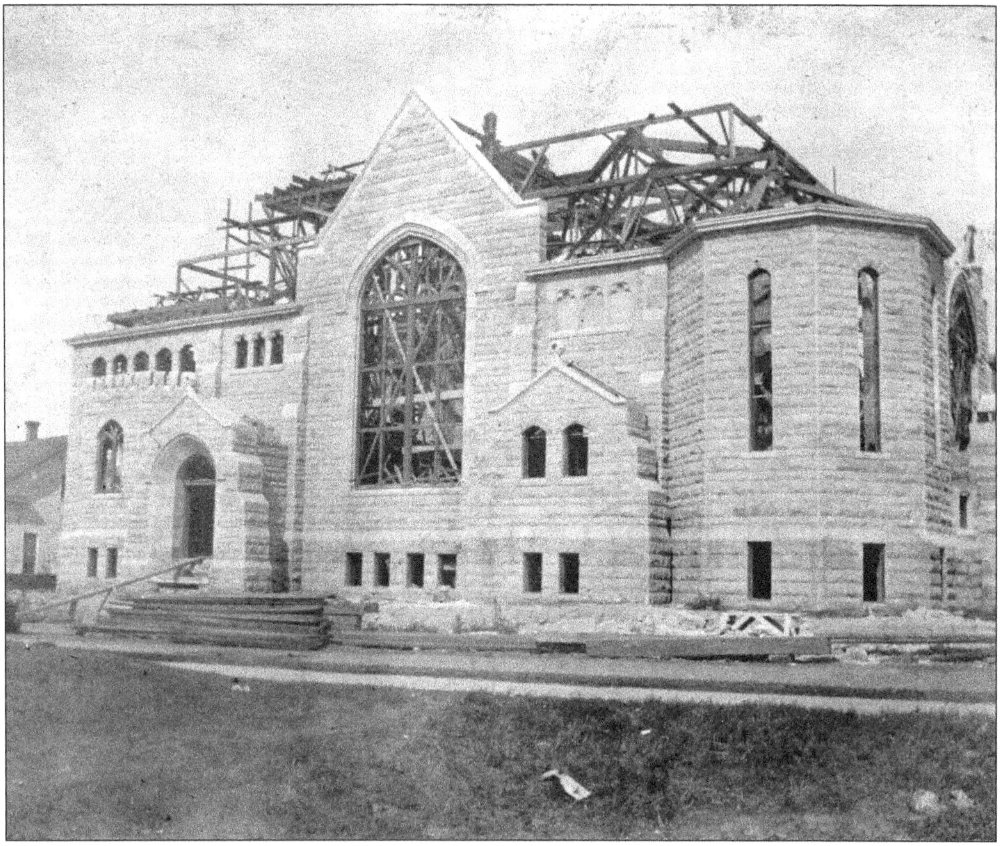

The First United Methodist Church of Elwood dates back to the mid-1800s, when parishioners met in a 36-by-50-foot, wood-frame structure, and membership numbered 14. By 1886, the membership had grown to 125, and the congregation erected a then modern, 40-by-70-foot, brick structure in its original location at South Anderson and North A Streets. Over the next 10 years, its Sunday school enrollment expanded exponentially and church membership doubled. In 1898, the brick building was razed, and the foundation was laid for a new church boasting a square footage that was two-and-one-half times larger than the building being replaced. The new sanctuary would seat 1,200 parishioners. That building was dedicated on April 7, 1901, and is still in use today. Deterioration of the church's distinctive dome necessitated its removal in the 1960s. (Both, courtesy First United Methodist Church.)

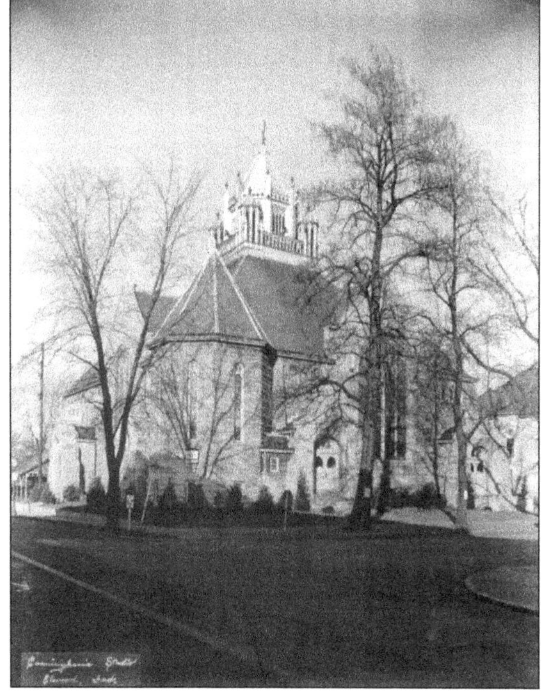

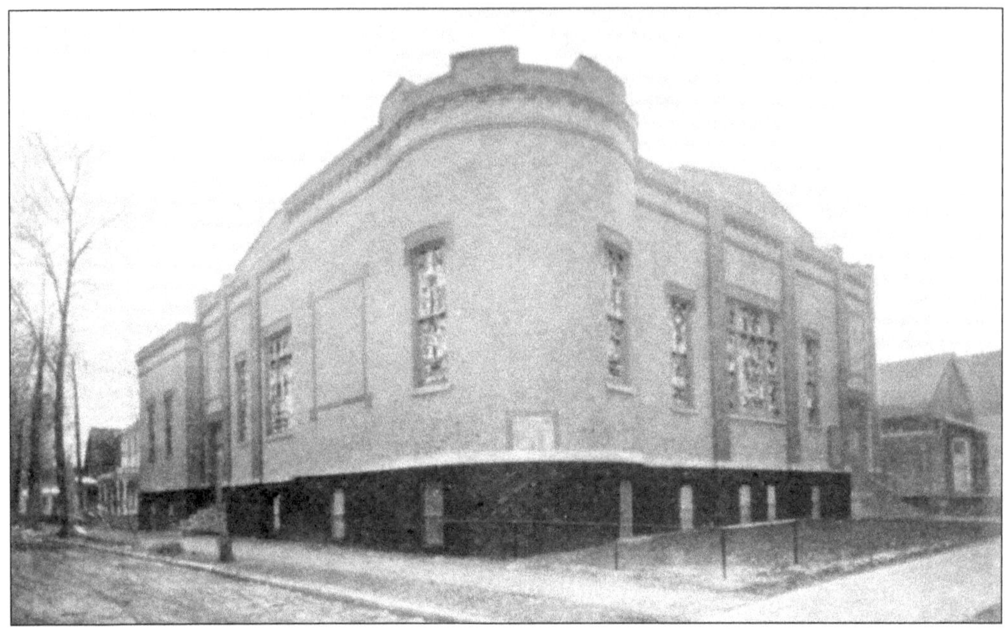

First Missionary Baptist Church organized in January 1890 with 20 charter members. They met in the house belonging to the Presbyterian Church. In 1893, the congregation moved to a new location on South B Street, but in 1915, it moved to its present site at 420 South Anderson Street. (Courtesy Eric Grogan.)

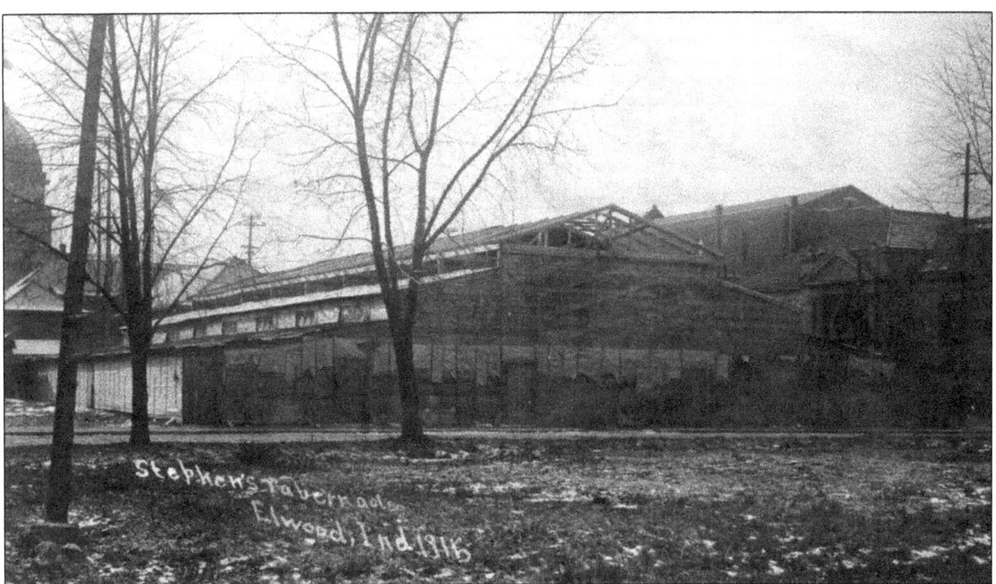

To accommodate a series of evangelical meetings in late 1915 led by nationally acclaimed evangelist George Stephens, Elwood churchgoers built a temporary 100-by-132-foot, wood-frame auditorium at the corner of North A and 16th Streets. Stephens's tabernacle stood for three months, and hundreds of souls reportedly were saved there. Before the building was razed in December, it also had housed numerous temperance rallies. (Courtesy Madison County Historical Society.)

Seven

COMMUNITY

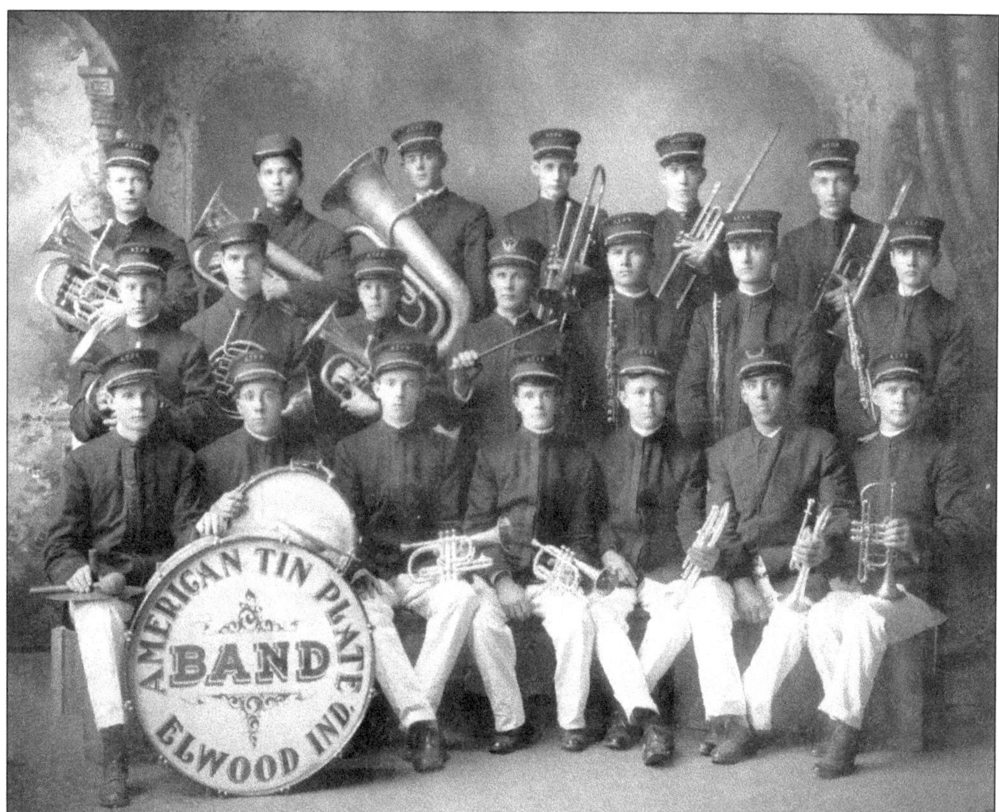

The American Tin Plate Band of Elwood, directed by Al S. Mygrant (center), organized in 1892 to perform locally and throughout the state, and won numerous awards. The band also performed summertime concerts from a bandstand at the corner of Anderson and South A Streets. The group disbanded in the early 1900s, but during its heyday it was one of Indiana's best bands.

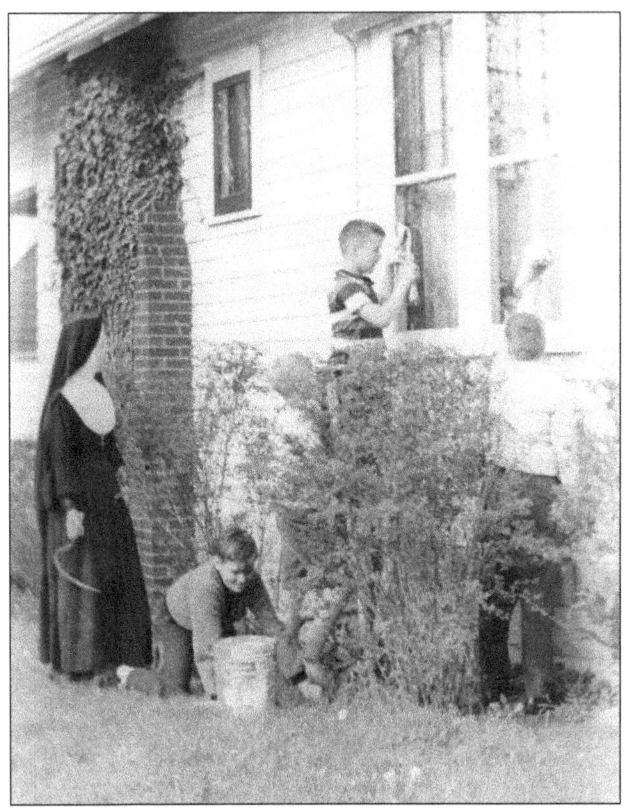

The 1966 Spring Clean-up, Paint-up, and Fix-up Campaign, sponsored by the Civic Affairs Committee of the Elwood Chamber of Commerce, proposed to "make the city a cleaner, healthier, safer, and more attractive place in which to live." At left, Sister Michael of St. Joseph's School supervises her sixth-grade students as they wash and shine the windows of an Elwood residence. Below, she keeps a watchful eye as the students clean the grounds and polish the monument in the Catholic cemetery. The entire city got involved in this annual event, which concluded in a festive downtown parade. The chamber entered the campaign in the National Cleanest Town contest. In December, a delegation of 13 Elwood citizens journeyed to Washington, DC, to accept a trophy on behalf of the city for its outstanding campaign.

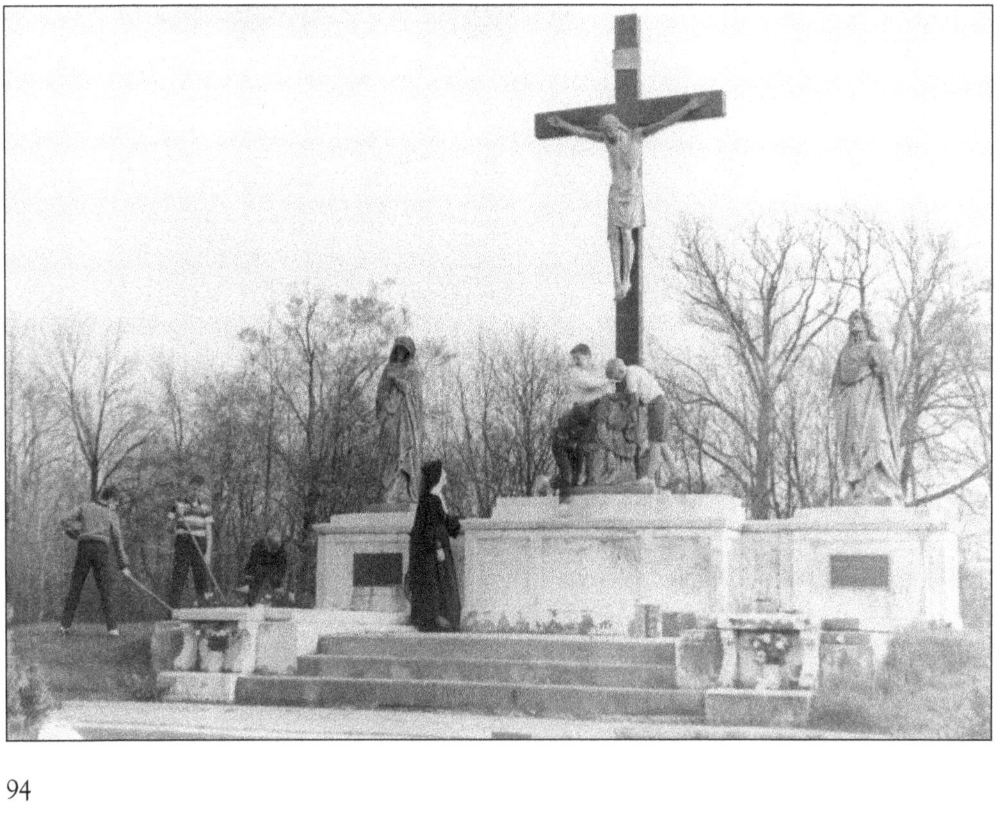

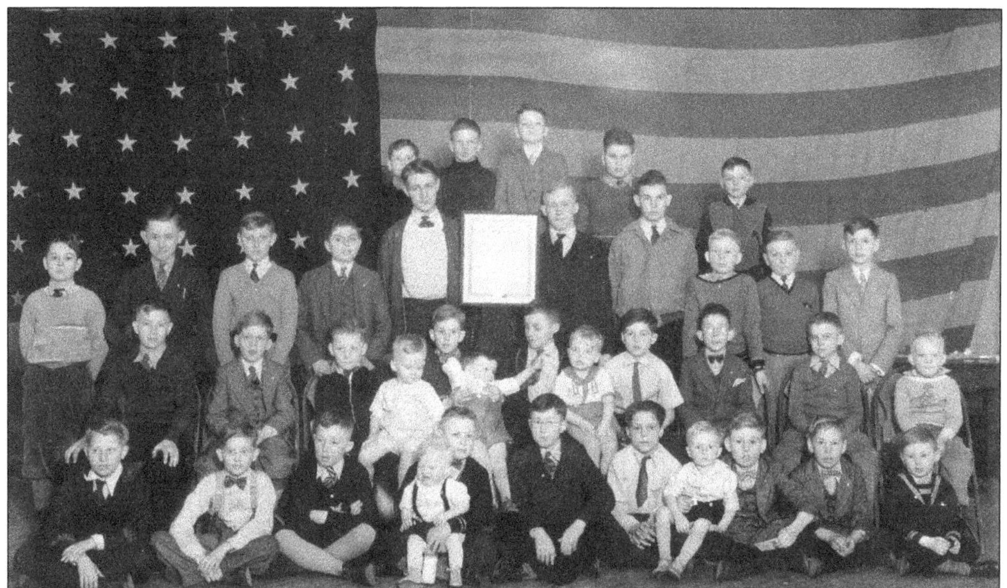

The Louis Monroe Post No. 53 of the Sons of the American Legion installed 34 charter members on March 26, 1934, at the Citizens Bank Building. The post was formed in 1919 after Congress chartered the national organization as a resource for World War I veterans. It was named for an Elwood soldier killed in France on November 10, 1918, just one day before the war ended. (Courtesy Elwood Public Library.)

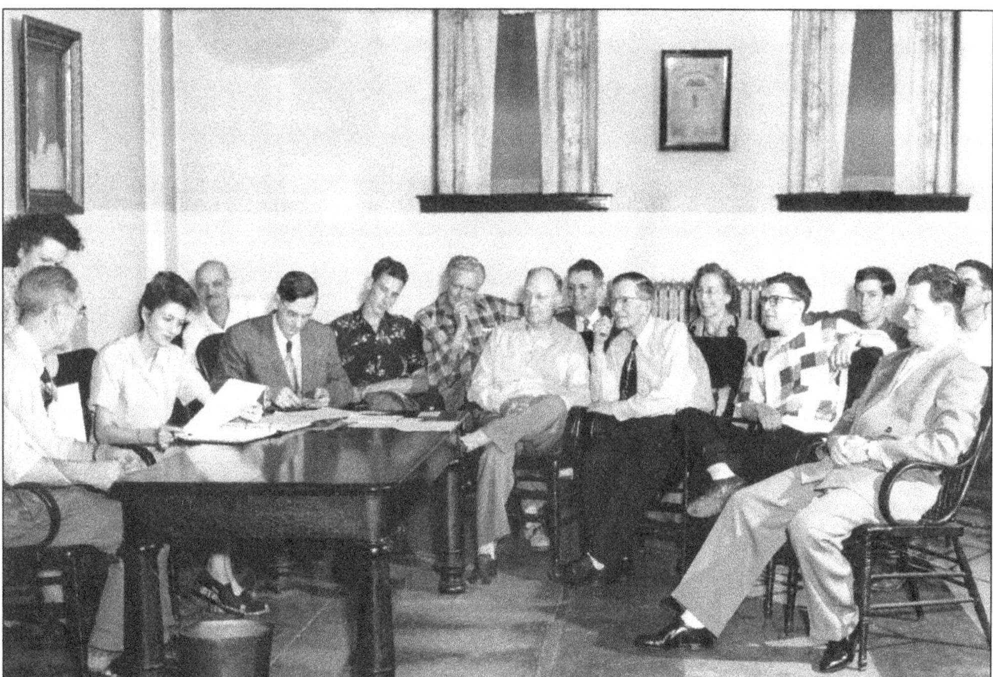

Members of the new Elwood Camera Club meet to organize on May 14, 1951, in the basement of the Elwood Public Library. The club brought the area's amateur photographers together to exchange knowledge, sharpen skills, participate in field trips, and to sponsor public shows and contests. The camera club was active into the 1960s. (Courtesy Elwood Public Library.)

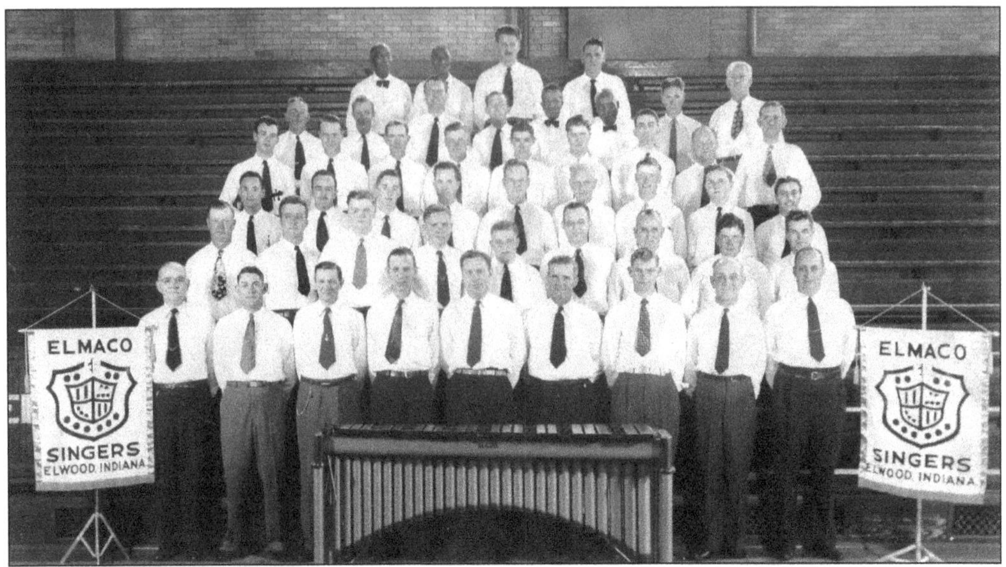

The Elmaco Singers organized November 11, 1946, with mainly local talent. Their first concert was June 29, 1947, in the high school gymnasium with the Foster-Hall quartet from Indianapolis. While reviews were mixed, the group earned rousing kudos for its enthusiasm. Identified are Eldon Floyd, fourth row, second from left; and former mayor Elmo Gustin, first row, second from right. The group disbanded in the early 1950s. (Courtesy Dorcas Floyd.)

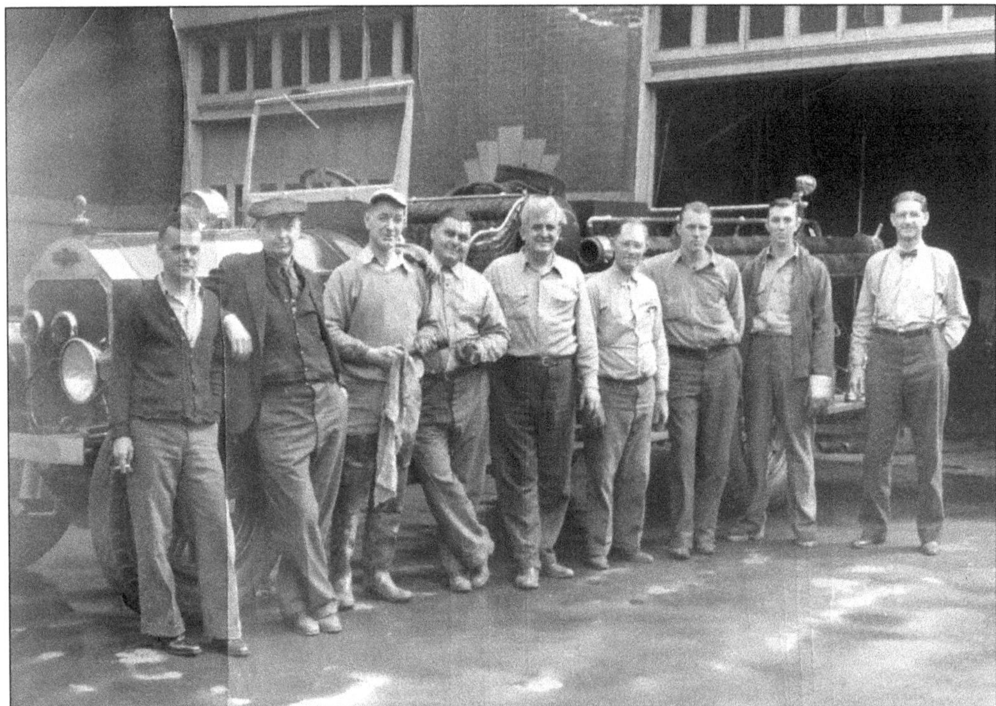

Nine members of the 1947 Elwood Fire Department posed for this photograph at the fire station, located at the City Building. From left to right, the men are Oliver "Pick" Leer, Chief John Brown, Laurence "Dutch" Goodknight, Theodore "Pete" Wilson, David "Di" Richards, Dewey Kelly, Harold Thomas, George Balser, and Ralph Clark. (Courtesy Sue Loser.)

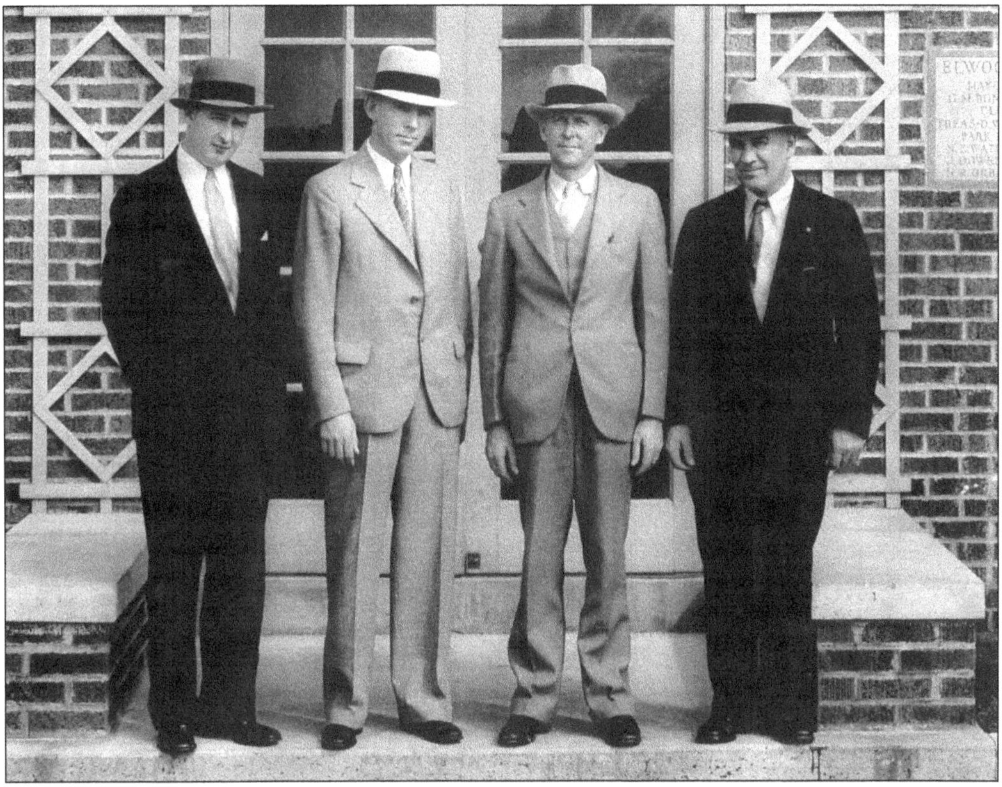

Standing in front of the newly built municipal swimming pool bathhouse in August 1932 is Mayor George Bonham, second from right. On his left are park board members Harold Orbaugh and Noland Watkins. John Dowell is on his right. (Courtesy *Elwood Call-Leader*.)

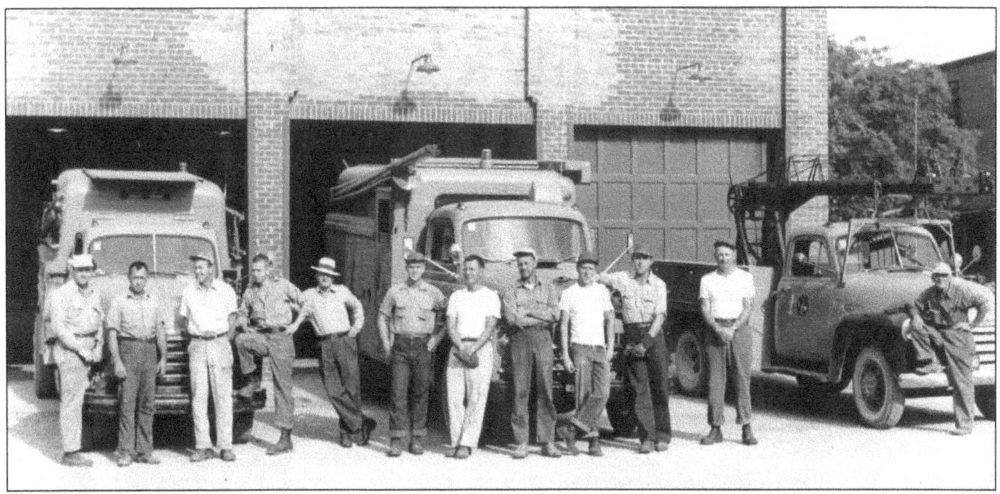

Members of the Indiana-Michigan Company line crew in Elwood are shown in this photograph dated July 1954. From left to right, the men are Ralph Saxton, C. Loser, R. Sparks, Donald Leever, George Rees, Donald Hill, Chester Perkins, Lester Alexander, W. Hobbs, C. Etchison, Bernard Cain, and Garth Venson. (Courtesy Bill Huntsman.)

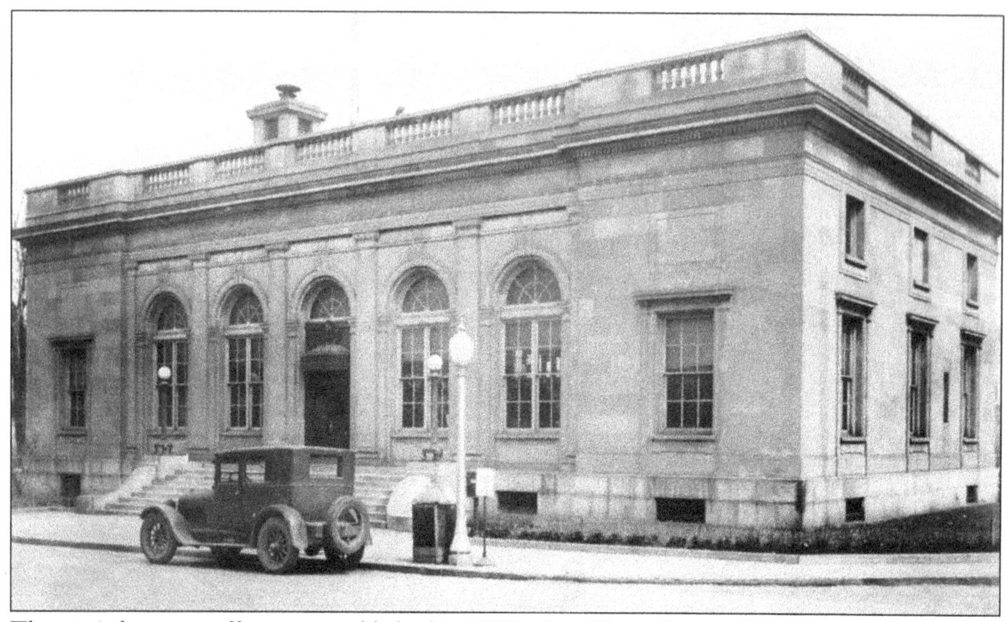

The city's first post office was established in 1855, when Elwood was still known as Duck Creek. From 1902 to 1913, the Elwood Post Office was located in the DeHority Building, across the street from the current office, which opened July 20, 1913. It was built by Cissel Construction Company of Washington, DC, for a cost of $57,500. At that time, the postmaster was E.E. Fornshell. (Courtesy Eric Grogan.)

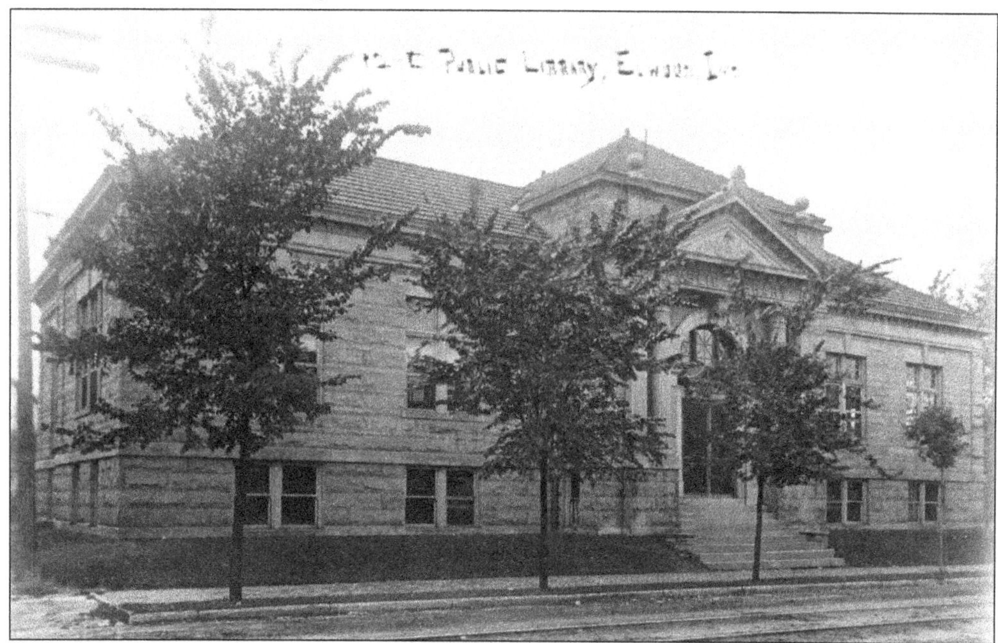

The Elwood Public Library opened a new, modern building complete with thousands of books, a reading and smoking room, a club room, and an auditorium on June 1, 1904. The building, located on 19th Street, was funded by Andrew Carnegie. The *Daily Record* called it a "marvel of beauty." Elwood's Carnegie library was in use until 1995, when the current facility was built. (Courtesy Eric Grogan.)

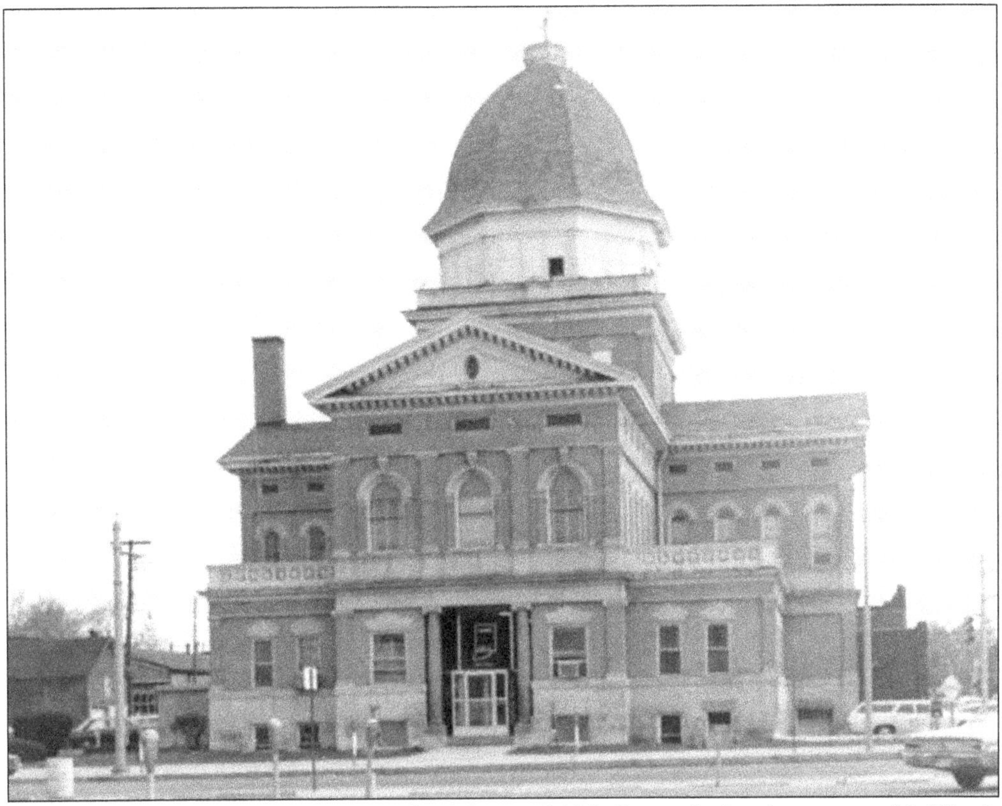

Elwood's first City Building was erected at Main and 16th Streets by local contractor J.J. Woods in 1899 for a price tag of $35,000. The building contained offices for city officials, the jail, a vault, the council chamber, the fire and police departments, a spacious hall for meetings, and a gymnasium. The building was retired in 2003, when a modern facility was built. (Courtesy Elwood Public Library.)

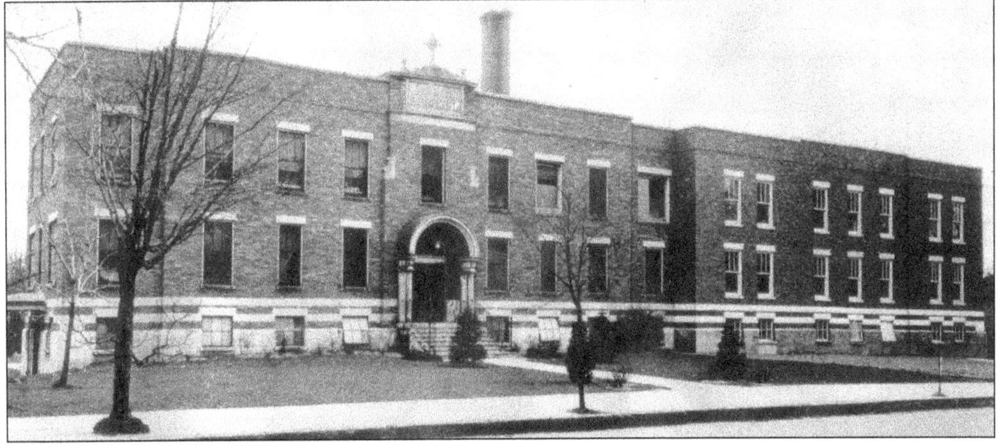

In 1916, Father Biegel asked the Sisters of St. Joseph to build a modern hospital in Elwood. Nine years later, ground was broken on a plot of land donated by the Elwood parish. When the 18-bed facility was completed in November 1926, the sisters dedicated it as Mercy Hospital. The hospital was expanded numerous times over the years and is one Indiana's finest today. (Courtesy St. Vincent Mercy Hospital.)

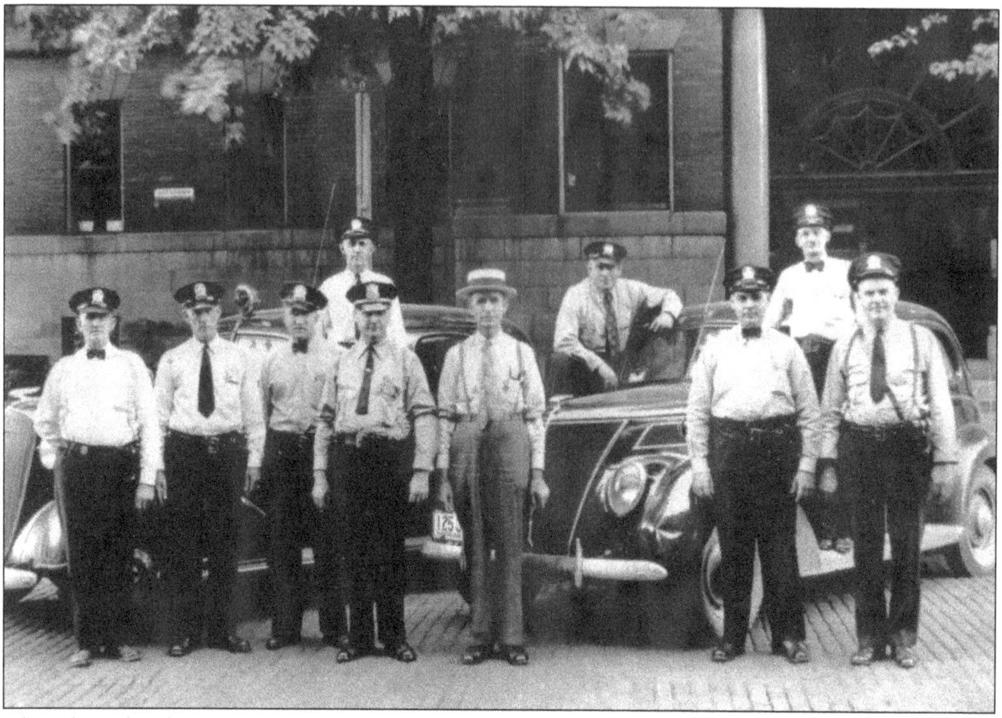

The Elwood Police Department lined up outside their offices at the City Building in August 1938 to pose for this photograph. From left to right are (first row) patrolmen Joe Edwards, L.E. Houser, and Clyde Loser, Sgt. David Overman, Chief Elmer Tunis, and patrolmen Pete Wilson and Clarence Van Horn; (second row) patrolmen Clyde Owen, Tony Monahan, and Harry Wann. (Courtesy Carl Ritter.)

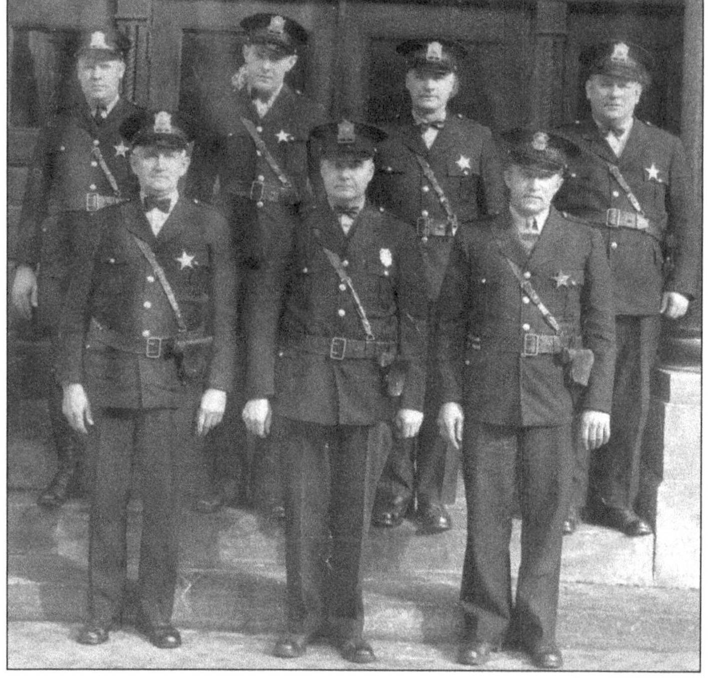

Members of the Elwood Police Department stood outside the City Building in 1935 for this photo. From left to right, they are identified as (first row) Joe Edwards, David Overman, and Clyde Loser; (second row) Clarence Van Horn, Frank McCall, Charley Fenstermaker, and Tony Monahan. Not pictured are night sergeant Joseph Hurlock and Chief Elmer Tunis. (Courtesy Elwood Heritage Center.)

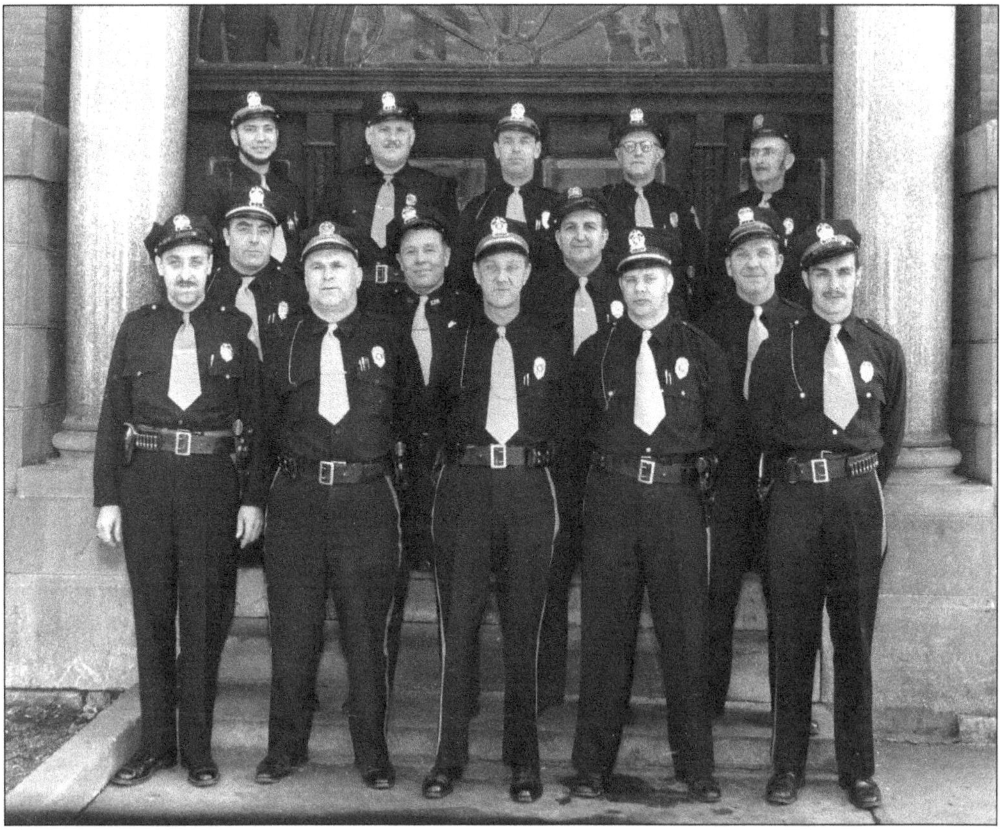

Elwood's finest gathered on the steps of the City Building in the spring of 1952. From left to right are (first row) Paul Stafford, Sgt. John Lowder, Chief Keith Dixon, Sgt. Hubert Call, and Verle Hartley; (second row) Harold Sherman, Wayne Jarrell, Sylvester Hahn, and Ralph Scott; (third row) Harley Shinkle, Joseph Hickey, W.L. Orbaugh, Clyde Owen, and A.C. Locke. (Courtesy Carl Ritter.)

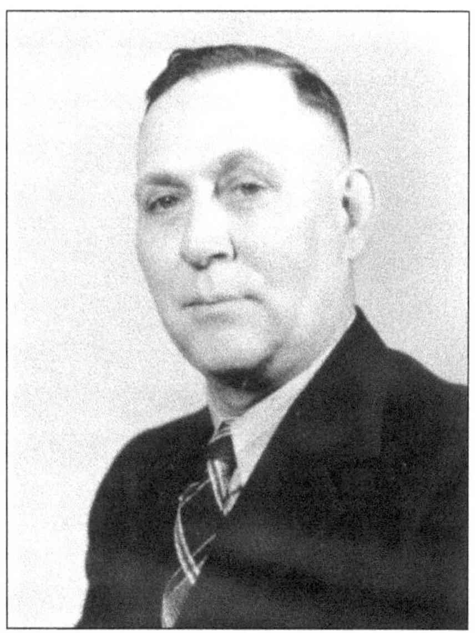

Charles "Vent" Sowash served 12 years as an Elwood merchant policeman, a precursor to today's private security officer. As such, he switched on the lights for downtown merchants, kept watch over their stores throughout the night, and occasionally made an arrest. It was a service he performed for a monthly fee of $3 per client. Born near Converse in 1882, Sowash died in Elwood in 1958. He was 75. (Courtesy Carol Dever.)

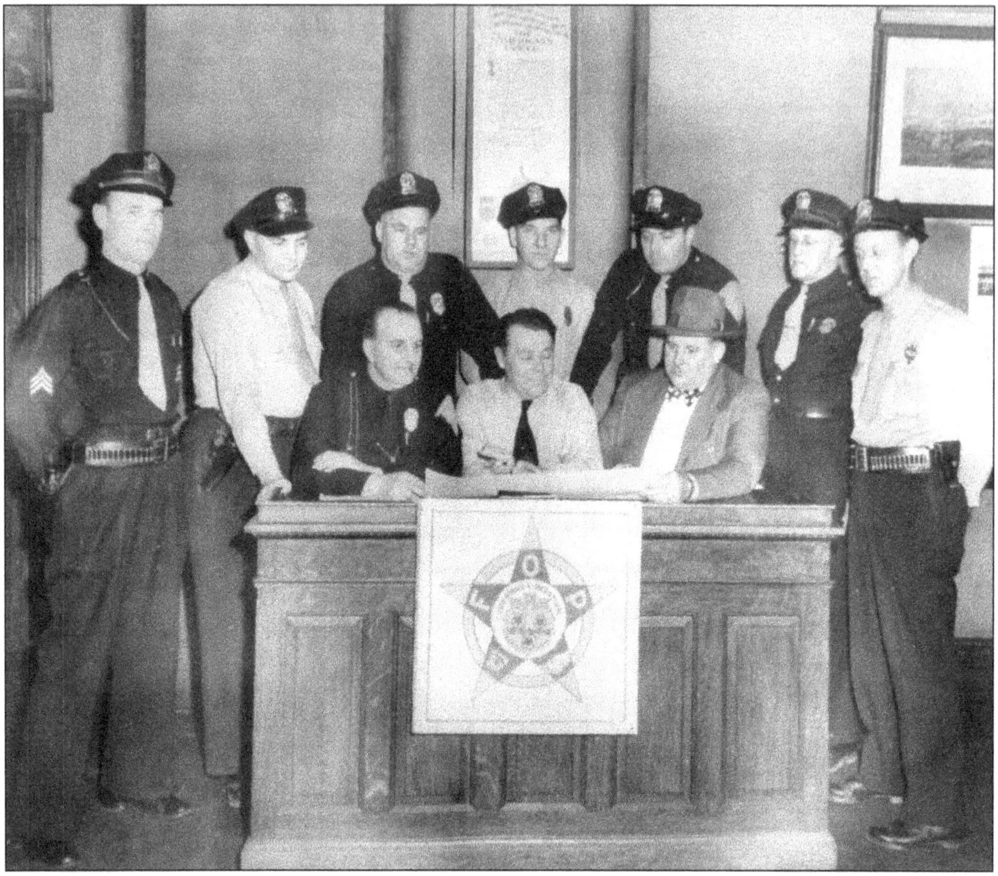

Members of Elwood's Fraternal Order of Police meet at the City Building on March 30, 1949, to make plans for their annual Policemen's Ball, scheduled for April 8 at the National Guard Armory. From left to right are (seated) Lloyd Hahn, Wayne Jarrell, and Chief Joe Hickey; (standing) Sgt. W. L. Orbaugh, Harland Shinkle, Sgt. John Lowder, Ralph Scott, Harold Sherman, Clyde Owen, and Keith Dixon. (Courtesy Carl Ritter.)

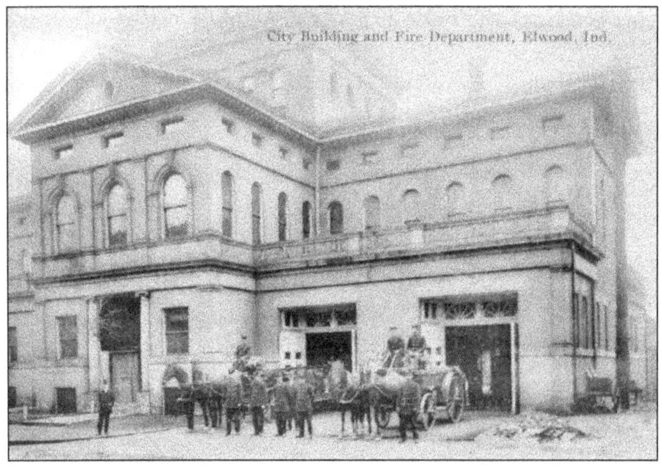

Elwood's first firehouse at 1411 Main Street operated with eight volunteers, two horses, and one wagon. In 1900, the station moved to the new City Building. The department acquired motorized trucks in 1918, and the horses were auctioned off. Two firefighters have lost their lives in the line of duty: "Pick" Lear in 1955 and "Pete" Wilson in 1962. Both suffered heart attacks. (Courtesy Eric Grogan.)

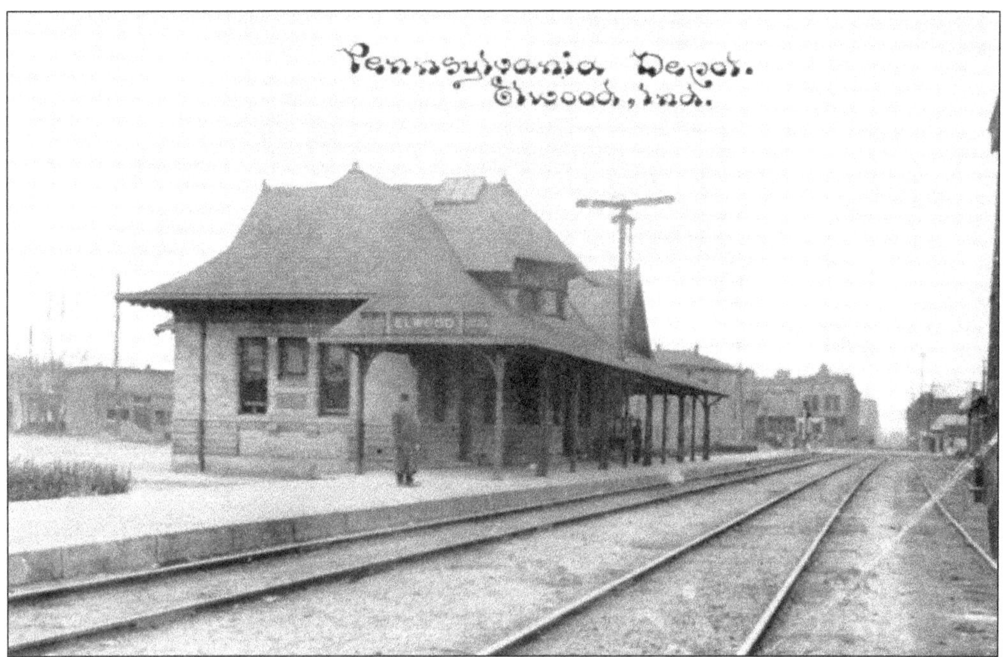

The first of the two railroads that ran through Elwood was the Pennsylvania, completed in 1888. From Elwood, northbound trains carried freight and passengers as far as Chicago. Southbound destinations included Anderson, Richmond, and on to Cincinnati. Below, four-year-old Pam Borum Savage and her grandmother, Vella Walker, wait for their train to Cincinnati at Elwood's Penn Station, located at South B and 16th Streets, in the spring of 1960. Elwood remained a busy hub until the Pennsylvania Railroad's passenger service was discontinued in 1965. The station was demolished in 1983, and the Elwood Fire Department burned its remains as a training exercise in 1990. (Above, courtesy Eric Grogan; below, courtesy Steve, Pam, and Mary Savage.)

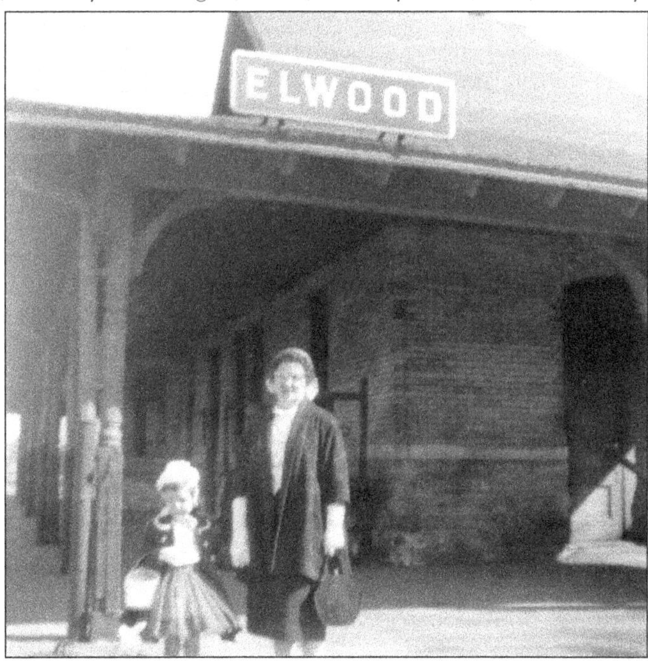

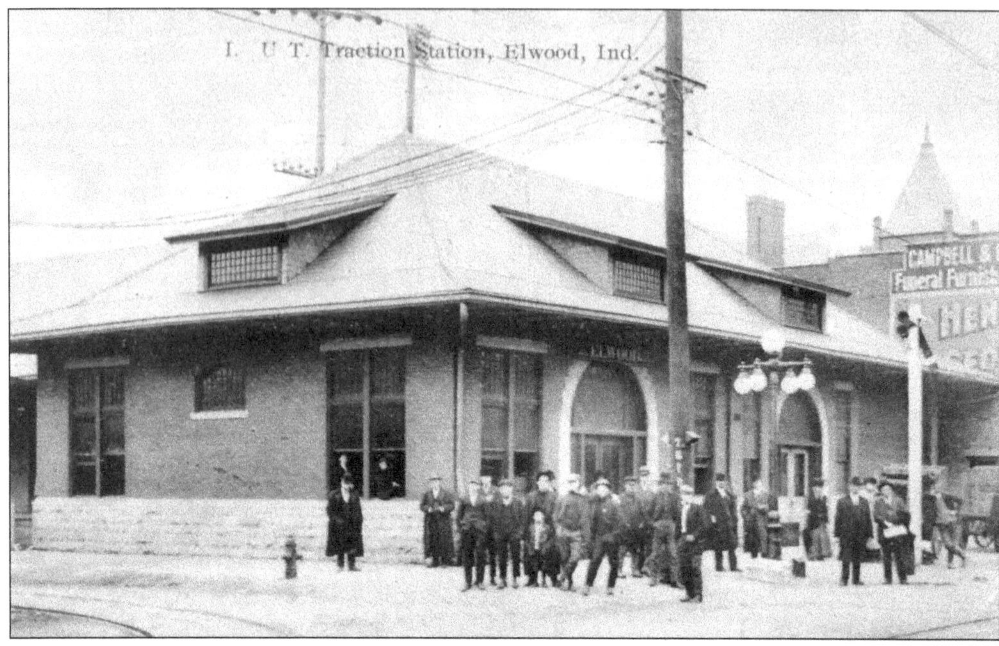

The Union Traction Company opened its Interurban line from Anderson to Alexandria in 1897, and the Elwood and Alexandria Railway Company was put into service 18 months later. Elwood soon became one of the system's busiest stops, and a station was erected at the corner of 16th and Main Streets, opposite the City Building, opening in 1910. The Interurban service thrived for years, but by 1931, with the growing popularity and convenience of private automobiles, the Interurban ceased operation. A high school gymnasium was later built on the property, and the depot served as a grocery store. In 1963, the one-time bustling station was razed, as pictured below. The land was paved and used as a parking lot. In 1996, the city's library was constructed on the site. (Above, courtesy Eric Grogan.)

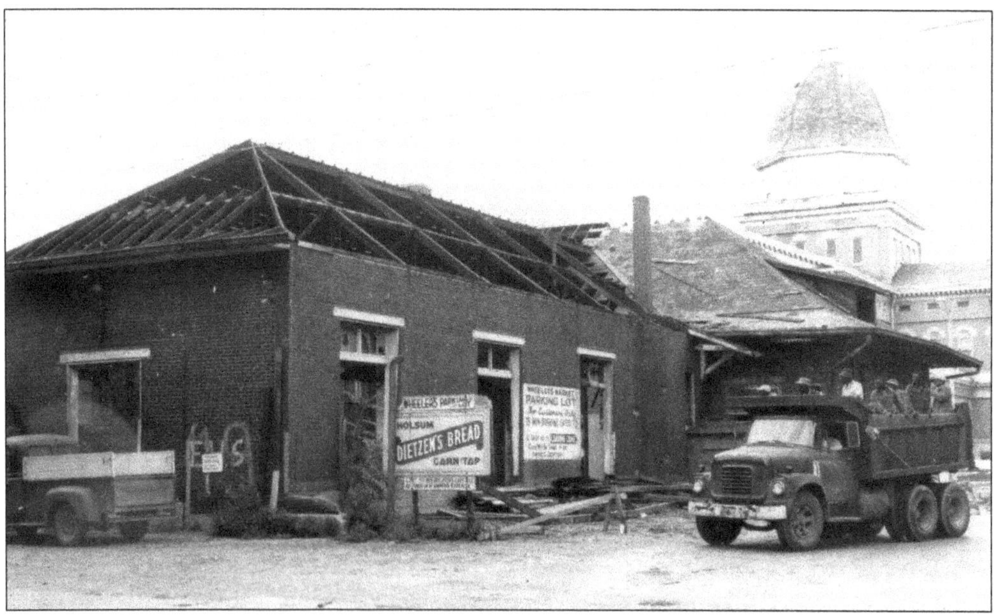

Eight

Hometown Heroes

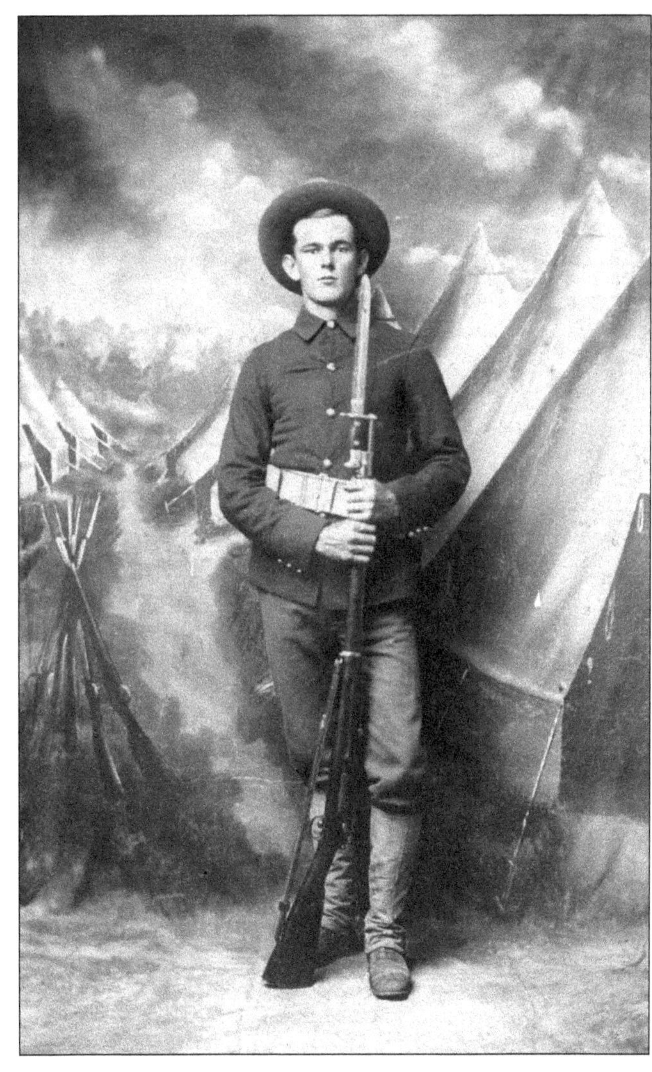

Daniel Delavou Redmond was 21 when he entered military service to do his duty during the Spanish-American War. Redmond was born in 1879 near Rensselaer. He and his wife, Minnie, moved to Elwood around 1912 and lived the rest of their lives on North F Street. He died in 1957 at the age of 77. (Courtesy Sue Loser.)

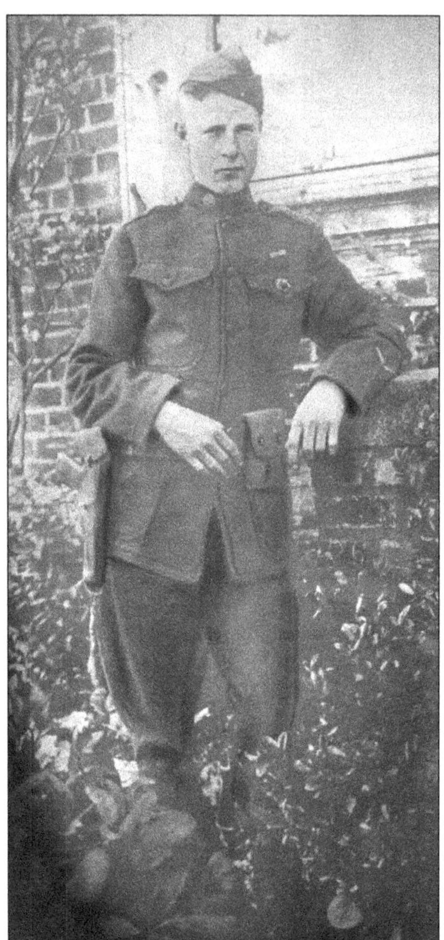

Russell Baugher joined the US Army in the spring of 1918 and served with Company D, 16th Infantry, in Germany during World War I. After returning home to Elwood in late 1919, he resumed his job at the Tin Plate. He was the father of five children, including Elmer, who made national news in January 1942 in Ripley's *Believe It Or Not*. Baugher died in 1977. (Courtesy Lisa Baugher.)

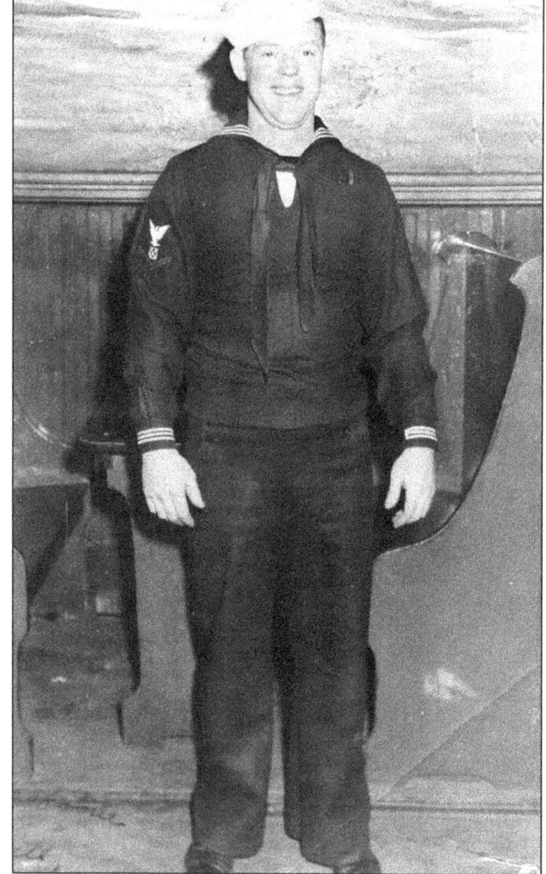

King Zebedee "Red" Gosnell lived in Elwood most of his life. He was a World War II veteran, joining the US Navy in 1942. He was a catcher and slugger for several Elwood softball teams in the 1940s and 1950s. He died in 1977 at the age of 60. (Courtesy Bobby Taylor.)

This January 25, 1945, Ripley's *Believe It Or Not* cartoon claims Cpl. Elmer Baugher, a Marine medical technician serving on Bougainville Island, had no rations until he found a can of food that had washed ashore. Miraculously, stamped on it was the name of the canning factory located in Elwood, Indiana, his hometown. Son of Russell and Mary Baugher, he died in 2015 at the age of 96. (Courtesy *Elwood Call-Leader.*)

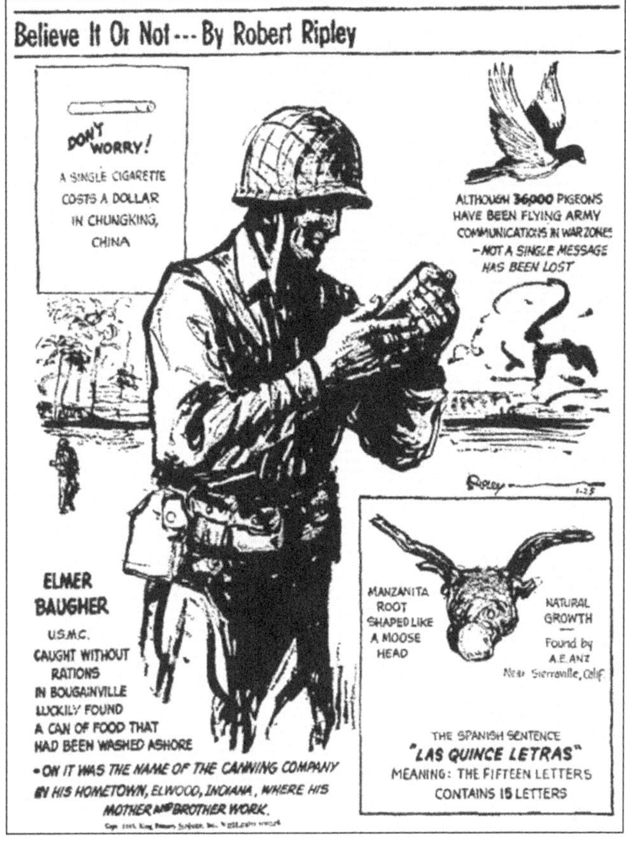

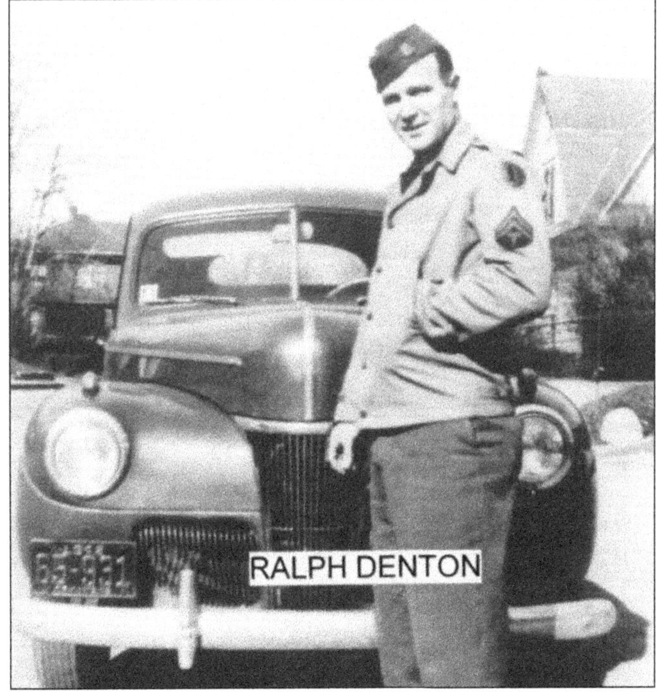

Ralph V. Denton was a World War II veteran, serving in the US Army. He was a charter member and first life member of the Veterans of Foreign Wars Post 5182 in Elwood, as well as the American Legion. He lived most of his life in Elwood and died in 1991. He was 79. (Courtesy Elwood VFW.)

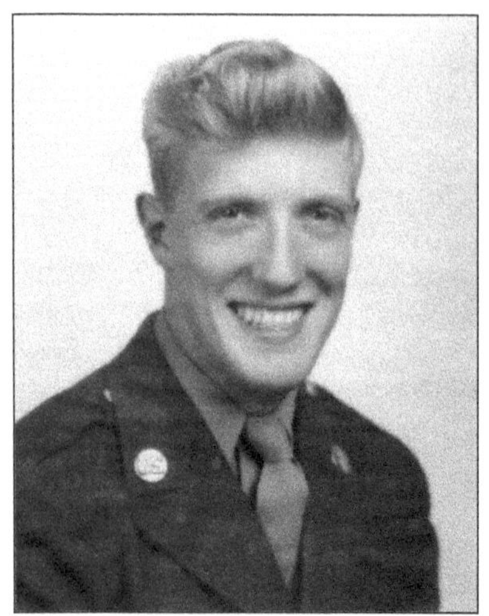

Lifelong Elwood resident Sam Laudeman enlisted in the Army in December 1941. After training as a medic, he joined the 318th Infantry Regiment in France, where he engaged in several battles with German forces. After suffering a wound at Manoncourt, he was awarded the Silver Star for his heroic acts. Upon discharge in November 1945, he returned to Elwood and started his longtime dental practice. (Courtesy Marla and Sam Laudeman.)

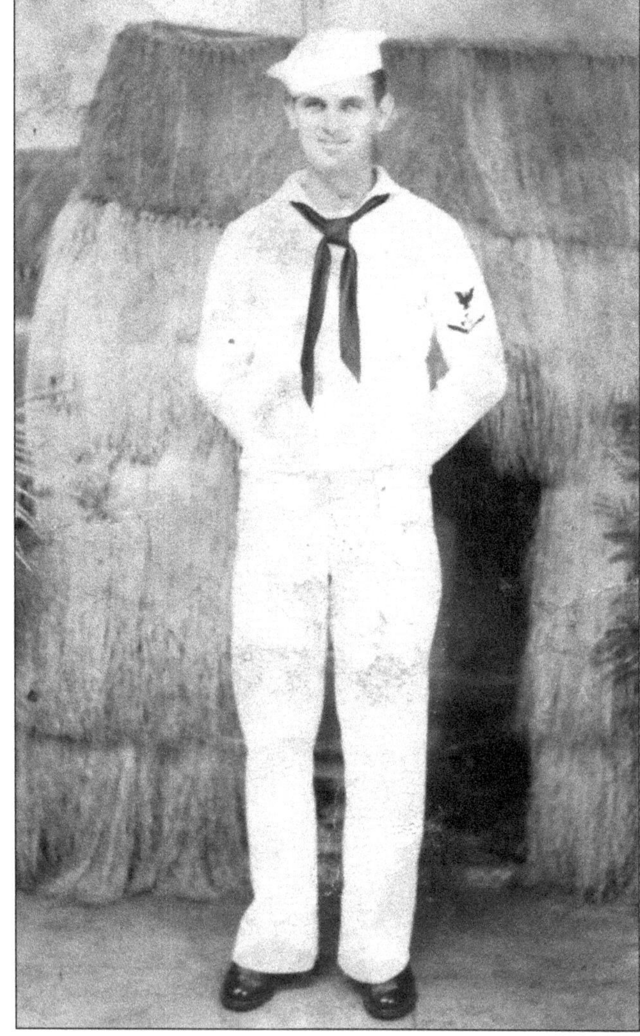

World War II veteran Hugh Gordon served in the Pacific as a US naval fireman first class aboard the USS *Moctobi*, one of the first US ships to enter the Yokosuka Naval Base in Japan. Gordon was honorably discharged in April 1946. Upon his return to Elwood, he resumed farming. Gordon died in January 1991 at the age of 72. (Courtesy Ann Brewer.)

Hubert L. Call was born in 1917 in Elwood. A 1935 Elwood High School graduate, he joined the Army in 1941 at the start of the war and served in Europe as an engineer. Attaining the rank of sergeant, he was honorably discharged in 1945. He was an officer with the Elwood Police Department from 1946 until his retirement in 1968. He died in 2002. (Courtesy Elwood VFW.)

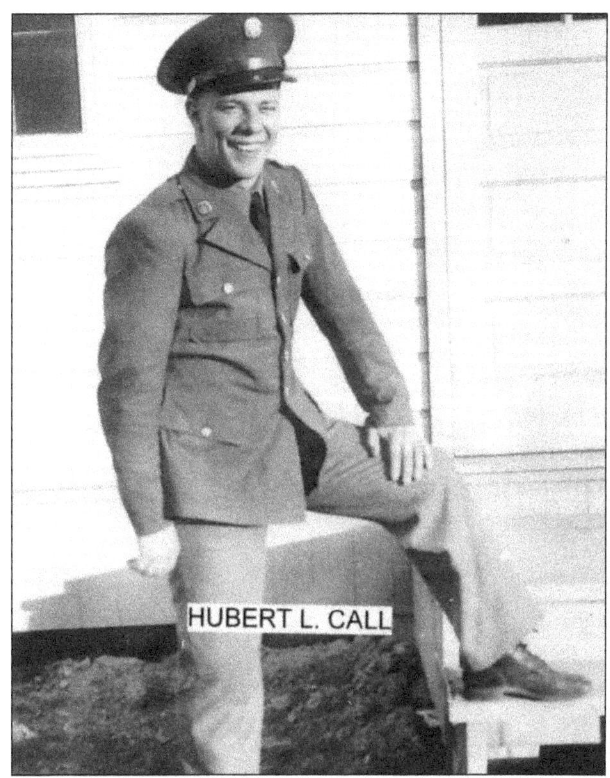

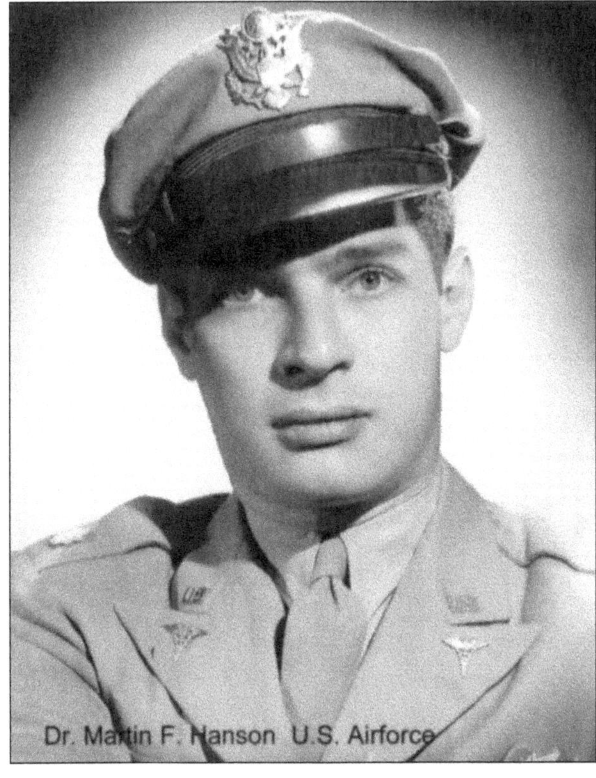

Martin F. Hanson was an Elwood physician for 40 years. He opened his office on South Anderson Street in November 1945, shortly after his honorable discharge from the US Army. He had served four years during World War II and attained the rank of lieutenant colonel. Dr. Hanson chaired Mercy Hospital's first cardiac unit. He was born in 1914 in Illinois and died in Elwood in 2003. (Courtesy Elwood VFW.)

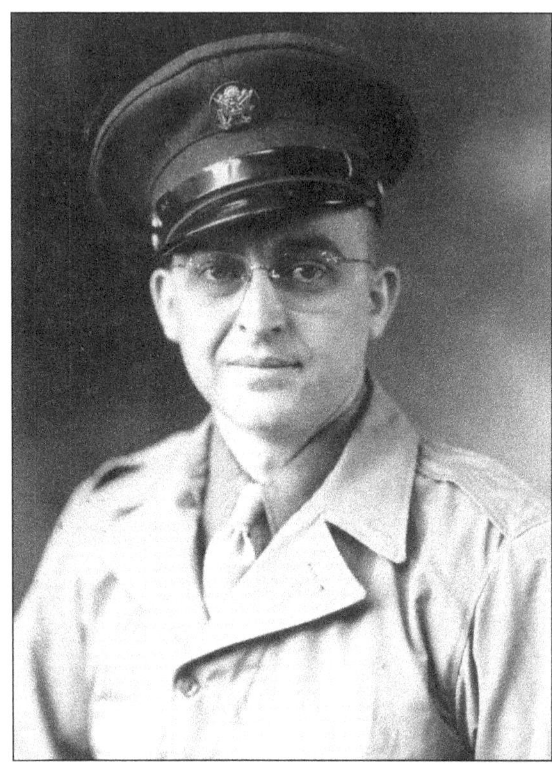

Leonard Etchison served the US Army 1943–1945 with a medical unit throughout Europe during World War II. After returning to Elwood, he resumed his profession as a barber at the shop on South 16th Street that he owned with his brother, Lester. Etchison was born in 1911 in Tipton County and died in 1998. (Courtesy Ann Brewer.)

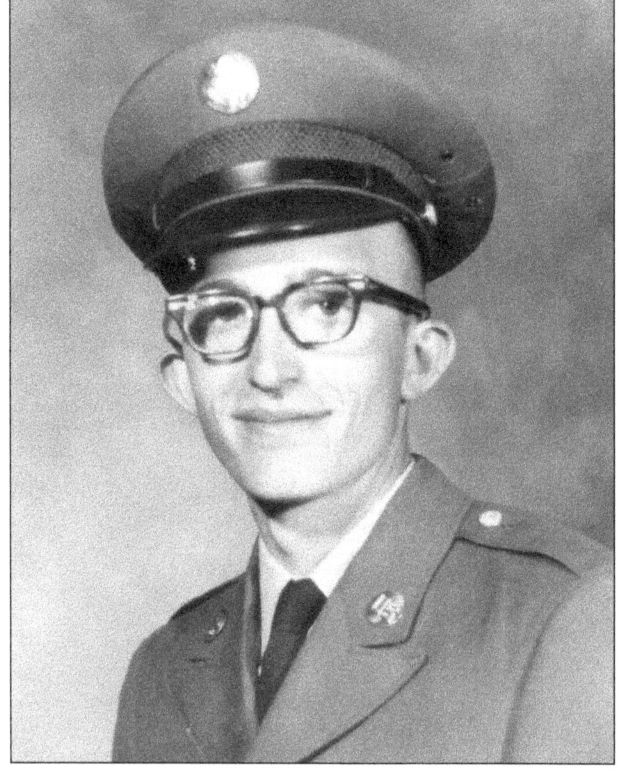

Elwood native Duane Etchison graduated from Wendell Willkie High School in 1964 and joined the US Army in February 1966. In August that year, he was sent to Germany, where he was stationed at Heilbronn until 1968. Following his return home, he joined the Elwood Fire Department and served as chief in 1980 and again in 1985–1987. He retired from the department in 1992. (Courtesy Duane Etchison.)

Nine

The Hope of Our Country

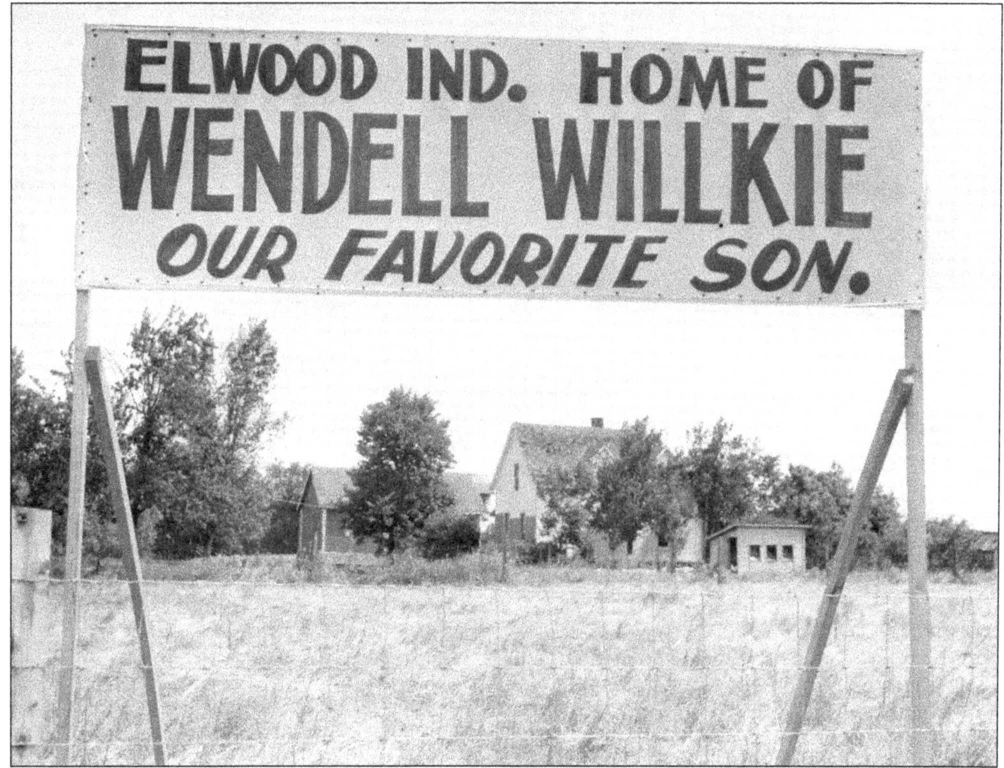

Signs such as this one were posted all around Elwood's perimeter to greet motorists arriving to witness Wendell Willkie deliver his historic notification speech on August 17, 1940. Willkie was born and raised in Elwood, and even today he is considered the city's favorite son.

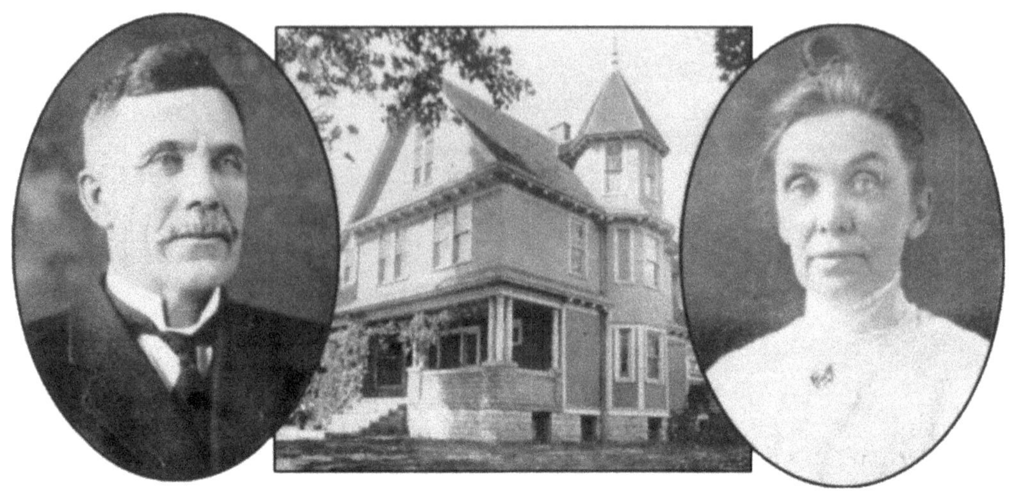

Herman and Henrietta Willkie moved to Elwood from Lagro, Indiana, with their four children in 1888, when Herman became superintendent of Elwood schools. Both Herman and Henrietta were practicing attorneys. In 1887, she became one of the first women in Indiana admitted to the bar. Their fifth child, Lewis Wendell, was born in Elwood in 1892. (Courtesy Elwood Public Library.)

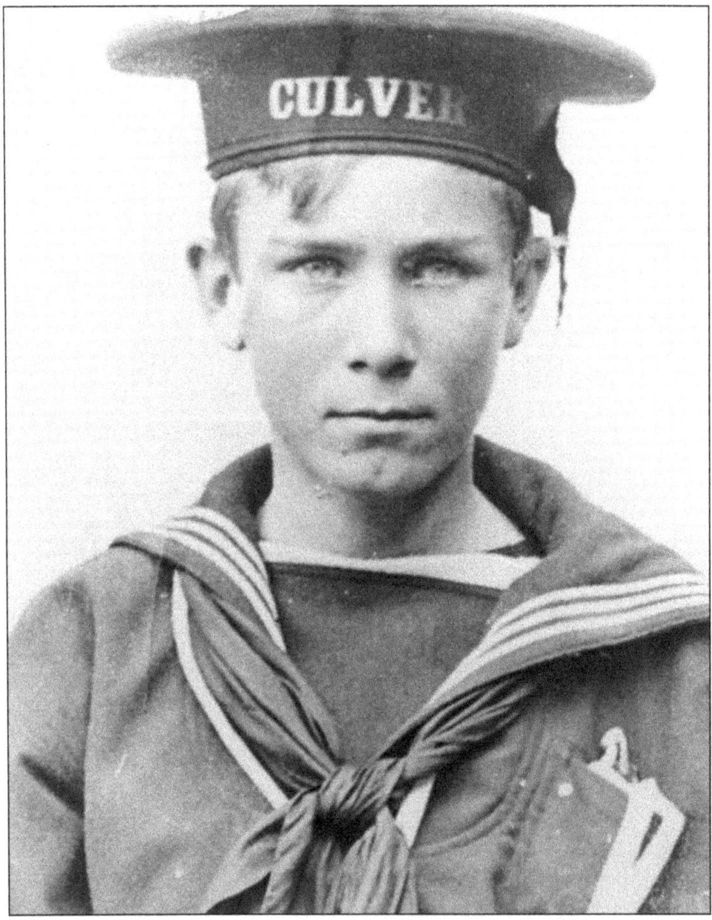

Wendell Willkie attended 1st through 12th grade in Elwood's Central School but attended Culver Military Academy for the summer of 1906. Willkie graduated high school in 1910 and earned his AB degree from Indiana University (IU). After working briefly in Kansas and Puerto Rico, he returned to IU and graduated from its School of Law in 1916. He then moved home to Elwood and practiced law with his father. (Courtesy Lilly Library, Indiana University.)

The day America entered the war, Willkie joined the Army. In January 1918, he and Edith Wilk, a young woman he had met in Rushville, said, "I do." That same year, shortly before the armistice, he sailed to France and spent the remainder of his service giving legal representation to enlisted men. He was honorably discharged in February 1919 with the rank of captain. (Courtesy Dave Berkemeier.)

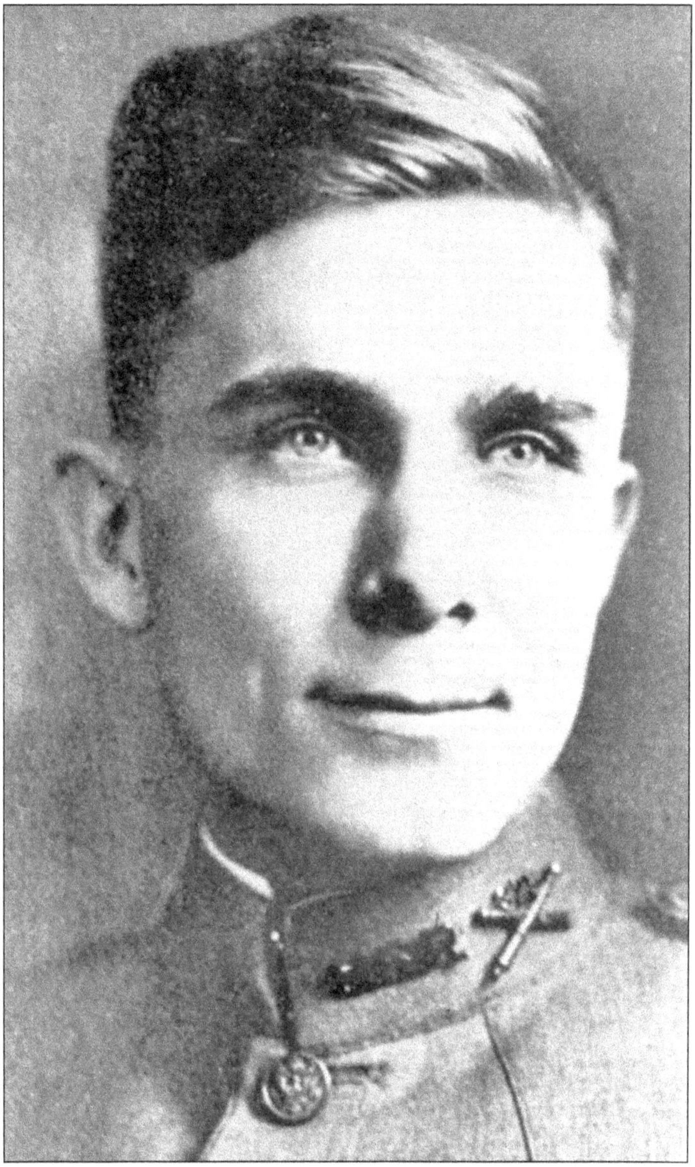

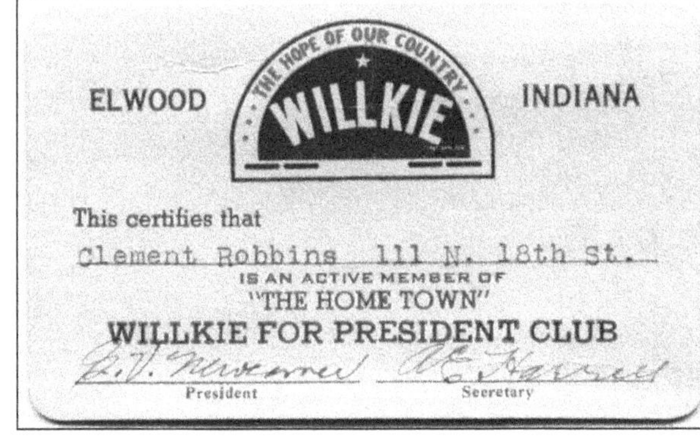

ELWOOD THE HOPE OF OUR COUNTRY WILLKIE INDIANA

This certifies that

Clement Robbins 111 N. 18th St.

IS AN ACTIVE MEMBER OF

"THE HOME TOWN"

WILLKIE FOR PRESIDENT CLUB

President Secretary

In May 1940, residents of Willkie's hometown sent him a petition bearing more than 2,000 signatures urging him to accept the nomination for US president if it were offered at the Republican convention in June. Shortly after that, "Willkie for President" clubs began to form around the nation, generating support and campaign paraphernalia. (Courtesy William Huneke.)

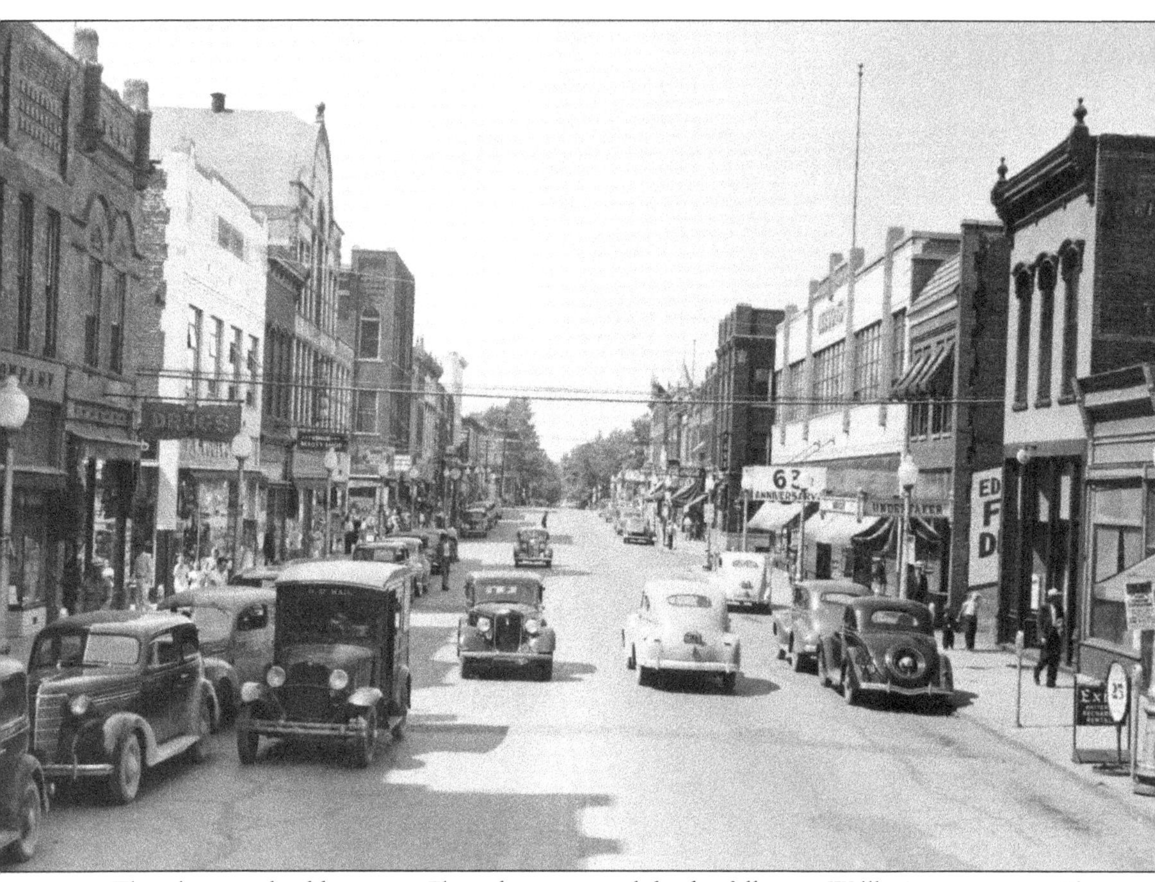

This photograph of downtown Elwood was snapped the day following Willkie's nomination. The cutline on the back reads, "Wendell Willkie's hometown did some celebrating when the Republican convention selected him as the GOP standard bearer in the presidential race, but the next day, June 28, the center of the city presented this quiet scene." Willkie dominated page one of the June 28, 1940, edition of the *Call-Leader*. A page-two column aptly describes the city's mood as "all Willkie." "At every street corner," it stated, "in every corner drug store, at every cigar counter, and in every restaurant—the talk was Willkie. It was as if some Messiah had come to roost on our front porch. It was grand." (Courtesy Eric Grogan.)

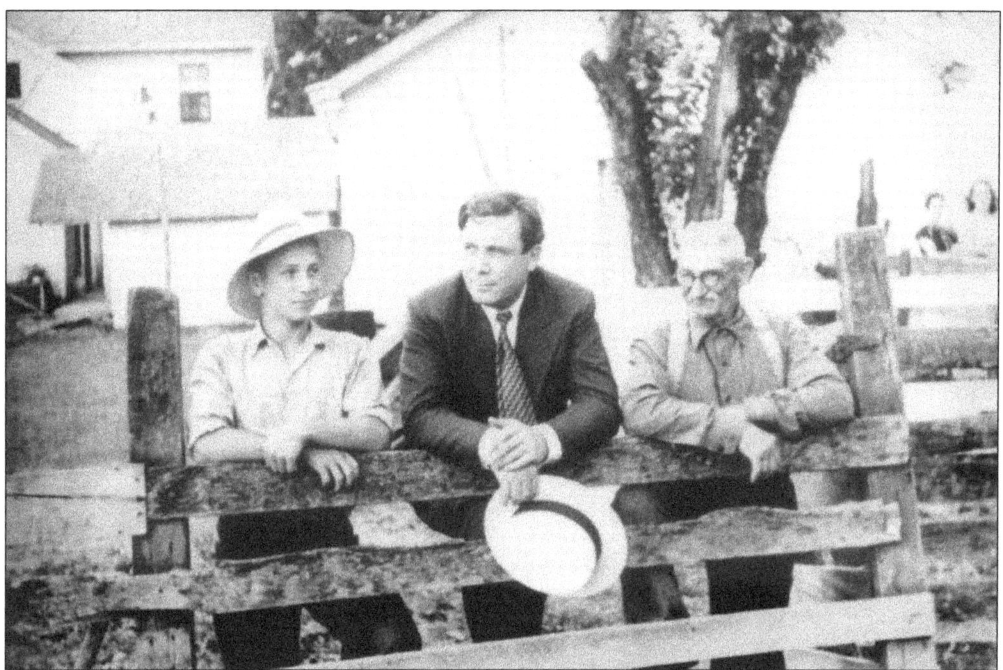

During one of his many trips home to Indiana, Willkie, center, visits with employees at the Willkie family farm in Rush County, Indiana, home of Willkie's wife, Edith Wilk, located about 50 miles southeast of Elwood. Pictured with Willkie are Bob Berkemeier, left, and his grandfather Frank Berkemeier, who are the father and great-grandfather of Dave Berkemeier, the 2014–2016 Elwood Chamber of Commerce director. (Courtesy Dave Berkemeier.)

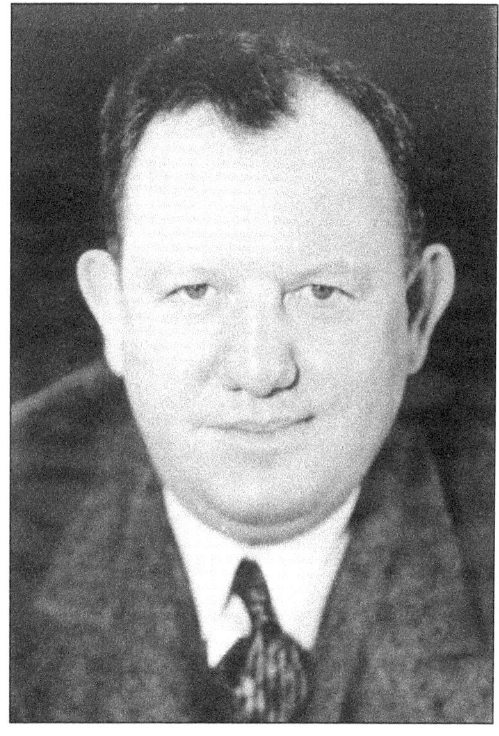

Shortly after Willkie snagged the Republican nomination for president, a campaign advisor suggested that, in keeping with his everyman persona, Willkie deliver his acceptance speech in his Hoosier hometown. Indiana businessman and future US senator Homer Capehart, right, took charge of the monumental task of readying Elwood for the historic event. Capehart estimated that 20,000 Willkie supporters would converge upon Elwood. His estimate was off by more than 200,000.

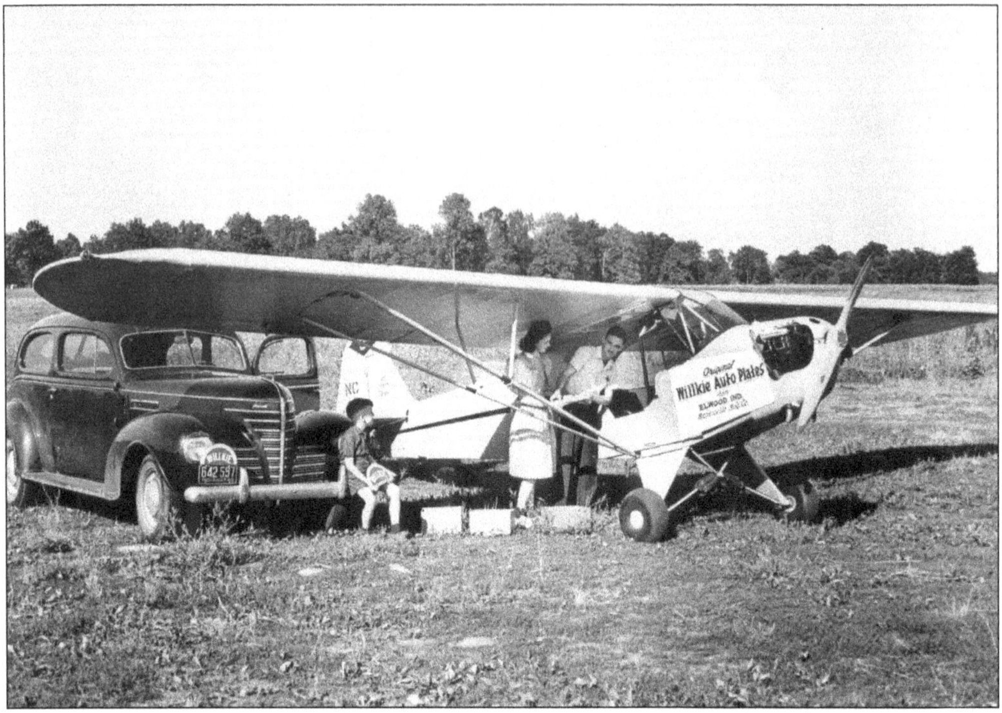

Pilot Wally Hobbs and his assistant load up his lightweight, Piper Cub airplane with Wendell Willkie metal auto plates during the summer of 1940 at the Hobbs, Indiana, airstrip. The plates were designed and produced by Francis E. Melvin, president of Monticello Manufacturing Co. of Elwood. Hobbs flew the plates to Washington, DC, for distribution to all 96 US senators. The boy is Melvin's son Mick. (Courtesy Mick Melvin.)

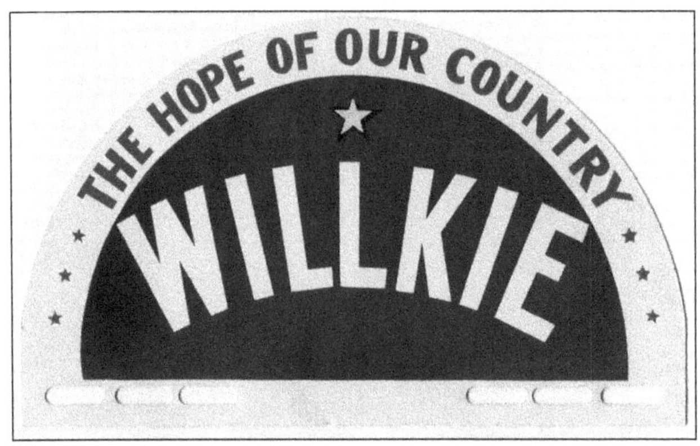

The plate in the boy's hands in the above photograph was made to fit above an automobile's front license plate. The words, "Hope of Our Country," incorporated into the plate's top curve, were inspired by the phrase inscribed on the arch over Elwood High School's front door. The plates were sold to Willkie supporters during his 1940 campaign for president. (Courtesy Elwood Heritage Center.)

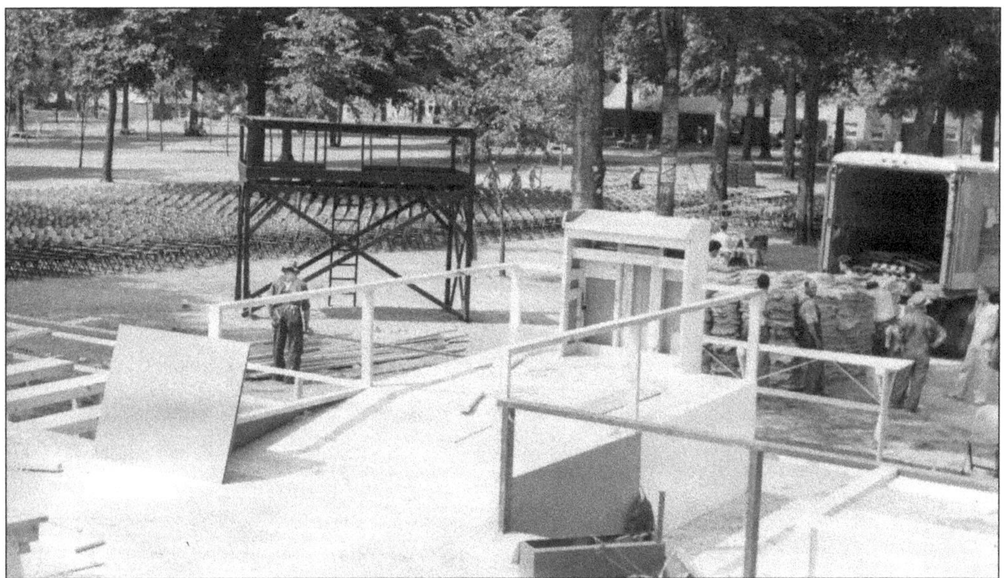

By August 1, the renaissance of Callaway Park, the site of Willkie's notification ceremony, was underway. Workers were leveling hills, filling holes, and beautifying the park. Fences were removed, trees and shrubs trimmed, stumps lifted, public restrooms (although far too few) renovated, and athletic fields cleared to accommodate concession stands. The stage was built, and electricity, water, telephone lines, a public address system, and broadcasting equipment were installed. Fields were turned into parking lots, and 30,000 rented folding chairs were set up in the center of the park, not simply for seating but as barriers in case the crowd grew too excited and rushed the stage. (Courtesy Elwood Heritage Center.)

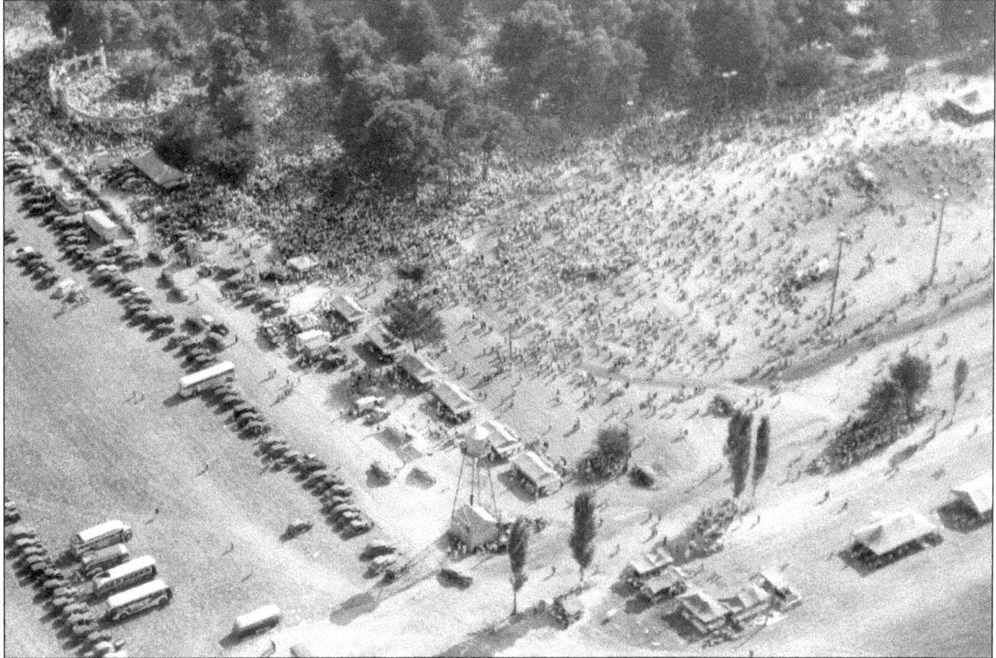

This aerial view of Callaway Park validates that the city could not have over-prepared for the massive crowd that converged there for the historic event. (Courtesy Elwood Heritage Center.)

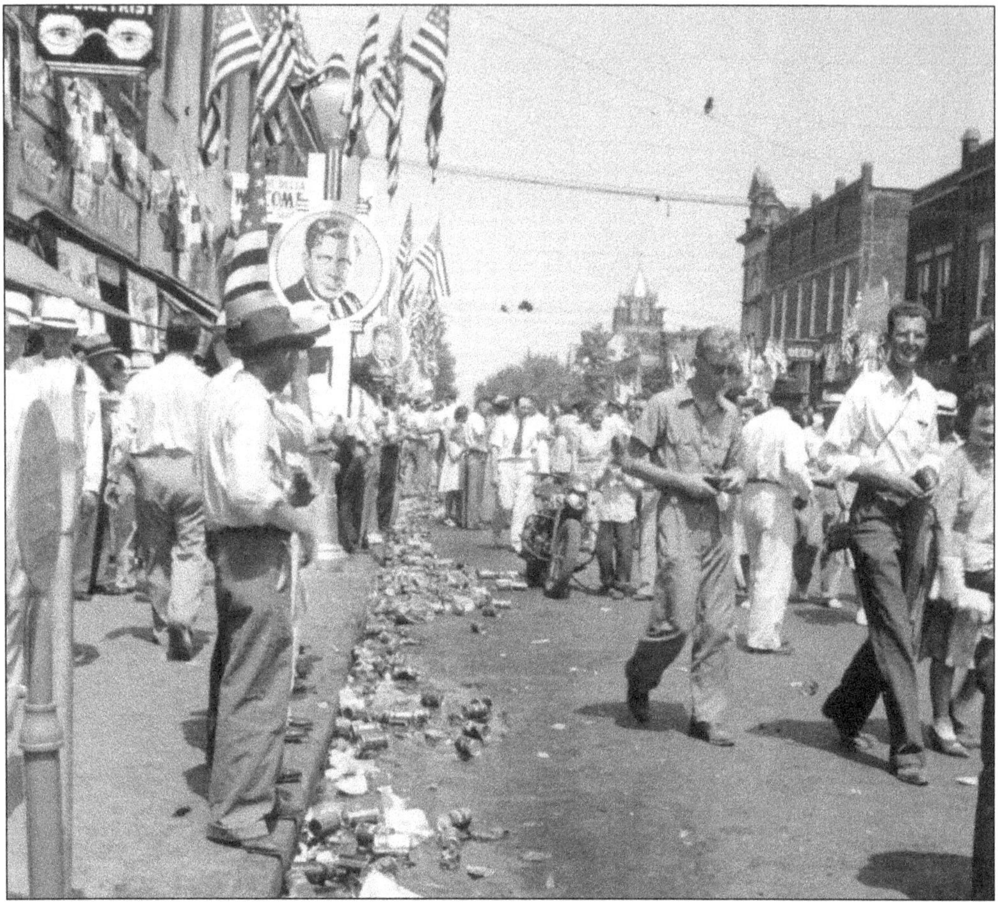

Special trains pulled into the stations carrying approximately 20,000 people. Busses brought in another 15,000. Some 60,000 more drove directly to the parking lots via private cars. Dietzen's bakery made 400,000 buns for the occasion, and the Elwood Coca-Cola Bottling Works stocked up with 192,000 bottles of Coke. Beer flowed freely, as attested by the empty cans cluttering the gutters, but police reportedly arrested only 37 drunks. (Courtesy William Hueneke.)

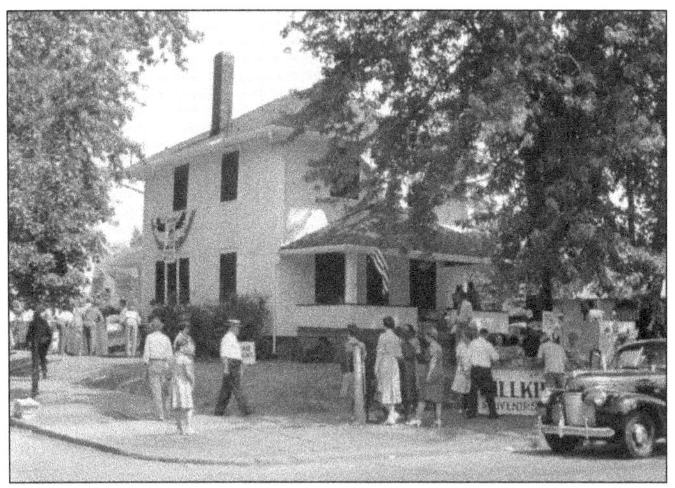

Willkie's birthplace on South A Street, Elwood, attracted hundreds of visitors. The homeowner had maximized its potential by selling refreshments, as well as postcards depicting a sketch of Willkie's birthplace. For a small, additional charge, tourists could have their cards mailed. The house stands yet today but attracts little attention. (Courtesy William Huneke.)

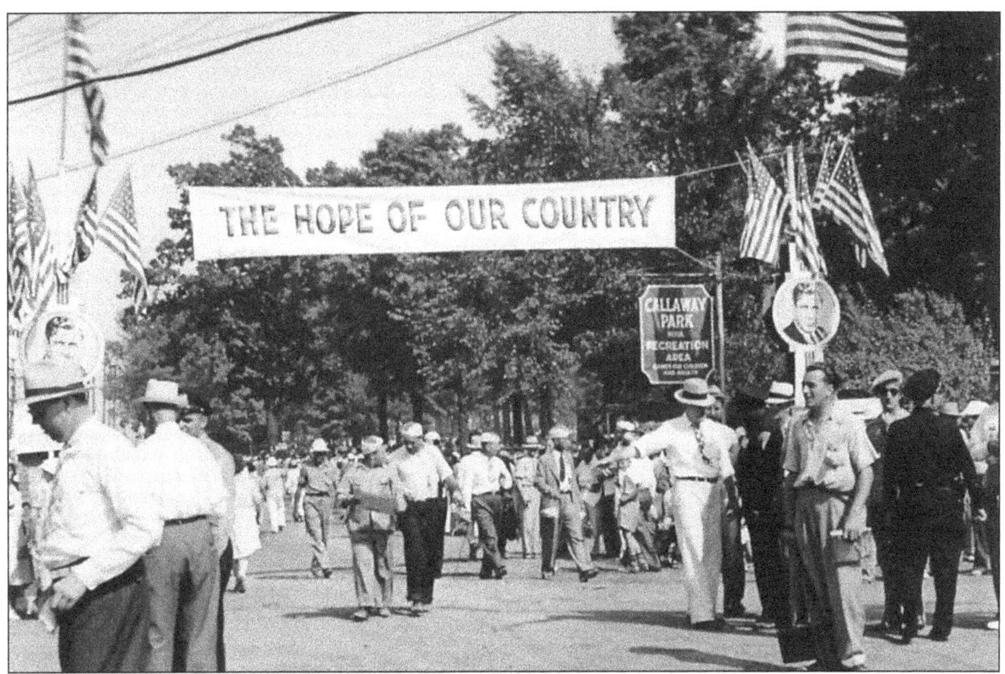

Throughout the city, hundreds of American flags had been mounted on light poles next to Willkie portraits. A banner referring to Elwood's favorite son as "The Hope of Our Country" was strung across the main entrance to Callaway Park, where Willkie would deliver his long-awaited speech. (Courtesy Madison County Historical Society.)

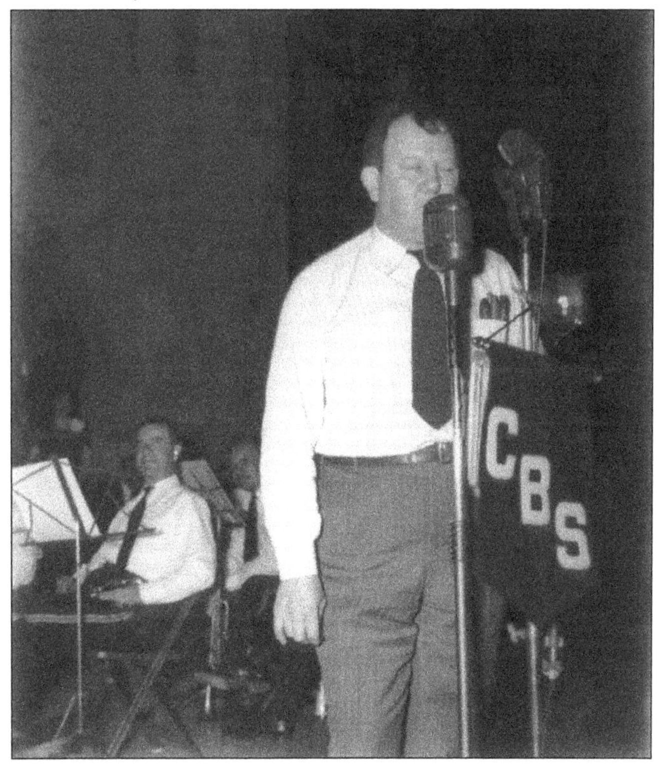

The Willkie Day event officially began Friday outside the high school under a bright, full moon. Radio legend Walter O'Keefe hosted a CBS broadcast featuring event organizer Homer Capehart (pictured), a community sing of "America," the Foster Hall Quartet's rendition of "We Want Willkie," William Herschel's poem *Ain't God Good to Indiana?*, read by his wife, and a military tap dance. (Courtesy Ball State University Archives and Special Collections.)

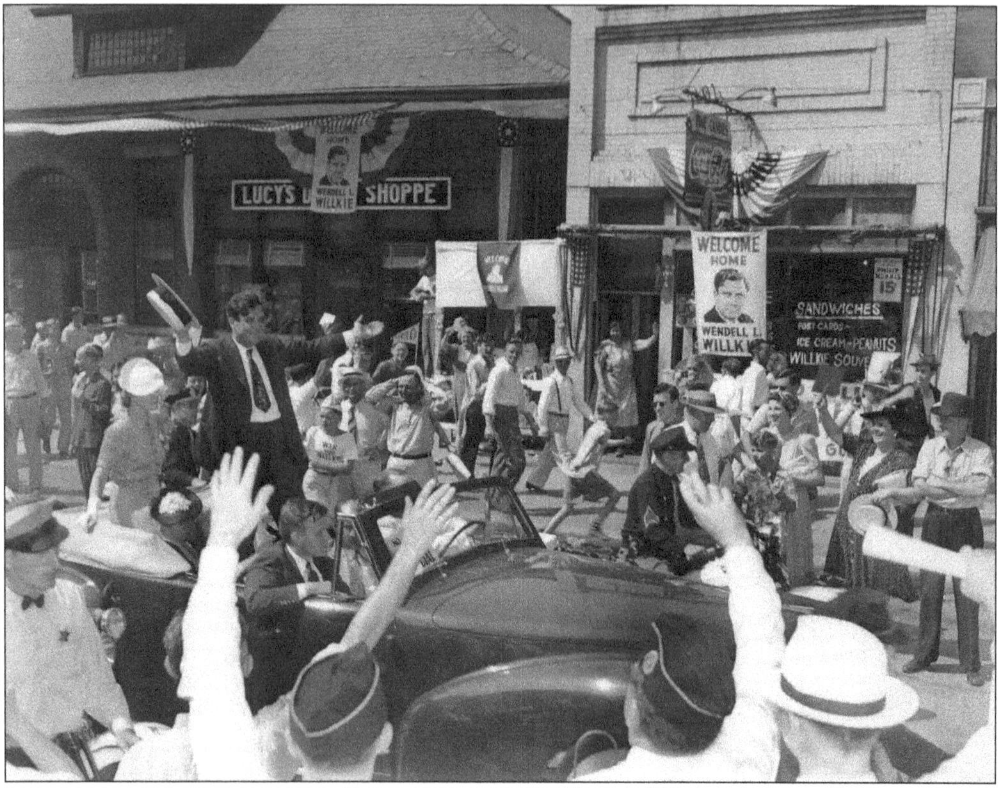

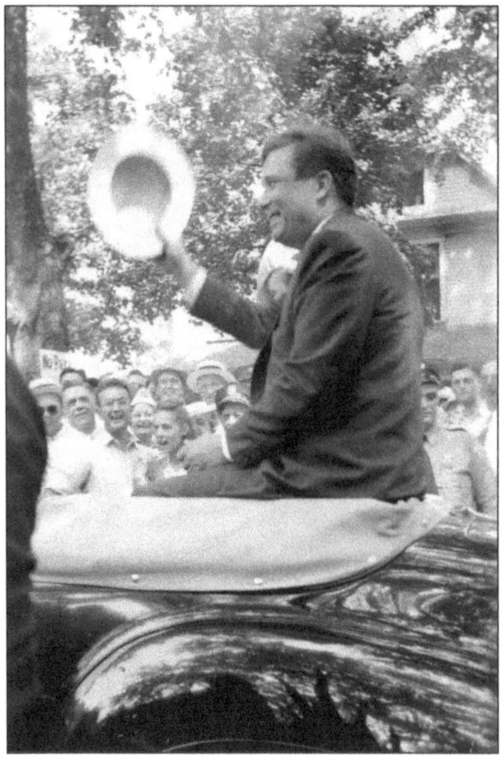

Willkie and his entourage rolled into Elwood's Pennsylvania Station from Rushville shortly after noon and proceeded to the campaign headquarters at 1113 South Anderson Street, the current location of Dunnichay Funeral Home. At 1:30 p.m., the Willkies climbed into the backseat of a Lincoln Zephyr convertible for the celebration parade. Heading north on Anderson Street through downtown Elwood, Willkie grinned broadly and waved his trademark straw hat at thousands of cheering onlookers. Reaching Main Street, the parade turned east (above) and proceeded to Elwood High School, where a massive crowd jammed a five-block radius of the school and awaited Willkie's arrival. After his brief address under the arch of the school's entrance, Willkie's car processed along North 19th Street (at left) to Callaway Park, where he would deliver his historic speech. (Above, courtesy Madison County Historical Society; left, courtesy Elwood Public Library.)

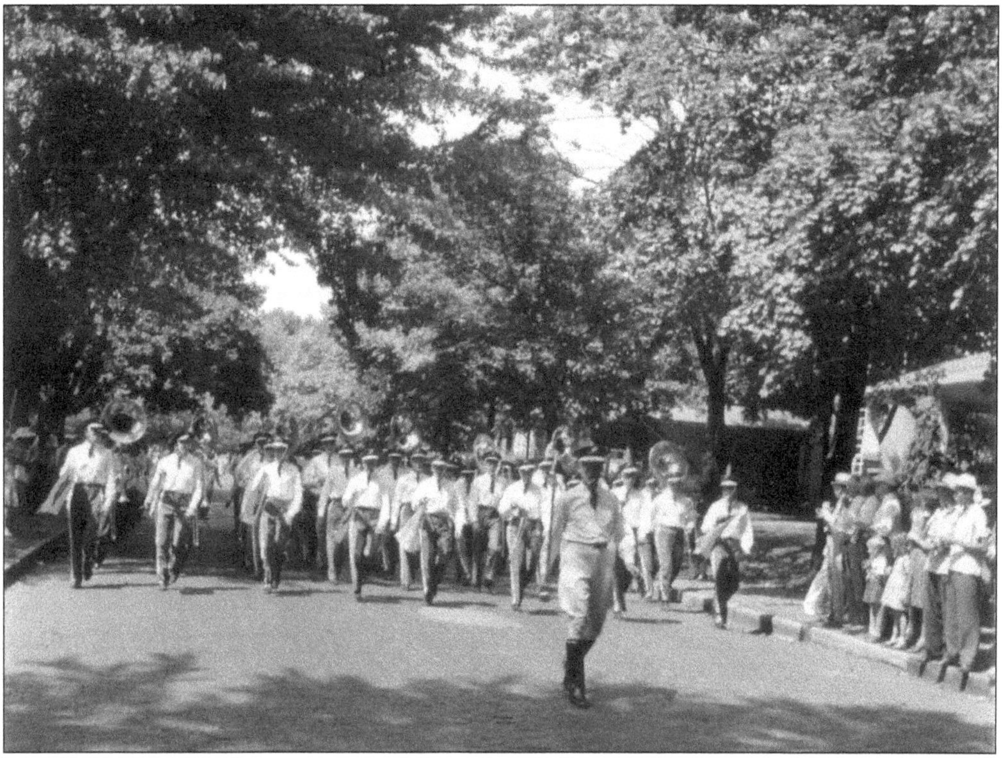

Bert Fenn, drum major, leads the famous Indiana University Marching Hundred north on 19th Street toward Callaway Park. Willkie, a 1916 graduate of Indiana University, chose the Marching Hundred as his official honor guard. The organization, founded in 1896, was and still is one of the nation's foremost marching bands. (Courtesy William Huneke.)

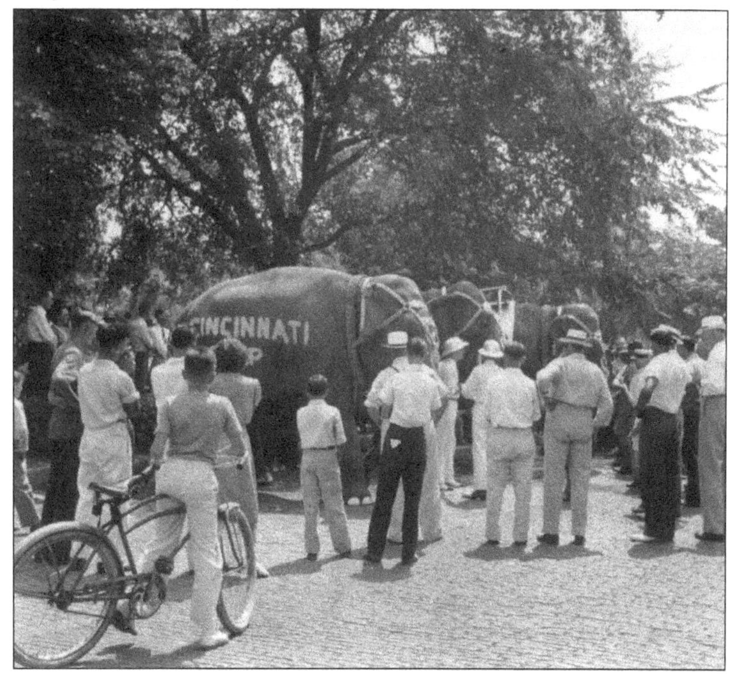

Four elephants, three from Hamilton County, Ohio, and one from Cook County, Illinois, arrived by separate trains. They attracted many visitors who had never seen elephants outside a zoo. All the elephants took part in the procession from the high school to Callaway Park. Sen. Robert Taft, who opposed Willkie for the presidential nomination, marched alongside the animals. (Courtesy William Huneke.)

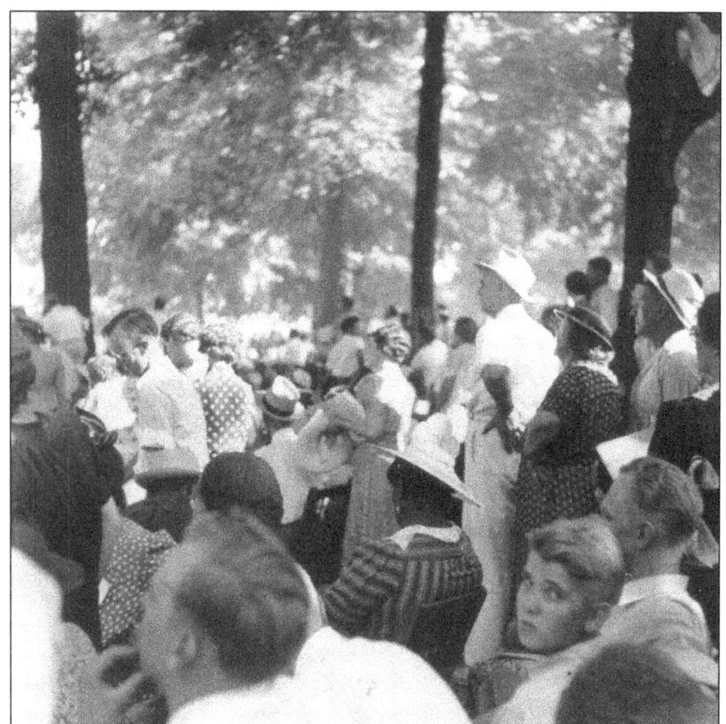

Supporters were waiting for Willkie at Callaway Park. They had been gathering since before dawn. By 2:00 p.m., the crowd had grown to more than 200,000. Loudspeakers had been set up so the program could be heard for a mile in all directions. Until that day, such a massive grassroots movement had not been seen in American politics. (Courtesy William Huneke.)

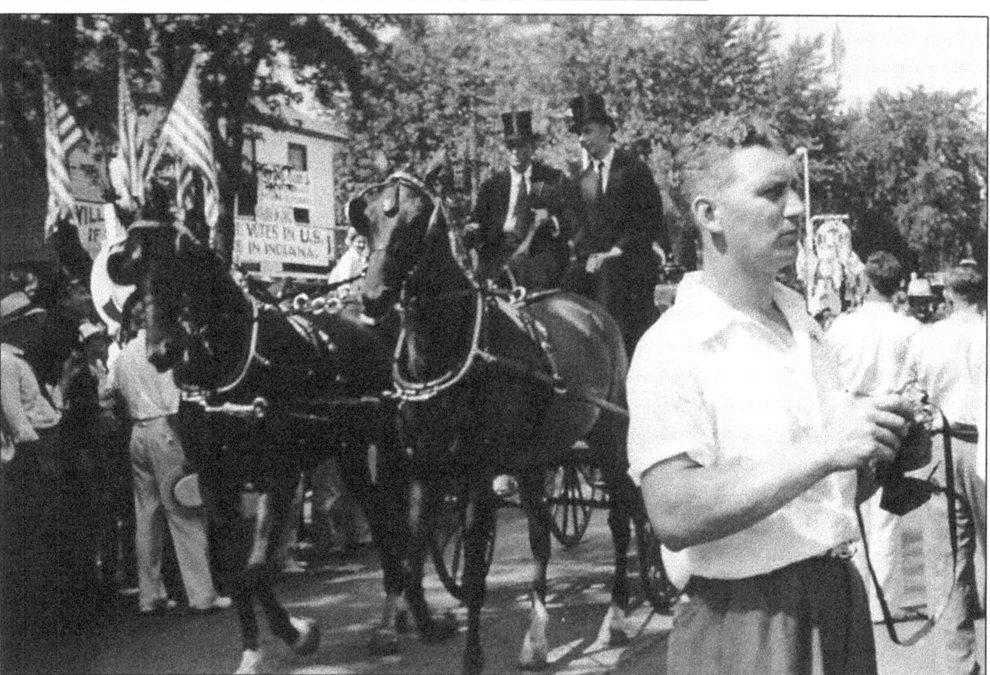

Temperatures soared to nearly 100 degrees in Elwood that day. The majority of men who witnessed the historic event dressed in short-sleeved shirts, proper attire for a blistering, hot day in Indiana, while the women donned dresses and silk stockings. Miraculously, of the thousands of supporters who endured the unrelenting sun, only 350 cases of heat prostration were treated at the first-aid tent. (Courtesy Madison County Historical Society.)

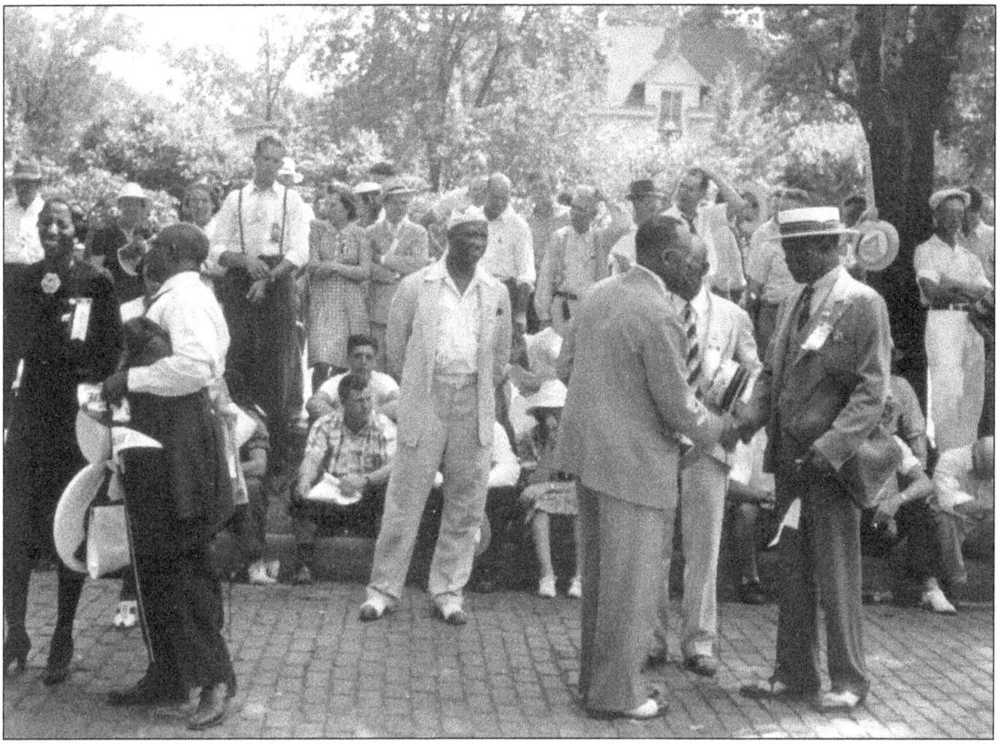

More than 2,500 African American Willkie supporters attended the notification. Later asked if he would continue the Republican Party's tradition of segregating "negroes and similar groups," Willkie answered, "It's my basic philosophy that there's no such arbitrary classification of American voters. We are all Americans." Elwood opened its doors to its African American visitors, and not a single incident of racial discourtesy was reported, according to the *Indianapolis Recorder*. (Courtesy William Huneke.)

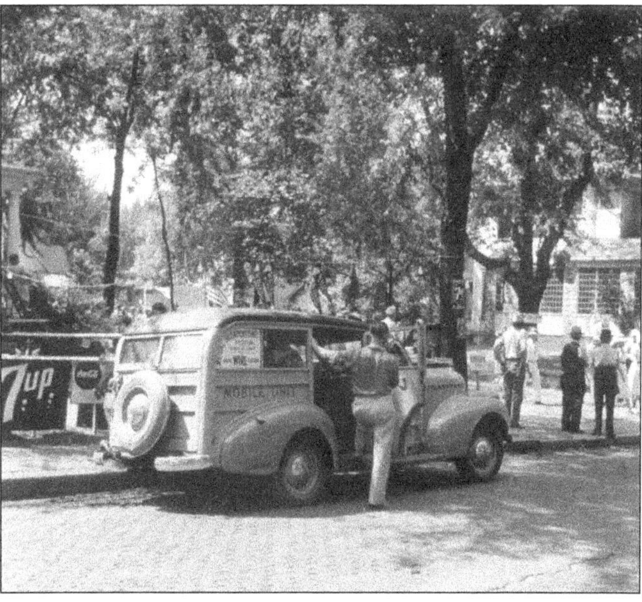

Besides the *Call-Leader* and other newspapers from Indiana, print media covering the Willkie notification firsthand included *New York Herald-Tribune*, *Providence* (Rhode Island) *Journal*, *Detroit News*, *Newark* (New Jersey) *Evening News*, *Chicago Daily News*, *San Francisco Chronicle*, Scripps Howard, *Pittsburgh Post Gazette*, United Press, Associated Press, and the *Chicago Times*. Radio networks that broadcast the events live, including Willkie's speech, were NBC, CBS, and MBS (Mutual Broadcasting Systems). (Courtesy William Huneke.)

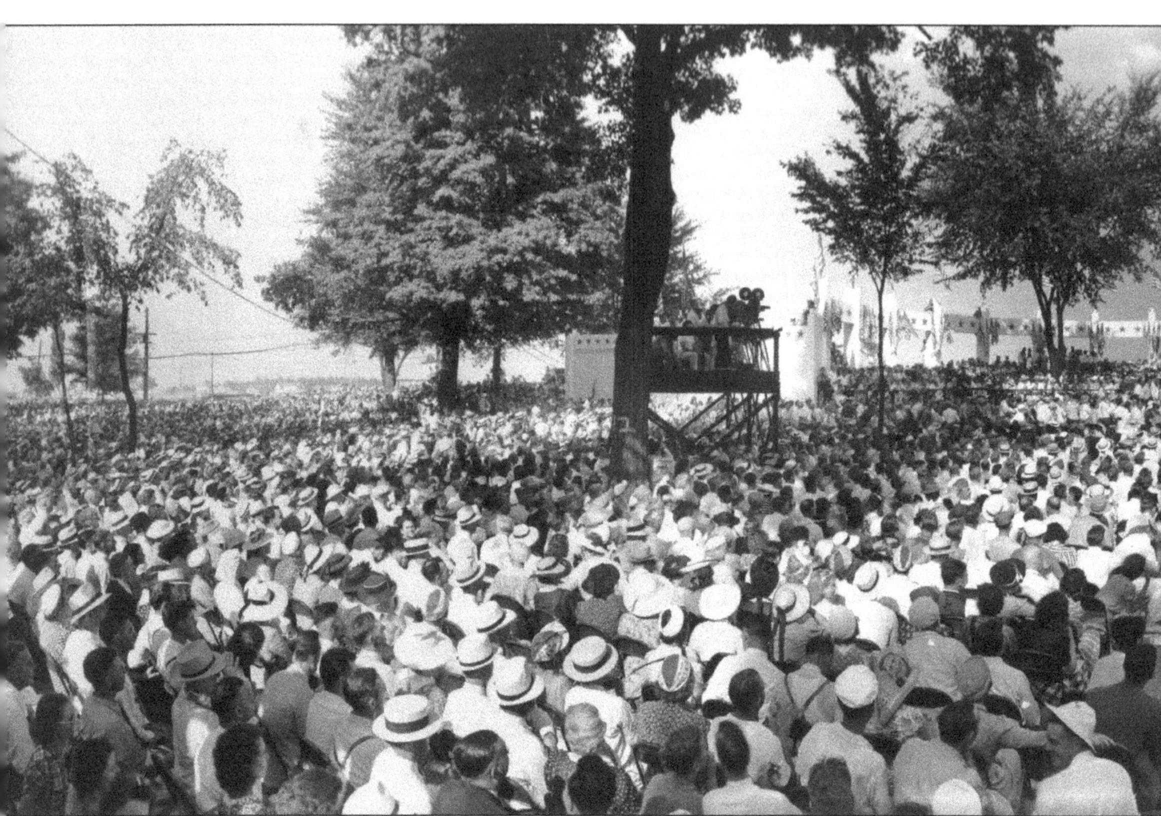

Willkie stepped onto the platform at 3:00 p.m. to the cheers of his waiting audience, 250,000 strong. Sipping water and wiping perspiration from his brow, Willkie told the enthusiastic crowd, "This young man was born and raised in Elwood. He attended the Elwood public schools. He worked in your factories and stores. He started the practice of law in your courts. . . . And he knew without any doubt that the greatest country on earth was the United States of America."

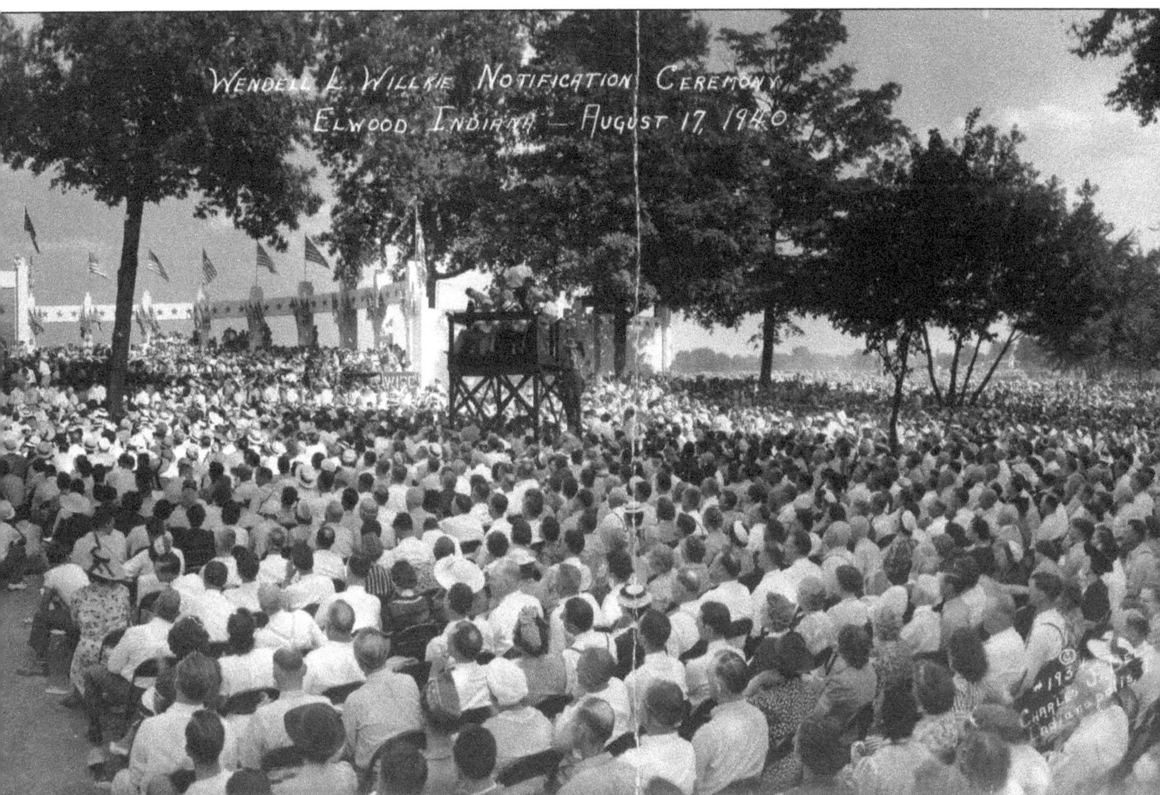

The Willkie event was deemed "the greatest outpouring of people in the political history of the United States." He so completely captured the public's imagination that he was regarded as the leader of the "people's movement." For the record, the number that turned out for Willkie's acceptance speech was reportedly twice the number that attended Franklin Roosevelt's.

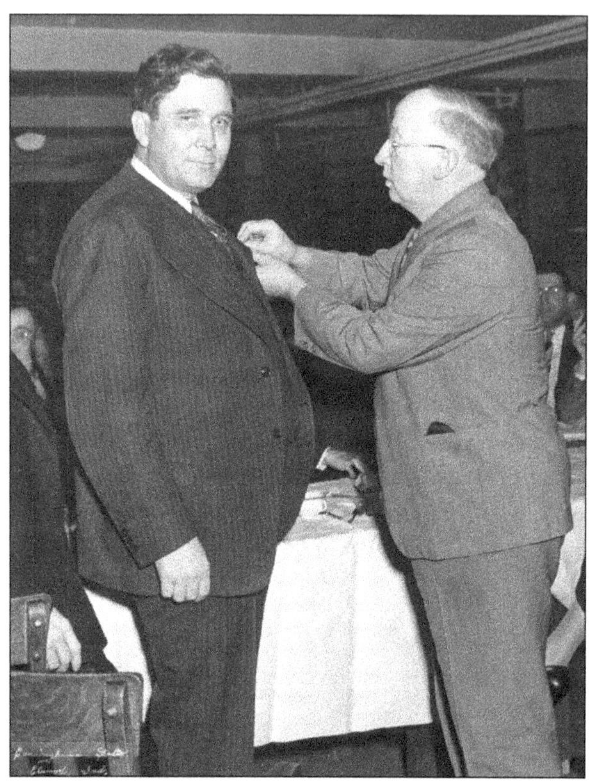

Willkie did not win his bid for president, but the defeat did not discourage his optimism for America. He returned to Elwood May 1, 1941, as a guest of the Kiwanis. Although he insisted the dinner be "nothing big or elaborate," 200 of his closest friends packed the First Presbyterian Church basement. After O.D. Hinshaw presented Willkie with a Kiwanis pin (left), the statesman joked about pulling stunts with boyhood friends. But with war raging in Europe, Willkie turned somber, reminding attendees of the perils if Germany won. "I would rather be dead," he said, "than live under any system of government or economy that is not the democratic way." Below, Willkie poses with, from left to right, (first row) Hinshaw, Ben Arkin, and Milt York; (second row) Walter Allen, unidentified, and R.C. McDaniel. (Left, courtesy Elwood Public Library; below, Ron Hinshaw.)

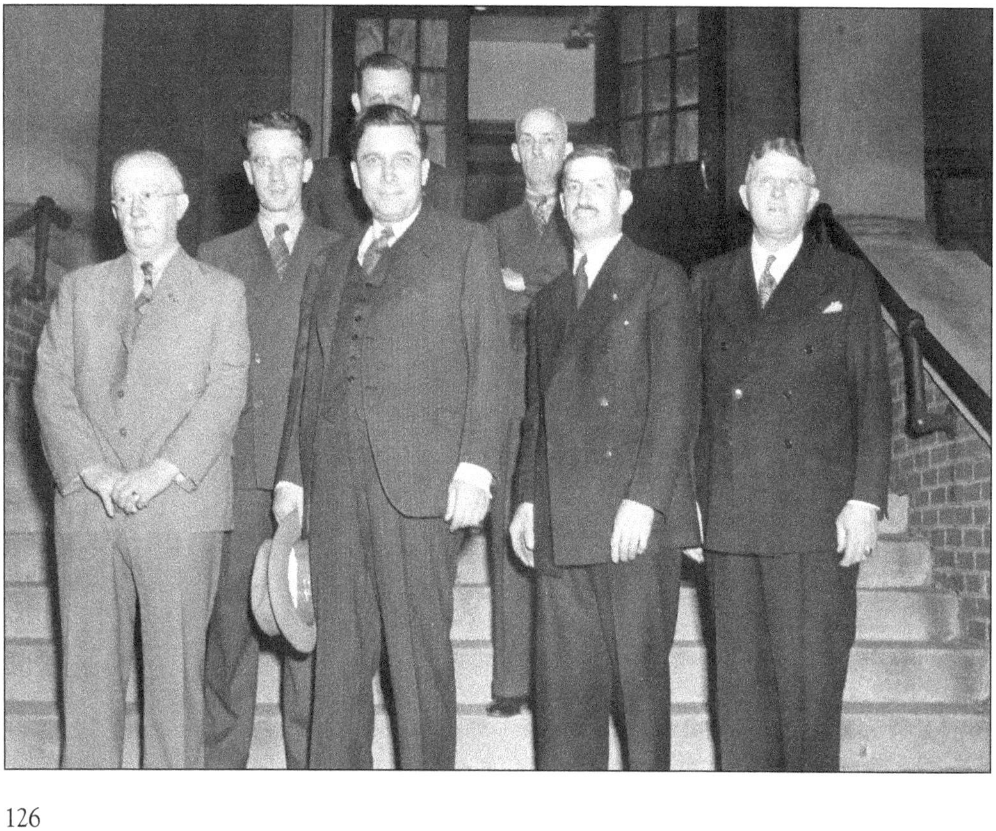

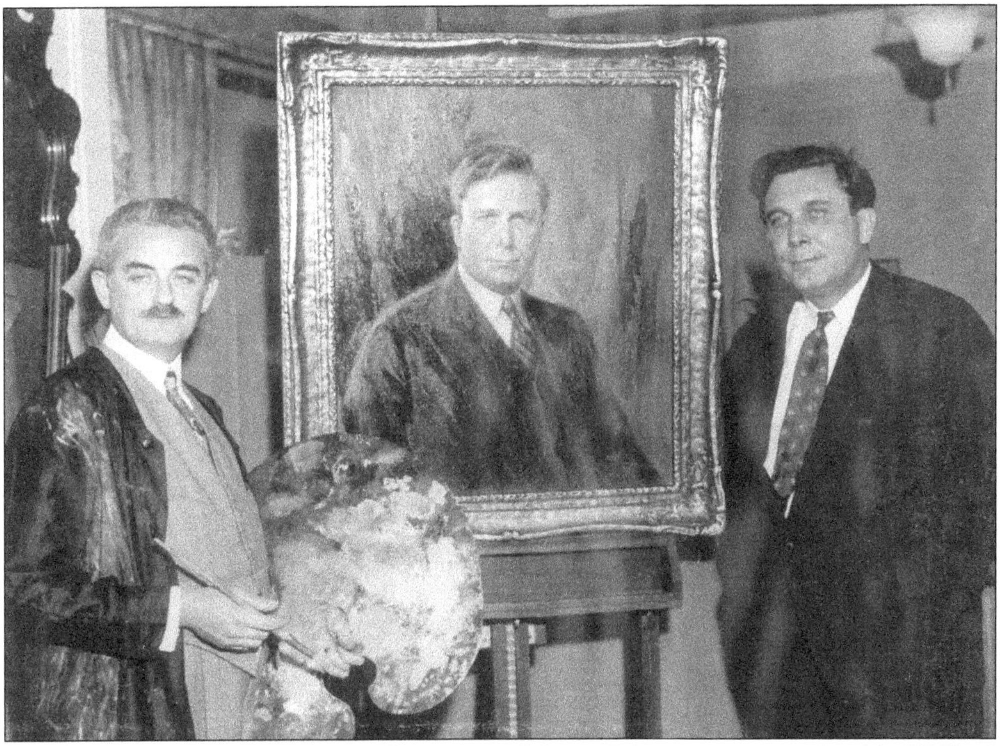

Willkie poses with renowned artist John Doctoroff alongside his painting completed for Willkie's 1940 presidential campaign. Doctoroff was known for his renderings of famous statesmen. Among his subjects were Calvin Coolidge, Clarence Darrow, and Winston Churchill. The Doctoroff painting is the only portrait for which Willkie sat. Elwood citizens purchased the painting in 1945 for the high school, where it still hangs today. (Courtesy Elwood Community School Corporation.)

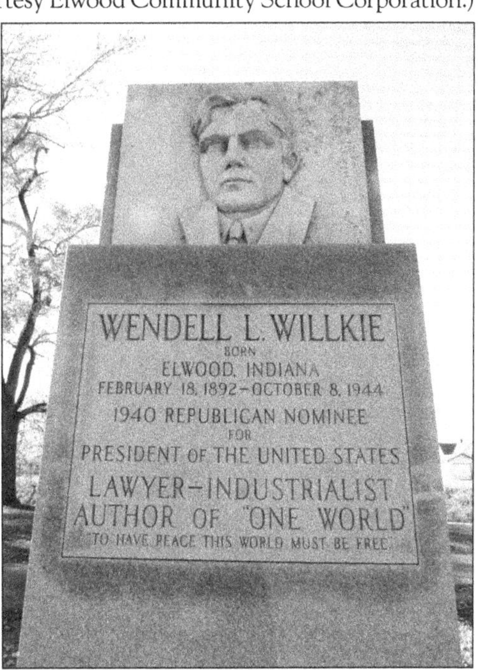

Willkie died suddenly on October 8, 1944. Reporting his death, the *Call-Leader* referred to Willkie as Elwood's Abe Lincoln and quoted Dr. G.V. Newcomer as saying, "Goodbye, Wendell. Elwood enshrines you and feels, indeed, you were the hope of our country." Elwood citizens erected this monument in Wendell Willkie Park in 2005 to commemorate Willkie and his outstanding achievements.

www.ingramcontent.com/pod-product-compliance
Lightning Source LLC
LaVergne TN
LVHW060625110826
845147LV00015B/937